Palestine
in the Time
of **Jesus**

Bet Netofa Valley, Galilee

This valley and these hillsides in Galilee have been farmed since ancient times. "And [Jesus] told them a parable, saying, 'The land of a rich man brought forth abundantly'" (Luke 12:16). (Photo by Douglas E. Oakman)

Palestine in the Time of Jesus

Social Structures
and Social Conflicts

Second Edition

K. C. Hanson &
Douglas E. Oakman

Fortress Press
Minneapolis

PALESTINE IN THE TIME OF JESUS
Social Structures and Social Conflicts, 2nd Edition

Cover image: Roman Aqueduct, Caesarea, Israel, © iStockphoto / Kreicher. Two bronze coins—Coin of Antigonus, Last Hasmonaean King of Israel, and coin from the period of John Hyrcanus II, © Erich Lessing / Art Resource, NY. Used by permission
Cover design: Kevin van der Leek Design, Inc.
Interior design: James Korsmo

ISBN 978-0-8006-6309-4

Library of Congress Cataloging-in-Publication Data
The Library of Congress catalogued the first edition as follows:
Hanson, K. C. (Kenneth C.)
    Palestine in the time of Jesus : social structures and social
conflicts / K. C. Hanson and Douglas E. Oakman.
      p. cm.
    Includes bibliographical references and indexes.
    ISBN 0-8006-3470-5 (alk. paper)   ISBN 0-8006-6309-8
    1. Sociology, Biblical. 2. Bible. N.T.—Social scientific
criticism. 3. Bible. N.T.—Criticism, interpretation, etc.
4. Jews—Social life and customs—To 70 A.D. 5. Palestine—Social
life and customs—To 70 A.D. I. Oakman, Douglas E. II Title.
BS2545.S55H37 1998
225.9' 5—dc21   98-18073
                                                              CIP

Manufactured in the U.S.A.

For Alice

and

Deborah, Jay and Joanna, and Jon,
with gratitude for all your support
and encouragement along the way

Sheep

"Which one among you, having a hundred sheep, if he has lost one of them, does not leave the ninety-nine in the wilderness and go after the lost one until he finds it?" (Luke 15:4). Palestinian shepherds were selling these sheep outside the "Sheep Gate" in the Old City of Jerusalem. (Photo by K. C. Hanson)

Contents

M.1 Map of Greater Palestine

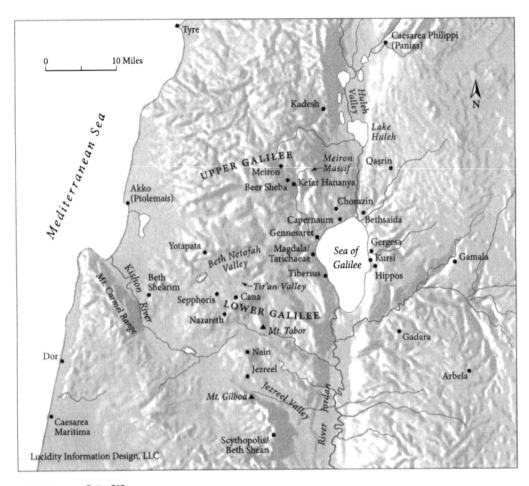

M.2 Map of Galilee

Maps, Figures, Illustrations, and Sidebars

Maps

Figures

Illustrations

Sidebars

Abbreviations

Ancient

Cicero

Ag. Verr.	*Against Gaius Verres*

Josephus

Ag. Ap.	*Against Apion*
Ant.	*The Antiquities of the Judeans*
Life	*Life of Josephus*
War	*The War of the Judeans*

Philo

Ag. Flacc.	*Against Flaccus*
Hypoth.	*Hypothetica*
Laws	*Special Laws*
Vir.	*On the Virtues*

Pliny

Nat. Hist.	*Natural History*

Pseudepigrapha

Jub.	*Jubilees*
T. Levi	*Testament of Levi*
T. Mos.	*Testament of Moses*

Rabbinic Literature

b.	Babylonian Talmud (*Babli*)
j.	Jerusalem Talmud (*Yerushalmi*)
m.	Mishnah
t.	Tosefta

'Abod. Zar.	*'Abodah Zarah*
'Abot	*'Abot*
'Arak.	*'Arakin*
B. Bat.	*Baba Batra*
B. Qam.	*Baba Qamma*
Bek.	*Bekorot*
Ber.	*Berakot*
Beṣ.	*Beṣah*
'Erub.	*'Erubin*
Giṭ.	*Giṭṭin*
Ḥag.	*Ḥagigah*
Ḥal.	*Ḥallah*
Ḥul.	*Ḥullin*
Ker.	*Keritot*
Ket.	*Ketubbot*
Lam. Rab.	*Lamentations Rabbah*
Ma'aś. Š.	*Ma'aśerot Šeni*
Mak.	*Makkot*
Menaḥ.	*Menaḥot*
Mid.	*Middot*
Ned.	*Nedarim*
Neg.	*Nega'im*
Pe'ah	*Pe'ah*
Pes.	*Pesaḥim*
Šabb.	*Šabbat*
Sanh.	*Sanhedrin*
Šebi.	*Šebi'it*
Šeqal.	*Šeqalim*
Soṭ.	*Sotah*
Sukk.	*Sukkah*
Ta'an.	*Ta'anit*
Ter.	*Terumot*
Yeb.	*Yebamot*
Yoma	*Yoma*

Noncanonical Gospel

Gos. Thom.	*Gospel of Thomas*

Modern

ABD	Anchor Bible Dictionary. 6 vols. Edited by David Noel Freedman. New York: Doubleday, 1992
ABRL	Anchor Bible Reference Library
AmAnth	American Anthropologist
ANRW	Aufstieg und Niedergang der römischen Welt
ARA	Annual Review of Anthropology
AusBR	Australian Biblical Review
BAR	Biblical Archaeology Review
BASOR	Bulletin of the American Schools of Oriental Research
BETL	Bibliotheca ephemeridum theologicarum lovaniensium
BibInt	Biblical Interpretation
BibIntSer	Biblical Interpretation Series
BJS	British Journal of Sociology
BJS	Brown Judaic Studies
BSJS	Brill's Series in Jewish Studies
BTB	Biblical Theology Bulletin
CBQ	Catholic Biblical Quarterly
CBR	Currents in Biblical Research
CIJ	Corpus inscriptionum judaicarum. Edited by Jean-Baptiste Frey. Vatican City: Pontificio istituto di archeologia cristiana, 1936–52
CPSA	Cambridge Papers in Social Anthropology
CRINT	Compendia rerum iudaicarum ad Novum Testamentum
CSCS	Cambridge Studies in Cultural Systems
CSSH	Comparative Studies in Society and History
FMAS	Foundations of Modern Anthropology Series
GBS	Guides to Biblical Scholarship
HSCP	Harvard Studies in Classical Philology
HTS	Hervormde Teologiese Studies

IDB	The Interpreter's Dictionary of the Bible. 4 vols. Edited by George Arthur Buttrick. Nashville: Abingdon, 1962
IDBSup	The Interpreter's Dictionary of the Bible: Supplementary Volume. Edited by Keith R. Crim. Nashville: Abingdon, 1976
IEJ	Israel Exploration Journal
Int	Interpretation
JAR	Journal of Anthropological Research
JBL	Journal of Biblical Literature
JDS	Judean Desert Studies
JESHO	Journal of the Economic and Social History of the Orient
JJS	Journal of Jewish Studies
JPS	Journal of Papyrological Studies
JRE	Journal of Religious Ethics
JSHJ	Journal for the Study of the Historical Jesus
JSJ	Journal for the Study of Judaism
JSJSup	Journal for the Study of Judaism Supplements
JSNT	Journal for the Study of the New Testament
JSS	Journal of Semitic Studies
LCL	Loeb Classical Library
LNSAS	Leicester-Nottingham Studies in Ancient Society
Matrix	Matrix: The Bible in Mediterranean Context
NovTSup	Novum Testamentum Supplements
NTL	New Testament Library
NTS	New Testament Studies
NTTS	New Testament Tools and Studies
PEF	Palestine Exploration Fund
PEQ	Palestine Exploration Quarterly
PHC	A People's History of Christianity
P&P	Past and Present
PRR	Princeton Readings in Religions
RBL	Review of Biblical Literature

RevExp	*Review and Expositor*	SPAAA	Special Publications of the American Anthropological Association
RSR	*Recherches de science religieuse*		
SBEC	Studies in the Bible and Early Christianity	*TBT*	*The Bible Today*
		ThTo	*Theology Today*
SBLSP	*Society of Biblical Literature Seminar Papers*	*ThZ*	*Theologische Zeitschrift*
		TSAJ	Texts and Studies in Ancient Judaism
SCJ	Studies in Christianity and Judaism		
SFSHJ	South Florida Studies in the History of Judaism	WUNT	Wissenschaftliche Untersuchungen zum Neuen Testament
SJLA	Studies in Judaism in Late Antiquity	*ZDMG*	*Zeitschrift der deutschen morgenländischen Gesellschaft*
SNTSMS	Society for New Testament Studies Monograph Series		
SocInq	*Sociological Inquiry*	*ZNW*	*Zeitschrift für die neutestamentliche Wissenschaft*

Judean cave

"Is it not written, 'My house shall be called a house of prayer for all peoples'? But you have made it into a cave of bandits" (Mark 11:17). Caves dot the Palestinian landscape and have been used as sheepfolds as well as bandit retreats. (Photo by K. C. Hanson)

Preface to the First Edition

While many books describe the world of first-century Palestine, the originating home of Jesus and the Gospels, most of the existing ones do so from the perspective of history, literature, or theology. Only recently have biblical scholars begun to apply social-scientific models to the Jesus traditions in any systematic way. While isolated observations and conclusions of a "social" or "anthropological" character have been made for years, what has been lacking are clearly conceived models of social relationships to organize this material. The problems have been compounded by the lack of cross-cultural comparisons. Another difficulty has been the failure to provide any systemic overview showing the structure of the social domains, the institutions that embody them, and the relationship between those institutions.

In reading the New Testament and contemporaneous works, it is fundamental to understand both the social values and the social institutions of ancient Palestine. The following pages focus on social institutions with a view to how they are reflected in or had an impact upon Jesus and traditions within the Gospels.

Since we intend this book for the undergraduate, seminarian, pastor, or generally educated reader, we have had to assume some things for the sake of clarity and emphasis. Beyond what is said in chapter 1 and in our glossaries, the reader should consult some of the many introductions to the biblical literature or the history of this period. We hope that our book, despite its limitations, will help readers to sort through complicated material and issues in comprehensible and readable form. We have the following general goals in mind throughout our work:

- To examine the primary social institutions of first-century Palestine through a social-scientific methodology
- To present testable models of society that can be employed when studying the Bible and therefore be refined or modified as the reader acquires more information
- To relate the systemic analysis directly to New Testament passages in each chapter in order to demonstrate how this material is applicable

Chapter 1 presents an overview of the use of models (or scenarios) and why they are important in doing social analysis. Especially important here is to make clear that models are instructive tools to help us visualize meaningful configurations, not pigeonholes into which one forces the data. Chapter 1 also covers social domains and how the world was perceived and organized differently in the ancient Mediterranean. The relationships and interactions of social domains are investigated. Finally, we compare, on a large scale, the differences between a preindustrial society (such as first-century Palestine) and a postindustrial society (such as the twentieth-century United States).

Our persistent aim is to employ the lenses of our models to help the reader of the New Testament Gospels to imagine institutions and scenarios more appropriate to first-century Palestine than those into which we were socialized. In each major chapter we examine materials related to Jesus as we address a different social domain. Chapter 2 focuses on kinship, chapter 3 on politics, chapter 4 on political economy, and chapter 5 on political religion. We take pains to show the reader how these social domains interact and interpenetrate through specific social institutions. Chapter 1 explains why the chapters and institutions unfold in this order. Each chapter then follows the same structure:

- Identification of central biblical passages or other texts
- A list of questions the passages raise
- The construction of meaningful models or scenarios
- Application of the models and scenarios to the focal texts, with consideration of the initial questions
- Highlighting of aspects of the Jesus tradition through the models and scenarios
- Identification of material for further reflection and suggested applications of the chapter's perspectives
- Recommended readings

We have summarized important technical discussions through graphical aids (pictorial conceptual models). While pictures are not always worth a thousand words—we often require quite a few to explain our charts—these can be helpful to the reader as orienting maps for the social-scientific discussions. The general model of chapter 1 is elaborated for specific institutional domains in subsequent models.

The reader will also find helpful the three glossaries at the end of the volume, which include terms relevant to Palestinian culture (for example, "tetrarch"), identification of ancient authors and documents (for example, Josephus), and modern social-scientific terms (for example, "institution"). The first time a technical term is used in each chapter, it will be highlighted in boldface type to indicate that it is defined in a glossary and followed by a number in brackets to give its location in the glossaries following the main text.

We have adopted a number of terminological conventions within our book. *Palaestina* was the Roman designation for the area (including Judea and Galilee) in which the early church and rabbinic Judaism emerged. Roman Palestine in this book refers primarily to Palestine in the Herodian period (37 B.C.E. to 70 C.E.). We adopt consistently "Israelite" or "Judean" rather than "Jew" for reasons that will be discussed, and the scholarly temporal indicators B.C.E. (Before the Common Era) and C.E. (Common Era). Biblical and other translations are usually our own, although we have checked these against standard versions of the Bible, the Loeb Classical Library, and other authoritative resources (see the first bibliography, which follows the glossaries). We have also checked the original languages of quoted translations wherever possible, since older translators were not as sensitive to their own "social-structural inexperience" as we are attempting to be.

We think the reader will also find our Web site helpful in using this book and in doing further research. The Web site includes a variety of helps organized by our chapter headings: links to photos, ancient documents, maps, archaeological information, the discussion questions from each chapter, full quotations of the ancient sources cited in each chapter (Josephus, the Mishnah, etc.), the authors' publication lists, and e-mail links to ask questions of the authors. It is available at: http://www.fortresspress.com/hansonoakman

Our presentation does not intend to be comprehensive in the sense of treating all aspects of every social institution. The archaeological data alone would swamp the reader. We intend to focus on central institutions in each chapter, to provide the reader sufficient argumentation to support our understanding of the institutions and domains, and sufficient data (ancient documents or archaeological materials) to lead the reader to examine the case for herself: to read the New Testament Gospels with fresh eyes, to test models and scenarios against the data, and to search for more data that will bring light on the constructs, confirming or disconfirming. In this way, the reader is brought into a new type of dialog with this sacred heritage. Out of dialog will hopefully emerge new insights into the mysteries of which the Bible speaks.

This book has gestated over a fairly long period, since we have both been heavily involved in teaching responsibilities. It was written in the spaces of our lives, but that (we hope) has permitted a maturing of the ingredients, like a fine beer or wine.

We owe many debts of gratitude. Fortress Press, the Evangelical Lutheran Church in America, and Pacific Lutheran University provided money to support our work along the way. Drafts of material have received occasional critical comment by colleagues in our institutional departments. The Context Group, an international group that meets annually to discuss the application of the social sciences to biblical studies, for several years has given us steadfast encouragement as well as discerning feedback. Bruce J. Malina, Dennis C. Duling, David Weidkamp, Eliesev Hansen, Ryan Fletcher, and Deborah Oakman and Justin Oakman served as readers for penultimate drafts. We thank them for the problems they helped us to identify and the suggestions for improvement they made. Of course, the synthetic perspectives and faults of this book remain our responsibility alone.

Deborah, Justin, and Jonathan Oakman played a significant role in encouraging this project to fruition. They worked around us when we had our annual work sessions, putting up with papers and books strewn all over the house. Part of the joy of seeing this book finally in print is sustained by the memories of those who have shared with us in its writing. To these friends and family, we dedicate our efforts with gratitude.

Finally, we salute Marshall Johnson for his encouragement and patience during earlier years of the project. And we thank

Michael West, David Lott, Debbie Finch, and other members of the dedicated Fortress staff for their indispensable assistance in pro- ducing a finished volume. May this book be as stimulating for biblical students as it has been for us in the writing.

Preface to the Second Edition

Ten years have now passed since the first edition of *Palestine in the Time of Jesus* was originally published. The book has been remarkably well received by its intended audiences, having found frequent use in university and seminary classrooms, service in pastors' studies, and positive responses from general readers. Indeed, the first edition was awarded "Book of the Year" by the Association of Parish Clergy in 1999. Even more remarkably, the book has received appreciative critical reviews by professional scholars and frequent employment in graduate seminars. This range of use commends the clarity of the writing as well as the accuracy of content.

At the request of the publisher, the authors have undertaken some necessary or desired revisions to both the form and the content of the original book. We hope that this second edition will be as widely used and helpful to scholar, student, pastor, and general reader alike. Besides a more reader-friendly format, we have added sidebars, new or revised models, new photos, key terms and a chapter outline at the beginning of each chapter, additional study questions, updated suggested readings, and updated bibliographies. We have also responded in various places to scholarly criticisms of the original edition. The authors have been blessed to enjoy a twenty-year friendship, and our collaboration on this new edition has marked again the joy we share in scholarly insight into the life and times of the enormously important historical figure of Jesus of Nazareth.

While the introduction will give much more detail about the articulated approaches of this book, it will be helpful to remind the reader here of several points. The first relates to methodology. This book is in many senses a congeries of models of the ancient world of Jesus of Nazareth. The book may be thought of as a metamodel of the social structures and social conflicts of that first-century period. Any model, as John Kautsky reminds us, is a simplification of reality in order to facilitate understanding. Hopefully, a model does not oversimplify nor distort reality. Many critics of what has come to be called social-scientific criticism of the Bible complain that modeling "forces" the data into predetermined forms. These critics are unreformed historians who believe their inductive generalizations are adequate to the data. By working without explicit models, they fail to surface their implicit categories (models) for scrutiny and run the danger of inappropriate, anachronistic, or ethnocentric inferences. Conversely, the materials of this book make models explicit from large-scale down to smaller-scale, while testing these models against a variety of textual, documentary, and archaeological data. Models actually facilitate the "seeing" of data or evidence ("seeing out of"). This modeling procedure has proven its worth in winning the assent of many scholars. Often, these scholars accept our general conclusions while taking issue with specific details. This is probably the result of the book's review by traditional historians, who glory in individuals and data, who, while recognizing the validity of the bigger picture, eternally caution against "overgeneralization." Indeed, some critics actually try to play off differences of detail against the big picture, all the while missing the validity of the big picture in the midst of all the details. More will be said about our procedures in chapter 1, but some of the criticism leveled at the first edition of this book was rooted in the ideological differences implicit in the approach of modeling the typical versus the historian's focus on the individual detail.

Second, we point out in chapter 1 that we have combined systems and conflict approaches precisely better to comprehend *the endless conflict within Jesus' environs that never led to any significant social change.* Ancient agrarian or peasant societies were static over long periods of time. Another way to say this is that major families assumed preeminence within static, pyramidal political-economic structures legitimated by powerful rituals of political religion. Not until the modern commercial, industrial, and communications revolutions were values and social forces set in motion to produce the revolutionary social changes associated with democracy and capitalism.

Finally, this book is best appreciated when it is understood that the systems it attempts to understand and explicate for the reader unfold in hierarchical fashion: Mediterranean societies, organized at the core around dominant families, issued in politics and political arrangements (treatment of all other families and clans) that structured both economic life (especially within households but also between households) and religious institutions (beliefs, rituals, practices). We have attempted to instruct readers on using compound terms like "political family" or "domestic religion" to capture these hierarchies of social institutions. In other words, religion and economy are embedded in household or political life; politics is embedded in the lives of dominant families.

As this new edition of *Palestine in the Time of Jesus* encounters a new millennium, we hope it will continue to challenge and inspire its readers to appreciate the distance of Jesus' social context from our own. In a world increasingly disrupted by cultural misunderstandings, and a world in which many are enthralled beneath rather mindless and solipsistic religious extremisms, we hope that this book will also help to free readers from thoughtless absolutisms and to move them toward a greater appreciation of both the social meaning of Jesus of Nazareth and his enduring significance as a human liberator.

Palestine
in the Time
of **Jesus**

The aqueduct at Caesarea Maritima

"The city itself was called Caesarea, and is beautiful in both materials and construction. In addition, he also built a theater of stone in it. And on the south side of the harbor, further back, an amphitheater sufficient to seat a large crowd of people and conveniently located with a view of the sea" (Josephus, *Ant.* 15.340–41). The aqueduct at Caesarea was important for supplying the freshwater needs of the city. A first-century aqueduct was constructed under Herod, and this additional aqueduct was built during the reign of the Roman emperor Hadrian. (Photo by Douglas E. Oakman)

CHAPTER 1

Catching the Drift

Introduction to the Social System of Roman Palestine

Key Terms	agrarian society anachronism cultural system domain ethnocentrism	honor institution Israelite Judean model	norms peasant shame values
Chapter Outline	Growing Awareness of the Biblical Social World / 3 Developing More Adequate Scenarios / 6 Addressing Critiques / 14 Applying the Perspectives / 17 Suggested Reading / 17		

A model is an outline framework, in general terms, of the characteristics of a class of things or phenomena. This framework sets out the major components involved and indicates their priority of importance. It provides guidelines on how these components relate to one another. (Carney 1975:7)

If the purpose of generalization is to simplify one's view of a complex reality and thereby to make it more comprehensible, this can, of course, be done only at the cost of ignoring certain specific elements in the phenomena about which generalizations are being developed. (Kautsky 1982:xii)

The Bible has been a familiar book in American life, although growing biblical illiteracy is making it less so these days. Its stories and metaphors still remain fundamental to knowledgeable discourse within our society. But while we may have been raised from childhood on the birth stories of Jesus or sayings from the Sermon on the Mount, the very familiarity of these texts may instill in us a misleading sense of identification with the Bible's characters and situations.

In the scholarly world, it is common knowledge that a number of serious obstacles stand in the way of our understanding the

1

Bible. Some of these have been obvious for centuries. The fact that the New Testament was written in a foreign language, a form of Greek known as *koine* (common), has been addressed since the early centuries of the Christian era. Even before Jerome translated the Vulgate (the whole Bible in Latin) in the fourth century, New Testament books had been translated into Coptic (an Egyptian language highly influenced by Greek), Syriac (a Semitic language related to Hebrew and Aramaic), and an earlier Latin version.

While learning the biblical languages is fundamental, however, it is far from the only interpretative barrier to an informed reading of the text. The further one stands from the original situation of a document, the more discipline one needs to bridge the gaps. The rise of modern exegetical methods may baffle, enrage, or appear irrelevant to the beginning student; but they have developed, especially since the European Enlightenment (seventeenth to eighteenth centuries), as systematic approaches addressing the gaps between the situations of modern readers and those of the ancient documents.

Research Tip 1

Access our accompanying Web site for this volume at:

www.fortresspress.com/hansonoakman

There you will find additional maps, photos, chronologies, ancient documents, and Web links that complement each chapter.

We study history to help account for the distances in time and historical experience. Historical geography helps us imagine the physical world of the text: the terrain, rainfall, vegetation, natural resources, political boundaries. Archaeology helps to place the Bible within a real material context. A whole range of literary disciplines examines both the shape of the present text (for example, narrative and poetic forms) and its development through oral and written processes: tradition history, form criticism, source criticism, redaction criticism, narrative criticism, literary criticism.

While all of these methods of study are important, it is fundamental to recognize that the biblical texts convey meanings derived through a specific culture and particular social arrangements. For the most part, ancient documents refer to their contemporary social systems only indirectly. They assume that their readers share their world and know what they mean by **patron** [3.40], what sort of taxation is in effect, or how a certain **faction** [3.19] fits into the social matrix. Our difficulty as modern Western readers is to relate meaningfully to documents that are the products of a radically different world in terms of **institutions** [3.30] and **values** [3.56]. We do not share important social understandings with the writers of these texts. Because our social and cultural experiences do not match those of the biblical authors, we can be seriously misled about what they mean (Malina and Rohrbaugh 2003:6–8).

Growing Awareness of the Biblical Social World

While the social sciences have their roots in the nineteenth century, it was not until the twentieth century that they began to emerge in the forms recognizable today: psychology, sociology, anthropology, and all their subdisciplines. It is macro- and systems sociology, together with anthropology, that inform us in this volume. The experiential gaps bridged by these disciplines have to do with culture and social institutions. Not only do we live in a different linguistic environment, historical period, and physical space, but we live in a substantially different social world. At the most obvious level, we live under a different form of government, and this affects our perspective significantly. Even the various forms of modern Judaism and Christianity are significantly different from the **movements** [3.36] that gave them birth in the first century. Industrial capitalism was unknown in ancient societies. But this barely scratches the surface of differences between modern U.S. culture and first-century Palestine.

1. Most of us have never encountered some of the most common first-century Palestinian social institutions, for example, patronage/clientage, household slavery, a resident foreign army. And conversely, first-century Palestinians would not share some of our most common institutional experiences, for example, voting, public education, free choice of spouses and careers. The challenge, then, is to imagine ourselves "into" the world of the people we encounter in the New Testament. This requires conceptualizing scenarios—ways of acting, thinking, valuing, perceiving, and structuring the world—appropriate to their life-world.

2. First-century social institutions were configured and related in ways different from our own. In U.S. society, **religion** [3.48] and **economics** [3.13] are explicit **domains** [3.11] (groups of institutions), while in Palestine, indeed, most of the ancient world, religious and economic institutions were embedded in **kinship** [3.31] or **politics** [3.42]. By embedded we mean that they did not exist substantially apart from the larger domains. They were conceived and they operated as particular manifestations and subsets of political and kinship institutions. Kinship relations interpenetrated political, economic, and religious institutions; **power** [3.44] relations structured village, economic, and religious life.

To illustrate the last point, Herod the Great not only expanded the Jerusalem Temple Mount with tax monies, but built temples in **honor** [3.25] of Roman **emperors** [1.21] and gods. The emperor of Rome was not only supreme commander of the government and military *Princeps* (head man), but was *Pontifex Maximus* (highest "priest") of Roman religion and posthumously voted divine **status** [3.53] by the **Senate** [1.73]. Successive political rulers of Palestine—Macedonians, Ptolemies, Seleucids, and Romans—appointed the Jerusalem **high priests** [1.38]. And immediately before the Roman era, the **Hasmoneans** [1.34] ruled Judea as both **kings** [1.13] and high priests.

By contrast, one of the things that sets U.S. society apart from much of the rest of the world (throughout history!) is our "separation of church and state"; this would have been incomprehensible to people of any religious **group** [3.23] in the ancient Mediterranean. The United States Constitution guarantees that Congress shall not institute a state religion, support any religion with taxes, or prohibit the practice of religion. Because social institutions are interactive, this right (and the laws, regulations, and public policies that enact it) has been a matter of bitter contention within government and the courts throughout U.S. history, for example, in cases involving school prayer, nativity scenes on public property, state support for parochial schools, and Native American use of peyote in religious rites.

In the United States, education as a whole is regulated by the government: the federal Department of Education, the state departments of education, and local elected school boards. But actual schools may be specifically run in any of the four major social domains (family, politics, economy, religion). The majority of K–12 schools are operated by local political bodies—local boards of education, which may be connected to a township, city, or county. But schools may also function as an arm of a religious group—"parochial schools." They may also be run in the economic domain by a private corporation or individual—"proprietary schools," including "virtual" schools online. And children may be educated by their parents or a surrogate in "home schools," a rising phenomenon in the United States since the 1980s.

3. The values-orientation in U.S. society is quite different from first-century Palestine.

One can determine a society's foundational values by asking what criterion of decision-making comes up most often, what dominates the value-vocabulary, and what is threatened the most if it is lost. In the ancient Mediterranean as a whole, and Palestine in particular, scholars have focused upon the "honor/shame complex" as the base values (Peristiany 1965; Peristiany and Pitt-Rivers 1992; Gilmore 1987; and Malina 2001a:27–57). Briefly, the honor/shame complex implies that the maintenance of honor—for one's self, one's family, and one's larger groups—is absolutely vital to life. This entails reputation, status, and sexual identity. The vocabulary of honor and **shame** [3.50] is extensive in Hebrew, Aramaic, Greek, and Latin.

In U.S. society it would be hard to place anything in the culture higher than economics. This does not mean that everyone in the society is a "money-grubber." But it does mean that economics is taken as a fundamental determinant in almost all social transactions, and our metaphors are dominated by economic references. A few examples will make the point:

- One of our most prevalent American phrases is "the bottom line"; referring literally to the final accounting total, it is used metaphorically to mean any central point or conclusion.
- Quality is often assessed in terms of cost: a house, a car, an education, a vacation.
- The most powerful committees in Congress are arguably the finance and budget committees.

- People often leave family, church, and friends to pursue better-paying jobs.
- Couples postpone marriage, and churches do not pursue ministries if they "can't afford it."
- A person's public status correlates closely with his or her income and assets; actors and athletes are given multimillion dollar contracts, while teachers are often laid off when school boards cannot even meet their very basic salaries.

4. The relationship of the individual to the group is significantly different in modern U.S. culture from that in the ancient Mediterranean. U. S. culture places an extraordinarily high value on the individual in a variety of ways (**weak–group orientation** [3.57]). Individual rights are held as not only constitutional, but sacred. Individualism, self-sufficiency, self-esteem, personal identity, self-determination, and autonomy are all highly valued, discussed, and sought after (note the magazine *Self*). Americans may act loyally, but we expect and exercise a high degree of freedom and liberty in our actions and associations. Workers change careers an average of five to seven times during a lifetime. We have a high divorce rate: approximately 45 percent of **marriages** [3.34] end in divorce. A typical Protestant congregation or parish is composed of members who grew up in different denominations. The American ideal is to attend college away from home and move out of one's parents' home. And we are highly mobile in terms of our housing, moving often both within a city and around the country to find employment or a suitable climate for retirement.

In **agrarian societies** [3.1] like that of ancient Palestine, the needs of the group take precedence (**strong–group orientation** [3.54]). Loyalty to family, clan, village, political faction, and religious group is fundamental. The integrity of the group is more important than self-reliance. This entails a highly limited degree of either geographical or social mobility; poor but ambitious farmers do not eventually become wealthy merchants, and farmers from one village do not move to another because they can purchase more productive vineyards. This does not mean that **peasants** [3.41] do not know what an individual is, or that the individual has no importance; rather, the social weight is placed on the group over the individual. This is rooted not in totalitarianism or Orwellian "group-think," but in survival; a peasant family or village cannot sustain itself if everyone "does their own thing." The precariousness of life among peasant subsistence farmers cannot tolerate radical individualism. And the attachment to the family land prohibits treating it as a commodity: it is where their honor has been established, it is their basis for livelihood, and it is where their ancestors are buried.

Modern scholarly treatments of the Bible are not immune from these misunderstandings, and important scholarly works available today on the background to the Gospels have not taken the perspectives offered by the social sciences adequately into account. The contemporary reader requires theory-informed **models** [3.35] or scenarios for reading the Gospels and enhancing the reader's knowledge and understanding of how major social institutions referred to there worked. Models and scenarios, as special glasses, help us to compensate for our own "inexperience" in the biblical world.

Developing More Adequate Scenarios

Social institutions make the value concerns of a social group operational. They are "fixed ways of realizing values. . . . A social institution is like a set of railroad tracks of a specific width laid out in a given direction toward a specific end or goal" (Pilch and Malina 1998: xvii). Institutions are specific sets of social relationships (for example, families, **banking** [1.6], the army, churches) that are concrete, even though they may take on different forms. In the United States, for example, financial institutions are quite diverse while overlapping in function: federal and state banks, savings and loans, thrift and loans, mortgage companies, credit unions, annuity funds, investment groups, moneylenders, and "loan sharks." In American life, the PTA (Parent-Teacher Association) acts as a formal institution that functions to facilitate the interface of two other institutions, the school and the family.

Social institutions can be grouped at a higher level of abstraction into "domains," or what Nolan and Lenski call "institutional systems" (2006). Sociology and anthropology identify four primary social domains: kinship, politics, economics, and religion (some additionally place education and law at this level). Each of these domains is usually

composed of several institutions. Once these domains take on concrete or specific form, they are identifiable as institutions; just as there is no such thing as "fruit" (an abstraction) apart from apples, oranges, pears, "kinship" does not exist apart from marriages and divorces, parent-children relationships, and **inheritance** [3.29] practices. These domains are not absolutely separate spheres of life; rather, they appear as different sets of institutions that may overlap or interact on an occasional or continual basis.

In the past century, the social sciences have centered around two major theoretical streams: structural functionalism and conflict theory. A *structural-functionalist approach* emphasizes the forms of a society, the functions its parts play, and assumes that the society seeks equilibrium among its different parts and groups. The goal is to understand why the social structures and relationships work the way they do and how each part contributes to the efficient working of the whole. Structural functionalism is part of the philosophical tradition of idealism. The major drawback of this approach is that it tends to accept social inequities and the domination of one group over others simply as "givens."

In many ways, the society in which Jesus lived was structurally dysfunctional, since it gave inordinate power and privilege to a very few. A *conflict approach,* therefore, attends to the tensions between social factions, institutions, and subcultures that are the product of power relations in which one group seeks to dominate, control, manipulate, or subdue the others for its own advantage.

	Functionalist	**Conflict**
1. Interests perceived as	Uniting	Dividing
2. Social relations viewed as	Mutually advantageous	Exploitative
3. Social unity achieved by	Consensus	Coercion
4. Definition of society	System with needs	Stage for class struggle
5. Nature of humanity	Requires restraining institutions	Institutions distort basic human nature
6. Inequality viewed as	Social necessity	Unnecessary, promotes conflict
7. The State	Promotes common good	Instrument of oppression
8. Social class	Heuristic concept	Objective social groups with different interests

Figure 1.1 A Comparison of Structural–Functionalist and Conflict Approaches

Conflict theory seeks to understand who benefits from the social structures and how conflict is managed: "lumping it," avoidance, coercion, negotiation, mediation, arbitration, or adjudication. This approach is identified closely with the materialist tradition, mindful that adaptive and economic pressures have shaped social relations. (Figure 1.1 is from Sanders 1977:9, based on work of A. E. Havens.)

The principal theoretical frameworks we employ are macrosociology (which focuses upon the major types of societies in terms of their primary modes of subsistence; Nolan and Lenski 2006); systems sociology, as represented in the work of Talcott Parsons and others (Parsons 1966, 1971, 1978; Bellah 1970; Turner and Beeghley 1974); and cultural anthropology (which focuses upon values and institutions; Keesing 1975; Gilmore 1987; Malina 2001a). First-century Palestine was an advanced agrarian society, and

only kinship and politics were explicit social domains. Economics, religion, and education were all "embedded" in kinship or politics.

The narrower foci of our social-scientific research will be Mediterranean culture and peasant studies and, more specifically, Palestinian society. Besides being an advanced agrarian society, first-century Palestine was shaped by several dominant forces: the Israelite tradition (linguistic, cultural, and religious heritage), the Roman Empire (political control), and **Hellenism** [1.36] (the pervasive cultural influence over the whole Mediterranean and Middle East).

We also take a comparative approach to be not only helpful but essential, since ancient social information is incomplete and social interpretation depends so heavily upon social type and context. Our work attempts to build upon analogies and comparisons to other cultures and societies in order to operate from the known to the unknown. These parallels will derive predominantly from "Third World" (or better: "Two-thirds World") cultures. At various levels of abstraction, cultures that share common characteristics with ancient Palestine inform our understanding of its parts:

- advanced agrarian societies that employ horticulture, plow-farming, viticulture, herding, and fishing;
- societies that are composed predominantly of peasant populations;
- societies that include household slaves but are not "slave economies";
- societies that have clearly demarcated social hierarchies set within aristocratic empires; and
- honor/shame societies.

The closer the analogies to Palestine in terms of time and space, the fewer cultural hurdles one needs to account for; but more distant parallels can also be of use as a result of their common characteristics. For example, sheep and goat herding may play different roles in different cultures, but the animals nonetheless pose similar challenges and requirements, whether in twenty-first-century Kenya or first-century Galilee—they have to be grazed, milked, protected, medically attended, sheared, bred, and exchanged (bought and sold or bartered); they are vulnerable to disease, theft, predation, and wandering. Particular techniques for dealing with these issues may vary, and comparisons are not only informative but vital.

The use of explicit models is vital to a social-scientific approach. This means articulating a clear configuration of how a social structure or institution fits together, what its dynamics entail, where the conflicts lie, and who benefits from it. The alternative to employing an explicit model is not working without presuppositions, but employing an implicit model. The goal of modeling is not to force data into a preconceived mold or pigeonhole. Rather, it presents a hypothesis of a meaningful configuration of the known data and the presentation of a believable scenario for human relationships. The idea is to account for the available data, not dispense with data that does not conform to a preconceived model. It also facilitates proposals to account for missing data. As new or non-comforming data come to light, the model may need to be adjusted, modified, or completely replaced. One must not become so wedded to a particular model that the maintenance of the model takes precedence over the data. Rather, one should work back and forth from data to model and back to data (Malina 1991b).

This book employs two major types of diagrams: (1) systems models that indicate how elements of an institution work or show relations of structural components, and (2) tabular charts that break out components of an institution to highlight their function or composition. Diagrams and models are deployed in chapters as needed, though more general comparative considerations are raised initially in each chapter's "Models" section.

While the social sciences predominate in our methodology, we are also aware that other methods must be taken into account. Since we deal with real life-worlds, history, archaeology, and historical geography come

---

The Mustard Seed

The disciples said to Jesus, "Tell us what the Reign of Heaven is like." He said to them, "It is like a mustard seed, the smallest of all seeds. But when it falls on tilled soil, it produces a large plant and becomes shelter for birds of the sky." (Gos. Thom. 20)

---

into play. Since we deal with texts that have emerged from oral tradition and have gone through a variety of literary processes, questions of tradition history, source, form, and redaction must also be attended to. Our concern, however, is not to focus primarily on literary history or the editorial perspectives of the evangelists, but on the social situation of Palestinian peasant life confronted by Jesus and the earliest groups of his followers.

We work with a number of critical hypotheses about the relationship between Jesus and the Gospels: Jesus died around 30 C.E., during the prefecture (**prefect** [1.61]) of Pontius Pilate (26–36 C.E.). Paul's letters were composed in the 50s C.E. Collections of Jesus material began to be made before the earliest gospel, with at least a first edition of **Q** [2.14] (a collection of Jesus' sayings used by Matthew and Luke) by 50 C.E. A strong scholarly consensus sees the first three New Testament Gospels, called "Synoptics" because of their similar presentation of the story of Jesus, as interdependent narratives.

Mark was written during or immediately after the **First Judean Revolt** [1.28] (66–70 C.E.). Sometime between 75 and 90 C.E., Mark was being used as one of the two major sources, along with Q, in the composition of Matthew and Luke. John, appearing after 90 C.E., formulates the latest Jesus traditions

within the New Testament. Another gospel outside of the New Testament requires mention. The **Gospel of Thomas** [2.5] (discovered in 1945 at **Nag Hammadi** [2.9], Egypt) is a fourth-century Coptic document emphasizing esoteric knowledge as the way to salvation. *Thomas,* however, likely originated out of first-century traditions: three Greek fragments of *Thomas* exist from early in third-century Egypt. Since the *Thomas* tradition originally came from Syria, time had to elapse for the tradition to migrate to Egypt. This puts the gospel's origins back before 200 C.E. Linkage to "Judah the Twin" (Judas Didymus Thomas) and similarity in genre and content to Q suggest an origin in second- or late first-century Syria. *Thomas* is comprised of Jesus' sayings, very much like those of Q, although the form of individual sayings and the order of sayings differ substantially (which speaks against direct borrowing from the completed Synoptics). Further, words of the historical Jesus occasionally seem more accurately preserved in *Thomas* (for example, *Gos. Thom.* 20). Therefore, modern social and historical assessments of Jesus have taken the Thomas tradition quite seriously (see Patterson 1993).

Besides these Gospels, we draw where appropriate or necessary from the **Old** [2.10] and New Testaments, the **Dead Sea**

Scrolls [2.3], the **Apocrypha** [2.1] and **Pseudepigrapha** [2.13], Egyptian papyri, the works of **Josephus** [2.7] and **Philo of Alexandria** [2.12], the **Mishnah** [2.8], the **Talmuds** [2.18] of Palestine and Babylon, and various Roman writers. Many of these writings are available in English translation (consult *glossary 2*: *"Ancient Documents, Collections, and Authors,"* and *bibliography 1*: *"Ancient Documents"*).

Aspects of the issues we discuss are still highly debated by scholars. For instance, contemporary scholarship has not reached substantial agreement on where authentic Jesus material lies within the Gospels or how to identify first-century material within the voluminous traditions from the **rabbis** [1.68]. Only within the past few decades have refined methods of tradition criticism emerged that will perhaps allow greater consensus. A number of recent books on the Jesus traditions have offered careful and detailed analyses of that material (for example, Crossan 1991; Kloppenborg 2000). Such work is extremely important.

Fortunately, we do not always have to decide exactly whether a tradition is "authentic" or how it has assumed the written form we have. We situate discrete narratives and sayings about Jesus within broader social systemic or structural relations so that typical meanings dependent upon knowledge of institutional structures can be recovered. In our perspective, there is significant difference between elite meanings and non-elite meanings, and we examine the Jesus tradition consistently with reference to non-elite interests. Likewise, the rabbinic traditions present a mostly idealized picture of the Jerusalem temple, and we have hazarded to use some of these where a harsher reality or less flattering picture comes through (as we shall discuss related to Hillel's *prosbul* or the sayings of rabbis regarding the high priestly families). These procedures depend upon two important conclusions: (1) **Scribes** [1.72] were embedded in elite interests that preserved both the Jesus and the rabbinic traditions. The formations of the biblical canons were the product of power **elites** [3.14] in both Judean and later Christian communities (Coote and Coote 1990). The Gospels do not obscure the perspectives and concerns of disaffected elites and non-elites. The ministry of Jesus in Galilee took place almost entirely in villages and the countryside among the peasants: farmers, fishers, **artisans** [3.3], and day laborers. His activity involved a serious critique of the "powers that be," a fact that is central, not peripheral, to the tradition. (2) Historians focus on dissonant elements in tradition as clues to historical reconstruction (since later communities tend to idealize their own origins). In the future, a more comprehensive social analysis of both scribal traditions needs to be undertaken (see Horsley 2007). For the present, our approach requires some simplifications and compromises if our study of institutions is to stay within a reasonable compass.

Scholars have worked diligently over the past three centuries to date, locate, and interpret all of these ancient documents. But often the continuities and connections of these documents' life-worlds in terms of cultural practices and social structures have been overlooked. While historians have often focused upon the fine nuances of difference between Judea and Galilee—or even between upper and lower Galilee—they have generally been less interested in seeing the unities at a higher level of abstraction. By comparison, one could reasonably focus on the many differences between Canadian and U.S. societies. The political form of Canadian government is parliamentary, while the United States employs a bicameral Congress; but at a higher level of abstraction, both are constitutional democracies. In anthropological terms, these two countries share a great deal in the way of language, cultural heritage, geography, education, law, religion, kinship patterns, communication, literature, and so forth. It all depends upon what level of abstraction one focuses on. A balance must be maintained between the general and the particular, between the typical and the unique. In social-scientific perspective, our primary focus will be on the typical and general in its application to understanding the particular and unique.

The Terms Judean and Israelite

It is common to read in translations of the Bible as well as in the scholarly literature the term Jew *where we have employed* Judean. *This does not derive from some prejudicial inclination to take something away from the historical Jewish community, but from an interest in being more precise when discussing the first-century scene. The issues are not, however, unambiguous or without problems.*

When comparing the Old Testament, writings of Josephus, New Testament, Philo, and others, one can see that context is everything. What was originally the kingdom of Judah was renamed Yehud as a Persian province. The Romans could refer to the geographical region as Palestina, and to all the inhabitants as Judeans. But they would also use the term Judean *for ethnic Judeans living in Greece, Italy, or Egypt. This is analogous to other ethnic designations. Inside the various regions of greater Palestine, a writer might distinguish a Judean from a Galilean. But in referring to all those with allegiance to the state religion in Jerusalem, they would often use the more encompassing term* Israelite *(for example, John 1:47; Acts 2:22).* Israelite *is also the most common term in the Mishnah.*

As Louis H. Feldman, renowned Josephus scholar at Yeshiva University, notes in his translation and commentary of Josephus's Antiquities: *"I normally translate the Greek term* Ioudaios *as 'Judean' rather than the more customary 'Jew/Jewish,' on the model of other ethnic designations (Egyptian, Babylonian, Athenian, etc.) of the period" (2000:xiii). It is on this basis that we use the terms* Israelite *and* Judean *in this book rather than* Jew.

In addition to Feldman, for the complexity of the historical and linguistic issues, see Schwartz (2005), John H. Elliott (2007), and Mason (2007); but see also Cohen (1999) and Marquis (2007).

A summary of some of the attributes of Palestinian society with which we will deal may help orient the reader to its cultural context (see also the glossaries):

- Foundational values complex: honor/shame orientation
- **Patriarchal** [3.39]: elder males' domination of public life
- **Gender divided** [3.21] in terms of **roles** [3.49] and social space
- Kinship patterns: patrilineal, patrilocal, endogamous, and complex **dowry-giving** [3.12]
- Group orientation: strong-group rather than weak-group
- Domination of cities over villages
- Government: **imperial province** [1.40] of Roman Empire combined with **client–aristocracy** [3.8]
- Patronage/clientage as a powerful mechanism in vertical social relationships
- Advanced agrarian subsistence: plow-farming, viticulture, herding, horticulture, fishing
- Economy: tributary economy in which "surplus" is consumed by a distant, elite minority
- Peasants: formed vast majority of population but were dominated by urban elites
- Life expectancy: approximately twenty years for live births and approximately forty years for those who lived past five
- Religion: centrally regulated by the state, hierarchical, and focused on sacrifice and communal ritual
- Time orientation: taking cultural cues from the tradition rather than merely present needs or anticipation of future exigencies
- Literacy: highly limited; culture passed on predominantly orally

The society of Roman Palestine was not static during this period. It is important to appreciate that institutions were sustained and contested by human agency as well as shaped by tradition and material factors and concerns. A systems model can illustrate major elements shaping all social institutions in the Palestine of Jesus as in figure 1.2.

This model provides an overview of the way Palestinian society in the time of Jesus was structured (see John H. Elliott 1993:64–65), attempts to overcome the problems of anachronistic **ethnocentrism** [3.16] identified above, and indicates why this book assumes the form and structure it has. The graphical aids and detailed discussions of the following chapters elaborate the general perspective offered here.

The *social system* is the general domain of human social institutions. The arrows in the diagram indicate how other factors condition the system; arrows in both directions indicate reciprocal influence. For Palestine in the time of Jesus, and Mediterranean culture generally, kinship institutions conditioned politics; both in turn conditioned (and are conditioned by) religion and economy. Elite families controlled society, which they tended to view as part of their "household." Caesar's "family" (clients, slaves) helped him to administer the far-flung Roman Empire. Education and religion were conducted

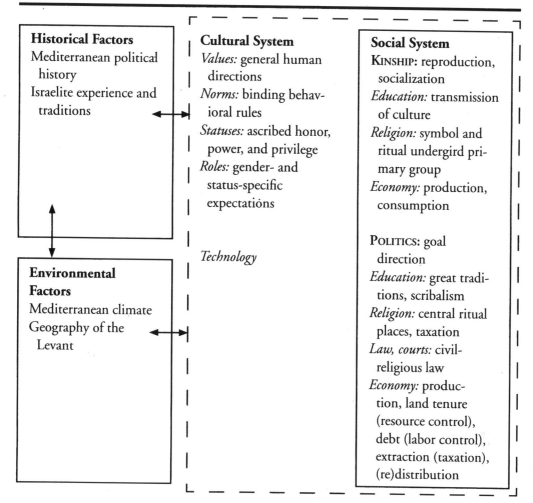

Figure 1.2. A General Model for First-Century Palestinian Society
The social system makes values, norms, and roles of the culture operational. In ancient Palestine, kinship provided the basis for all other institutions.

within both familial and political contexts. Domestic education and religion helped in the socializing of children and the transmission of culture. Domestic economy was concerned with provisioning the household, and its basic goal was consumption.

Political religion, evident in the Jerusalem temple, enforced loyalty to the deity and the payment of taxes ("offerings") through divine law (**ideology** [3.27]) or group pressure. Political education, carried on by organized schools of scribes, led to the authoritative accounts of social arrangements. Scribes also concerned themselves with law. Judean civil law had divine sanction through Moses and affected the operation of the law courts.

The Jesus Movement and Christianity

Just as we distinguish between Judean state religion (organized around the temple and sacrifices, led by priests) and later rabbinic Judaism (organized around the synagogue and the interpretation of the rabbis, codified in the Mishnah and Babylonian Talmud), it is also appropriate to distinguish between the Jesus movement and later Christianity. The movement led by Jesus and his earliest followers was focused on the renewal of Israel under the key phrase "the reign of God." It was solely focused on ethnic Judeans, primarily in Galilee, and one of the earliest designations for the movement seems to be "the Way" (as in Acts 19:23). Christianity is the world religion that developed in the late first century and early second century, spreading throughout Syria, Asia Minor, Greece, Macedonia, Italy, and then the world. It includes the later doctrines of the Trinity, the creeds, the sacraments, and the New Testament canon. The term Christianos *(Christian) is used three times in the New Testament (Acts 11:26; 26:28; 1 Pet 4:16), each time evidently as a derisive term by outsiders. See John H. Elliott (2007).*

However, at the time of Jesus, Hellenistic-Roman law also affected the lives of peasants. Political economy, managed by political kin, was concerned with what was produced, and its major goal was to control the distribution of what was produced.

Culture represents the accumulated symbolic social information necessary for the structuring and directing of the social system. The *culture* box is displayed with a dotted line because culture is borne within the social system by its transmission within the family or political society.

No social system is static, but all societies are conditioned by *historical factors.* For first-century Judea, Israelite experience and traditions were formative of the basic culture, especially of a strong sense of historical purpose (consider the eschatology of apocalyptic Judean writings). Political history, too, played an important role: in Jesus' day, **Judeans** [1.43] had lived under foreign rul-

ers for almost six hundred years. Technology, like tools, pottery, clothing, weapons, influenced the social system in terms of productive capacity or limiting the extent to which power could be projected at a distance.

Social scientists debate the role of ecological adaptation in the formation of human culture and social institutions. Without resolving that debate, it is important to recognize that *environmental factors* like climate and geography affect both culture and social institutions. For example, environmental adaptation in the rugged and climatically challenging eastern Mediterranean world has led to the prevalence of strong-group orientation there.

Addressing Critiques

In this revised edition of *Palestine in the Time of Jesus,* we have been mindful of critical reviews and communications about various aspects of the book. We appreciate that other scholars took the time to read the book and offer constructive criticisms. Perhaps the following remarks will not persuade all, but we will at least give a response.

Harold Hoehner and several others (private communications) have been concerned that the word "Palestine" is used anachronistically, since the Romans did not designate the area *Palaestina Secunda* until Hadrian's time in the second century, and that this usage obscures reference to the area as Judea. This is a fair criticism, but it fails in a number of respects.

The authors of this volume are extremely mindful of the difficulties around a number of emic/etic designations, for example, Judea/Palestine or Judean/Jew (see sidebar on p. 11). In this case, we needed to place emphasis on the etic, macroeconomic realities of a first-century region (the Roman Empire), as well as to characterize social-systemic realities pertaining to all areas. The more general term *Palestine* covers the whole area from the Negeb to Upper Galilee.

Even the emic (first-century) designations are not unambiguous. Ancient or emic usage of the word "Palestine," more as a regional indicator than designation of political/administrative units, goes back to the fifth century B.C.E.: Herodotus, *Histories* 1.105; 2.104, 106; 3.5; 7.89; Ovid in several works (Augustan period); Mela de Chorographia 1.63 (c. 40 C.E.); Pliny, *Nat. Hist.* 5.66 (before 79 C.E.); and even Josephus, *Ant.* 1.145; 8.260; *Ag. Ap.* 1.168–71 (Flavian period):

Nor, again, has our country been ignored even by Herodotus of Halicarnassus, who has an evident, if not explicit, allusion to it. Speaking of the Colchians in his second book, he makes the following statement: "The Colchians, the Egyptians, and the Ethiopians are the only peoples with whom the practice of circumcision is primitive. The Phoenicians and the Syrians of Palestine admit that they learnt it from the Egyptians. The Syrians on the banks of the rivers Thermodon and Parthenius, and their neighbors the Macrones, say that they have adopted it recently from the Colchians. These are the only circumcised peoples in the world, and it is clear that they all imitate the Egyptians. Of the two countries of Egypt and Ethiopia, I cannot say which learned the practice from the other." Herodotus thus says that the Palestinian Syrians were circumcised; but the Judeans are the only inhabitants of Palestine who adopt this practice. He must, therefore, have known this, and his allusion is to them. (LCL revised)

Of a similar nature are the difficulties around the words "Judean" and "Jew." A number of contemporary scholars have insisted that "Judean" is the right translation of *Ioudaios* for our period, as a designation of the way of life in this particular geographic area (see sidebar on p. 11).

Further, Jonathan Reed (in his review in *RBL* 1999) felt that we had obscured differences between Galilee and Judea. We wanted, however, to indicate the political parallels between client rule in Galilee and priestly rule in Judea, and to stress the fundamental similarities of elite and non-elite institutional arrangements in both contexts. Reed seems to want more historical discrimination, but this seems at a level of abstraction finer than we wanted to pursue.

Reed and Richard Demaris (in his *JBL* review) stated that we had overemphasized the Jerusalem temple as the locus of political religion and neglected either its positive features or features of non-elite religion. This is a just criticism until it is remembered that the Jerusalem temple was excoriated in the literature of Qumran and that the Talmud vividly recalls Pharisaic criticism of temple rituals. Moreover, we do investigate the political nature of non-elite religion as a response to this situation. And we read Jesus of Nazareth as active within the political force fields of the religion of the elites. In this edition, we have said a bit more about the synagogue, but we fail to see evidence that it was a dedicated "religious building" at this time (if ever in antiquity). The reader must keep in mind that this book's systems perspectives highlight through successive chapters the political nature of economy and religion as nondiscrete domains.

Pieter Craffert (in private communication) asked in a similar vein: "Do you assume that what applies for Judea also applies for Galilee? One cannot deny that the temple was an important institution in Judea, but is it also the case for Galilee? I ask the question because in your chapter it is not always clear what you mean/refer to. I get the impression that you also alternate between Judea and Galilee and Palestine in order not to ascribe everything to Galilee on an equal base with Judea. Is this the case?" Certainly this is a fair question. Two notions immediately come to mind: Jesus' conflict with the Pharisees, which we take to belong to his context as a conflict with temple-adherents (see below, p. 138), and the question about the temple tax (Matt 17:26). Part of the conflict in Roman Palestine, which the Romans probably happily encouraged under a prevalent divide and conquer (*divide et impera*) policy, was that between the Herods/Herodians and priests/Pharisees.

Mary Ann Sawicki (two reviews in *RSR* as well as in remarks in *Crossing Galilee*) is highly critical of our methodology. She thinks that we not only draw upon "outdated" social theory, but make a fundamental mistake in identifying "first-century Palestine as a 'Mediterranean' society with an 'honor-shame' ethos." The reader will have to decide whether this is a fundamental methodological flaw, in light of her book and the voluminous scholarship on honor and shame. She also mentions errors of historical fact but does not disclose where they are (234).

A number of these criticisms could be answered at great length. We still want our book, however, to remain within a manageable compass, in order best to serve the audiences envisioned. And we believe that theoretical modeling has helped us to get the emphases just right regarding the social structures and social conflicts of first-century Palestine.

Applying the Perspectives

1. What stands out for you as the largest cultural gap between your own experiences and those of a person from first-century Palestine? What steps are necessary to bridge that gap?

2. Do you agree or disagree with our point that economics plays a dominant role in U.S. values orientation? Provide reasons for your point of view. Can you think of specific indicators that would add to our list highlighting the centrality of economics in U.S. culture?

3. Identify ways in which U.S. culture is highly functional and highly dysfunctional. How would these differ from first-century Palestine?

4. If first-century Palestine was an advanced agrarian society, how would you characterize contemporary U.S. society? What are the distinguishing marks of this form of society? What are the most significant ways it differs from an advanced agrarian society?

5. What proportion of the U.S. population lives and works on farms? How does that compare with first-century Palestine? What difference does this make in the functioning of each society?

Suggested Reading

Our focus on institutions and social structure is distinctive. For perspectives on Mediterranean culture similar to those of this book, compare Neyrey (1991), Malina (2001), Malina and Rohrbaugh (2003), Pilch and Malina (1998), Rohrbaugh (2007), Pilch (2008), and Oakman (2008). The reader will find Duling (2003) to be an excellent introduction to the New Testament, with highly developed sensitivities to its agrarian social world.

For useful accounts of the development of social-scientific criticism of the Bible, the reader should consult John H. Elliott (1993) and Osiek (1992). Elliott's book has a fairly comprehensive bibliography of contributions to 1993 in this area. For reading guides on the New Testament and social science issues, see Rohrbaugh (1996).

For a comparative approach to U.S. culture, see Stewart and Bennett (1991).

Many excellent Bible atlases are available for help in locating places mentioned in this book. We recommend especially Aharoni et al. (1993). For basic information regarding historical geography, consult Avi-Yonah (1977). For information on the general archaeology of Palestine, see Murphy-O'Connor (1992), Finegan (1992), Rousseau and Arav (1995), and Meyers (1997). For specific issues relating to Jesus and archaeology, see the articles in Charlesworth (2006b). And for an excellent social history of the Jesus movement in the first century, see Stegemann and Stegemann (1999).

Jerusalem house (interior)

This elegant house belonged to an elite family in Jerusalem and dates from the Roman era. It is located in the Wohl Museum. "There was a rich man who dressed in purple and fine linen and who feasted sumptuously every day" (Luke 16:19). (Photo by Douglas E. Oakman.)

CHAPTER 2

All in the Family

Kinship in Agrarian Roman Palestine

The lineage record of Jesus Christ, son of David, son of Abraham. (Matt 1:1)

And his mother and his brothers arrived; and standing outside they sent to him, calling him. And a crowd was sitting about him; and they said to him, "Your mother and your brothers and your sisters are outside asking for you." And he replied, "Who are my mother and brothers?" And looking around at those who sat about him, he said, "Here are my mother and my brothers. Whoever does God's will is my brother, and sister, and mother." (Mark 3:31-35//Matt 12:46-50//Luke 8:19-21//Gos. Thom. 99)

Introduction

Questions

The Gospel of Matthew begins with a comment about Jesus' "lineage record" (1:1) followed by a **genealogy** [3.22] running from Abraham to Joseph and then Jesus (1:2-17). And in the Synoptic Gospels (Mark 3:31-35 and parallels) Jesus' saying seems to redefine family.

- What sort of family configuration was prevalent in Roman Palestine?
- Why would the Gospel writer want to begin his narrative about Jesus with such a lineage record?
- What sort of society was this that valued a person's genealogy?
- Why are David and Abraham emphasized as Jesus' key ancestors?
- How can Jesus be called "the Son of God" elsewhere in Matthew and also be a part of Joseph's genealogy?
- Can we tell whether Jesus himself was concerned with his ascribed, genealogical **honor** [3.25]?

- How does Jesus' saying on family relate to the traditional basis of Mediterranean honor rooted in one's family?
- Would Jesus' family hear this saying as praiseworthy or shameful?
- In what sense can "doing God's will" create a new kin-group?
- What was the traditional relationship between a mother and sons, between brothers and sisters, and between brothers in ancient Palestine?
- What was the expected relationship between the family and outsiders?

Models

In the simplest forms of society, hunter-gatherers and pastoral nomads (from prehistoric to modern times), all **institutions** [3.30] are embedded in **kinship** [3.31] (Nolan and Lenski 2006). The family's patriarch, matriarch, or clan elders are the only "political" structures. Together the family hunts game and gathers nuts, fruit, berries, and tubers for subsistence or herds sheep and goats; and trade is carried out on a barter basis between families. The religious structures are also formed around the family: worship of ancestral gods, clan leaders with sacramental functions, with the home, field, or camp functioning as sacred space.

In ancient Mediterranean societies during the first century, kinship was still the primary social **domain** [3.11]. That is to say, virtually no social relationship, institution, or **value** [3.56] set was untouched by the family and its concerns. But it was also no longer the only explicit domain. In these advanced **agrarian societies** [3.1], **politics** [3.42] had also contributed an identifiably separate set of institutions, even though heavily affected by kinship structures and relationships (see chapter 3).

The social domains (or institutional systems) addressed by cultural anthropologists (kinship, politics, **economics** [3.13], **religion** [3.48]) are never discrete entities that operate in isolation from one another; they are interactive in every society. But beyond interaction, one sphere may be embedded in another. By this we mean that its definition, structures, and authority are dictated by another sphere. As Malina has demonstrated, religion in the ancient Mediterranean (and specifically with regard to Israelite religion) was always embedded in either politics or kinship (1986; see chapter 5 below).

Kinship in ancient Israel and Judah, as well as in first-century Palestine, was affected by the political sphere especially in terms of law, for example, incest, rape, **marriage** [3.34], divorce, paternity, and inheritance. But kinship also affected politics, most notably in **patron/client relationships**

[3.40; 3.8] and developing **networks** [3.37] of **"friends"** [3.20] (see chapter 3). Kinship was affected by religion in terms of **purity** [3.45], for example, regulating who could have sex with whom and the ethnic

---

Research Tip 2

To find social-scientific interpretations of particular Gospel passages, good places to begin are Bruce J. Malina and Richard L. Rohrbaugh's two commentaries:

- *Social-Science Commentary on the Synoptic Gospels*, 2nd ed. (2003)
- *Social-Science Commentary on the Gospel of John* (1998)

Also see these three volumes of essays:

- Jerome H. Neyrey, editor, *The Social World of Luke-Acts* (1991)
- Richard L. Rohrbaugh, *The New Testament in Cross-Cultural Perspective* (2007)
- Douglas E. Oakman, *Jesus and the Peasants* (2008)

To find interpretations of particular values in social-scientific perspective, a good place to begin is the volume edited by John J. Pilch and Bruce J. Malina: *Handbook of Biblical Social Values*, 2nd ed. (1998).

---

and religious **status** [3.53] of one's spouse. And kinship affected religion (embedded in politics) in terms of **descent** [3.10], especially in the importance laid on the lineages of **priests** [1.62] and their wives, but also by regulating membership in the political religion for the laity. Finally, kinship was interactive with the economic sphere in terms of occupations, **dowry** [3.12] and inheritance, and land tenure.

Emmanuel Todd has constructed a social theory that attempts to define the basic family forms manifested in the world and to account for the correlation between family structures and social systems: political, philosophical, economic, or religious **ideologies** [3.27] (1985). He attempts to counter the Marxist claim that economics is the root of all ideology. He analyzes a set of three polarized variables: *liberty/authority* (What is the basis for spouse choice: freedom of choice, oldest generation chooses, custom decides, or no rules?); *equality/inequality* (Is the inheritance divided among the surviving children, or does only one child inherit, and do the married children reside with the parents?); and ***endogamy*** [3.15]/***exogamy*** [3.17] (Is the social ideal to marry a

	SOCIETIES	
Variables	First-Century Palestine	Twentieth-Century U.S.A.
Family Form	Endogamous community (multigenerational)	Absolute nuclear (dual-generational)
Spousal Choice	Controlled by custom and parents	Free choice by couple
Marriage Strategy	Endogamous (ideal)	Exogamous (by law)
Marriage Arrangement	Betrothal (families' negotiation)	Engagement (individuals' commitments)
Wedding Endowment	Formal: dowry, indirect dowry, and bridewealth	Informal: family gifts
Postmartial Residence	Patrilocal (with groom's parents)	Neolocal (new household)
Cohabitation of Married Sons with Parents	Yes	No
Economic Function	Producing and consuming unit	Consuming unit
Geographical and Social Mobility	Severely restricted, thus closed networks	Limited restrictions, thus open networks
Inheritance Distribution	Oldest son: double Other sons: single Daughters: dowries	No inheritance rules*

*While the U.S. has complex laws relating to inheritance, individuals are free to leave their money and possessions to whomever they choose and may include or exclude any or all of their children. (Adapted from Hanson 1994:184)

Figure 2.1 Comparative Kinship

close relative, or is this excluded by incest rules?) (1985:19–32).

The resulting possibilities are seven family types: absolute nuclear, egalitarian nuclear, authoritarian, exogamous community, endogamous community, asymmetrical community, and anomic. Todd's theory brackets out African family systems, which compose approximately 6 percent of the world's population. He does this because the large number of variables and the flux in their family relationships make it difficult for the researcher to integrate their family forms with the most common configurations.

If we employ Todd's **model** [3.35], it is helpful to keep three issues in mind. First, he is not arguing that every family in a given society follows the scenario precisely. Rather, he is constructing ideal types that the society values and a significant percentage of the population employs. Second, family forms are relatively constant over time and in **peasant** [3.41] societies in particular (1985:vii). Third, while an important aspect of Todd's hypothesis is that family types correlate one-to-one with ideologies (17), it is not necessary to concur in order to use his family model as a useful tool. We will focus here on the "endogamous community family" and the "absolute nuclear family."

The endogamous community family is the best description of the family type most common in ancient Israel as well as in Roman Palestine. Its characteristics are "1) equality between brothers established by inheritance rules; 2) cohabitation of married sons with their parents; and 3) frequent marriage between the children of brothers" (1985:133).

In Israelite and later Mishnaic law, polygyny (multiple wives simultaneously) was also permitted—up to four wives for "commoners" (Josephus, *Ant.* 17.14; *m. Ket.* 10.5) or even five (*m. Ker.* 3.7) and up to eighteen for a **king** [1.13] (*m. Sanh.* 2.4). And while Mishnaic law stipulates the rule of "double portion" for the oldest son, each child inherits (Luke 12:13; 15:12; *Gos. Thom.* 72; *m. B. Qam.* 9.10; *B. Batra* 8.1–4). This family type persists in the modern Arab world, as well as in Turkey, Iran, and surrounding regions.

The most common family form found in the United States is the absolute nuclear family. This is characterized by "1) no precise inheritance rules, frequent use of wills; 2) no cohabitation of married children with their parents; and 3) no marriage between the children of brothers" (1985:99). Besides the United States, this family form predominates in the Anglo-Saxon world (Great Britain and many of its former colonies), the Netherlands, and Denmark (Williams 1970:51–97).

Figure 2.1 summarizes some of the key variables in analyzing kinship configurations as they are manifested in first-century Palestine in comparison to contemporary practices in the United States. Both sides of the chart represent generalizations about the respective societies. Especially because the United States is composed of so many immigrants and includes such a variety of subcultures, variations certainly occur, even concerning those behaviors regulated by law. For example, the preferred "postmarital residence" (where a newly married couple resides) in the United States is "neolocal" (that is, a "new place"; they live in their own apartment or house). But due to financial constraints, a couple might choose to live with the bride's or groom's family for a limited time. The point of the generalizations is not to eliminate all variations, but to clarify the largest patterns of behavior.

Gender

At the heart of understanding any set of family relations are assumptions about gender: What are the social **roles** [3.49] and expectations for males and females in the society? These conventional configurations are the product of a society's worldview. Drawing boundaries, setting goals, and articulating fears emerge from this worldview. Some of these male/female differences may be stipulated in law, but for the most part, they have to do with the assumptions operating deep in the society's structures, arrangements, and habits. Moreover, most societies assume that their gender configurations are "obvious" and simply "natural": the ways in which males and females operate in society are established in nature, rather than in culture (1 Cor 11:4-16). This assumption could hardly be fur-

ther from the truth, as established by the last century of ethnographic and cross-cultural research.

First-century Palestine was no different. Palestine (and the ancient Mediterranean as a whole) was **patriarchal** [3.39] in its structures and assumptions, and this was a foundation stone in its worldview. This means that the public aspects of society were heavily controlled by males, and the older males over the younger. In these ancient patriarchal societies, the privileged status of the male stemmed from the assumption that his "seed" was what created a child (Wis 7:1-2); in other words, the mother provided the womb for the birth of his children. This male primacy was also legitimated through the Israelite creation story: God created males first; males, therefore, have the superior position (Gen 2:7-23; 1 Cor 11:7-9). **Philo** [2.12] (an Israelite philosopher, theologian, and diplomat who lived in Alexandria, Egypt, in the first century) went so far as to say that males and females have two different types of souls (*Laws* 3.178; see sidebar below), reflecting assumptions common among Greek philosophers.

Philo on Gender

There are two kinds of soul, just as there are two genders in humans. The first is a masculine soul, belonging to men; the other a female soul, as found in women. The masculine soul devotes itself to God alone, as the father and creator of the world and the cause of all things that exist. But the female soul depends upon all the things that are created and that may be destroyed, and which puts forth, as it were, the hand of its power in order that in a blind sort of way it may lay hold of whatever comes across it, clinging to a generation that has innumerable changes and variations, when it should cling to the unchangeable, blessed, and thrice-happy divine nature. (Laws 3.178)

But **gender division** [3.21] is also rooted in male fears of the female. Ancient Israelites did not simply construe females as different but as potentially dangerous. A man can be overpowered by a woman simply by looking at her (Philo, *Vir.* 38–40). A daughter's chastity is described as the "weak link" in the family's **shame** [3.50] (Sir 7:24; 42:9-11). And women are often categorized as fundamentally sinful, for example, in the proverbial statements of Ben Sira:

> Do not look upon anyone for beauty,
>   and do not sit among women.
> For moths emerge from garments,
>   and a woman's wickedness emerges
>   from a woman.
> Better is the wickedness of a man
>   than a woman who does good.
> And it is a woman who brings shame and
>   disgrace.
> (Sir 42:12-14; see also Philo, *Hypoth.*
> 11.14-17)

These negative statements must also be put in context with positive statements made about wives and mothers. A "good wife" is grand (Prov 31:10-31), and mothers are deserving of their sons' respect, honor, and attention (Exod 20:12; Prov 1:8; 6:20). A wife or mother, a daughter or sister is worthy of love, care, and respect, but she must also remain within the parameters set by the males and must constantly be kept in check by the adult males of the family. Males must guard the females within the family and continually be on guard against females from the outside.

A clear articulation of gender roles and social space in daily practice is also provided by Philo:

Marketplaces, and council chambers, and courts of justice, and large groups and assemblies of crowds, and a life in the open-air full of arguments and actions relating to war and peace are suited to men. But taking care of the house and remaining at home are the proper duties of women; the virgins having their rooms in the center of the house within the innermost doors, and the full-grown women not going beyond the vestibule and outer courts. For there are two types of states: the larger and the smaller. The larger ones are called "cities" and the smaller ones "households."

And the superintendence and management of these is allotted to the two genders separately: men having the governance of the larger, which is called a "polity," and women that of the smaller, which is called "economy" [household management]. Therefore, do not let a woman busy herself about those things which are beyond the province of economy; but let her cultivate solitude, and do not let her be seen going about like a woman who walks the streets in the sight of other men, except when it is necessary for her to go to the temple, if she has any proper regard for herself. And even then, do not let her go at noon when the market is full, but after the majority of the people have returned home, like a well-born woman, a real and true citizen, performing her vows and her sacrifices in tranquility, so as to avert evils and to receive blessings. (*Laws* 3.169, 171; see also *Ag. Flacc.* 89)

Division is accentuated in the prohibition for women to enter the inner courts of the Jerusalem temple (Josephus, *Ant.* 15.419) and such places as athletic games (Philo, *Laws* 3.178). Furthermore, garments were also strictly identified as gender-specific (Deut 22:5; *Ant.* 4.301; Philo, *Vir.* 18–21), as were hairstyles (1 Cor 11:14-15). From these passages, we can see that ancient Israelites replicated their perceptions of gender in social roles, behaviors, dress, spaces, times, and attitudes. To modern Western ears this may seem like simple male chauvinism. But our own assumptions about male and female roles are no less socially constructed and interpreted.

The results of ancient forms of gender division were heightened expectations that males and females would function differently. Household management was for females, field management for males. Public representation of the family in negotiations, in the making of contracts, and in court was for males. Informal familial connections to other families was for females (marriage plans, for example). Sacrificing at the temple was for males. Childrearing was for females. Only males functioned as priests. Only females functioned as midwives. Formal education was limited to males. Male and female clothing had to be carefully distinguished. These are all generalizations, and they are affected by status as well as gender. Education, for example, was primarily limited to **elite** [3.14] males; peasants had little time

or need for advanced literacy. Elite females seem to have had more flexibility in their marital arrangements than non-elites.

This division of the genders is also made clear in the fundamental Mediterranean values of honor and shame. Males are expected to embody the family's honor in their virility, boldness, sexual aggression, and protection of the family. This is symbolized in the male's penis and testicles. Females are expected to keep the family from shame by their modesty, restraint, sexual exclusivity, and submission to male authority; this is symbolized in the female's hymen. All the social roles of husband/wife, grandfather/grandmother, father/mother, son/daughter, brother/sister, uncle/aunt, male cousin / female cousin take their definitions from these assumptions about male and female roles, behaviors, dress, and attitudes.

Genealogy and Descent

Genealogical Systems and Genealogies

The particulars of ancestral background carry little practical importance within contemporary U.S. society. It is a commonplace that we are a "melting pot" culture, composed of every conceivable national, ethnic, and linguistic **group** [3.23] (although some have suggested "mixed salad" as a better image). We may have been raised with cultural stereotypes and prejudices about groups we consider "outsiders," whether based on race, ethnicity, regional origins, or economic status. But we seldom interpret the meaning of "insiders'" social status in terms of their long-term family lineage. If a job applicant from Senegal, for instance, listed her tribal group and clan and the genealogy of her family on a résumé and sent it to an American corporation, her potential employer would not know what to make of it. This information would only be meaningful and clearly communicate her status to those within the same kinship system.

Genealogies are a historical curiosity or a hobby in the United States, except in rare instances when they are ascribed importance within a particular group (such as the Mormons or the Daughters of the American Revolution). It is in traditional, honor/shame cultures that genealogies are of great importance—where oral tradition is the primary means of communicating culture and in which honor and shame are the foundational values. It is for these cultural reasons that the biblical genealogies are meaningless to most modern Western readers.

A "genealogy" is a particular type of "list" (note also in the Bible: king list, administrative list, booty list, itinerary). It is a list of relatives arranged by generation, but it may skip any number of generations for lack of information, to achieve schematic design, or to emphasize the importance of particular members. The social setting of the genealogy is the domestic group (family, clan, or tribe) that depends upon this information primarily for inheritance rights, marriage eligibility, and social status. But it is easily adaptable for use by the military, state, cult, or economic group. While the roots of genealogies are oral (Wilson 1977:11–55), they were also written down as institutional records or included as parts of literary works, such as those in the Bible. The intention of any genealogy

must be assessed in terms of its institutional setting, for one's genealogy may be used to establish religious purity, rights to political leadership, inheritance rights, marriage eligibility, and ethnic connections.

Genealogies appear in two basic forms: "unilineal" and "segmented." A unilineal genealogy traces one descendant per generation (father, son, grandson, great-grandson) from a prior generation. In its simplest form it consists of "*A* fathered *B*, *B* fathered *C*"; or "the son of *A* is *B*, the son of *B* is *C*." This can be made more complex by adding material, as in the genealogy of Adam in Genesis 5:1-32 and 9:28-29—birth report, length of life, and death report.

A segmented genealogy traces the descendants considered "relevant" from a prior generation (multiple brothers, sisters, cousins): "*A* fathered *B*, *C*, and *D*; *B* fathered *L*, *M*, *N*; *C* fathered *R*, *S*, *T*; *D* fathered *X*, *Y*, *Z*"; or "the children of *A* are *B*, *C*, and *D*." But both unilineal and segmented genealogies can easily be expanded into narrative form (Gen 5:1—9:29). The relevance of a particular member of a descent group to the genealogy is dependent upon the specific intention of its composition.

Genealogies do not have one simple meaning, function, or compositional form, even when they concern actual biological links; they are always complex social constructs. They may be unilineal or segmented; patrilineal (following the father's line), matrilineal (following the mother's line), or cognatic (following parts of the father's and mother's lines); include and exclude individuals or groups; lump descendants together without names (for example, "other sons," "two daughters"); and vary in breadth, depth, and fluidity. But genealogies may also be composed to demonstrate social links other than biology (for example, relationships between allied groups). These are all variables, and so how one composes a genealogy reflects one's social values, perspective, and specific goals. "All of them are accurate when their differing functions are taken into consideration" (Wilson 1975:182). But one must add to Wilson's insight that they are all "accurate" *given their particular construction of reality and cultural matrix.*

Written genealogies are less flexible in adjusting to the shifting honor of an individual or a segment of the lineage than are oral genealogies, which can be continually adapted to new situations. But both oral and written genealogies demonstrate fluidity. Once a genealogy is taken up into a piece of literature (Genesis, Matthew, Luke, or **Josephus's** [2.7] *Antiquities*), however, it can be employed by the author for any number of purposes, for example, to emphasize a narrative theme, claim social validation for the characters or narratives, provide historical or social context, bridge a gap in the narrative tradition, or facilitate chronological speculation about the "Great Year" or world cycles (Johnson 1988:77–82).

But what social functions may a genealogy serve on its own terms? Why mention one at all? We can list several interrelated possibilities:

1. To establish the significant kin-group to which one belongs, tracing a map of social relationships and the continuity of a particular family (2 Sam 9:6)
2. To embody the honor of the family in a list of names (1 Sam 9:1)
3. To identify potential marriage partners within the family: endogamy (Josephus, *Ant.* 17.12–16)
4. To identify the actual "outsiders" who were allowed to marry into the kin-group: exogamy (*Ant.* 18.130–41)
5. To make a political claim to leadership or office by identifying relevant ancestors (1 Kgs 13:2)
6. To assert inheritance or other family rights; thus gender, order of birth, and mother are all key issues (2 Sam 3:2-5; 5:13-16)
7. To establish membership in the religious group for which heredity is important (1 Chr 9:1; Ezra 2:59-63; 10:18-44)
8. To establish the right to hereditary offices (Exod 28:1; Lev 16:32)

Descent

Descent is related to, but not identical with, genealogy. While a genealogy is an actual list, **descent** [3.10] is a principle or set of principles that establishes the series of links that connects the members of a kin-group to a common ancestor. Three types of descent principles may be employed in any society:

patrilineal ("agnatic") descent, from an ancestor down through a series of male links (that is, through the ancestor's son, his son's sons, his son's sons' sons, etc.);

matrilineal ("uterine") descent, from an ancestress down through a series of females (through daughter, daughter's daughter, etc.);

cognatic descent, from an ancestor or ancestress through a series of links that can be male or female or any combination of the two (Keesing 1975:17).

Like genealogies, the descent principles employed mirror the social values of the society. The honor of kin-groups in traditional Mediterranean societies is virtually always based upon the patrilineal principle. This is the result of their social structures in which the males manifest and symbolize the kin-group's honor to the public world. This is rooted in a patriarchal system that normally gives males institutional precedence in terms of politics, kinship, economics, and religion, as well as the major substitutions of law and education. Since most traditional Mediterranean societies were (and are) patrilocal (the married couple resides in the home or neighborhood of the husband's family), the women and children come under the oldest male's authority and are embedded in his honor.

Carol Delaney (1986) has demonstrated that both fatherhood (paternity) and motherhood (maternity) are social constructs, variously expressed (see "Gender" above). In traditional, patriarchal, Mediterranean societies, the father's sperm is perceived to be the creative element, and the mother is the vessel that nourishes the seed. She notes that modern Islamic villagers in Turkey readily describe the mother as the "field" into which the father plants his "seed," based upon that metaphor complex in the Qur'an (Sura 2.233). This perception is that the father's seed determines the nature of the child (and thus the patriarchal social configuration of marriage, inheritance, living arrangements). This "monogenetic" view (everything from a single origin) of procreation is consistent with the broader cultural matrix and cosmology connected to monotheism (1986:496–98).

This is articulated further in the form of gender differentiation and body symbolization:

> In the Turkish village men are imagined to have creative power within them, which gives them a core of identity, self-motivation or autonomy. Women lack the power to create and therefore to project themselves. Men's bodies are viewed as self-contained while women's bodily boundaries oscillate and shift, for example, in developing of breasts and the swelling of pregnancy; they leak in menstruation and lactation, and are permeable in intercourse and birth. Physical attributes, filtered through this logic, take on moral qualities. (1986:499)

Delaney's research is focused on modern Turkish villages; she also makes a few random references, however, to biblical texts (Gen 1–3; 12:1-3). Delaney's conclusions, that the father is the sole creative force in childbirth and that the monotheistic God as creator and father is ideologically connected with this monogenetic view of birth, are reflected in

Old Testament [2.10] and New Testament passages (Jer 31:1-37; Wis 7:1; 1 Cor 15:35-58; *Gos. Thom.* 53; see Hanson 1989a).

That patrilineal descent is sometimes augmented with cognatic descent indicates that the establishment of women's honor is sometimes necessary to provide nuances within the patriarchal line (Keesing 1975: 20). This is especially important if the woman has increased the ascribed honor to the paternal family (for example, David's royal wife, Michal; 1 Sam 18:27) or has acquired honor through some virtuous or courageous act (for example, Ruth and Judith; Ruth 2:10-12; Jdt 13:18-20). In Israelite priestly families the wife's descent is important for purity reasons (for example, Elizabeth, the mother of John the Baptizer; Luke 1:5). But an additional motivation for including women in a genealogy is to differentiate the wife or concubine through whom the line is being traced over against other mothers (for example, David's sons: Adonijah from Haggith and Solomon from Bathsheba; 1 Kgs 2:13). Thus cognatic descent can indicate secondary lines of relationship, rights, or honor.

Marriage

Marriage is a sexual, economic, and (at times) political and religious relationship contracted between families (or segments of the same family) for a male and a female. In preindustrial, traditional societies, marriage is seldom (if ever) solely an arrangement between a man and woman; this is particularly true of first marriages. Herod the Great, for example, did not merely choose Mariamme, the

Hasmonean [1.34] princess, as his wife; he made a marriage contract with her *family* (Josephus, *War* 1.241). The parties involved do not act as individuals but as members of households. Thus we must pursue a social, rather than an individualistic, interpretation of marriage.

One implication of this is that it is not a matter of individuals who become "engaged." The U.S. custom of "engagement" is the period of dating, counseling, getting to know one another, and making plans together. In the ancient Mediterranean, "betrothal" was the practice (Matt 1:18). Like the U.S. custom, this describes the process prior to marriage. But it is not the period for the couple to get to know one another better; it is the period in which the male and female are promised to each other (usually by their families). It is also the process during which the families negotiate the dowry, **indirect dowry** [3.28], and **bridewealth** [3.5] arrangements (see below). And it may take place shortly before the wedding or even years before children are ready for marriage.

The **Mishnah's** [2.8] saying about the Israelite male's "times of life" indicates eighteen as the age for marriage (*m. 'Abot* 5.21), but no early legal traditions survive *regulating* the age of marriage. The first stage of the marriage was a betrothal, accompanied by a meal at the woman's home (*m. Pes.* 3.7) and the groom's payment of the indirect dowry (*m. Ket.* 5.2). The betrothal was a binding agreement, and a formal divorce was necessary to break it (Matt 1:18-19). The marriage itself was celebrated with a feast put on by the groom's father (Matt 22:2; 25:1-13; Luke 14:8-11; *m. Šebi.* 7.4; *Hal.* 2.7) that lasted seven days (*m. Neg.* 3.2) or longer (Tob 8:19-20). The basic parts of the wedding were

1) preparation of the bride, 2) transfer of the bride from her father's home to that of the groom, 3) the bride's introduction into the home of the groom, and 4) blessings and festivities within the husband's home. (Safrai 1976:757)

The impediments to a legal marriage for Israelites were descent (near relatives as defined in Leviticus 18 and 20) and purity (no Israelite/Gentile marriage, an adulteress could not marry her partner in adultery, a man could not remarry his former wife if she had remarried in the meantime, nor could a castrated man or an insane person marry) (Falk 1974:514–15).

Endogamy

Marriage between close kin-group members is known as "endogamy." In certain regions of the world (including the Middle East), marriage between the children of two brothers or two sisters (parallel cousins) or between the children of a brother and a sister (cross-cousins) ranges from 19 to 60 percent (Todd 1985:19). This relaxation of the "incest taboo" (restriction of close relatives as sex partners and spouses) may be the result of wanting to retain property and wealth within the kin-group, to consolidate **power** [3.44], to maintain cultic purity, and to protect the group from outsiders.

From antiquity to modern times, endogamy in its various forms has been one of the key characteristics of the eastern Mediterranean societies. Abraham, for example, was very concerned that Isaac take a wife from his kin-group (Genesis 24). But what evidence do we have for the **Hellenistic** [1.36] and Roman eras?

The books of Tobit and Judith (both third to second century B.C.E.) in the **Apocrypha** [2.1] mention that the marriages of all the main characters, Tobias and Anna, Tobit and Sarah, and Manasseh and Judith, were unspecified forms of endogamy (Tob 1:9; 3:15-17; 4:12-13; Jdt 8:2). In the book of *Jubilees* (an Israelite writing that retells the stories of Genesis; second century B.C.E.) in the **Pseudepigrapha** [2.13], several forms of endogamy are mentioned, while in Genesis most of these men are mentioned without specifying the wife's name or relationship to the husband. Note the following abbreviations used in the social sciences: B = brother; D = daughter; F = father; H = husband; M = mother; S = son; W = wife; Z = sister. An equal sign (=) indicates a marriage; thus read *FBS* = *FBD*: father's brother's son marries father's brother's daughter. See figure 2.2. By making these marriage identifications explicit, the author of *Jubilees* indicates that endogamy was the Israelite ideal prior to the first century C.E. (*Jub.* 41:2).

Information concerning marriages in the **Herodian** [1.37] family comes from Josephus. It is most helpful to us in studying first-century Palestine, because we can track this kin-group for more than eight generations. Thirty-nine Herodian family members

Brother/Sister (*B = Z* or *FS = FD*)

Cain = 'Awan (*Jub.* 4:9)

Seth = 'Azura (4:11)

Enos = Noam (4:13)

Kenan = Mu'aleleth (4:14)

Abram = Sarai (12:9)

Parallel Cousins (*FBS = FBD*)

Jared = Baraka (4:16)

Enoch = Edni (4:20)

Methusalah = Edna (4:27)

Lamech = Betenos (4:28)

Noah = 'Emzara (4:33)

Shelah = Mu'ak (8:6)

Serug = Melka (11:7)

Miscellaneous Forms of Endogamy

Mahalalel = Dinah (*FB = BD*; 4:15)

Terah = 'Edna (*MBS = FZD*; 11:14)

Arpachshad = Rasu'eya (*MFB = BDD*; 8:1)

Isaac = Rebecca (*FFBS = FBSD*; 19:10)

Jacob = Leah (*FZS = MBD*; 28:3)

Jacob = Rachel (*FZS = MBD*; 28:9)

(Adapted from Hanson 1989b:143)

Figure 2.2 Endogamous Marriages in *Jubilees*

entered into twenty-two endogamous marriages (accounting for multiple marriages); thirty-four of those individuals were Herodian blood relatives. Of those marriages, seventeen were between blood relatives, and five were between relatives by marriage. The marriages to blood relatives are all different types, although *FBS = FBD* and *FB = BD* marriages are the most prevalent. Marriage between maternal parallel cousins was evidently not practiced (Hanson 1989b:143–44).

Even when an endogamous strategy is held as an ideal, it cannot always be pursued; hindrances do exist. A "potential mate of the correct sex or age range simply may not exist, or poor relations between siblings may prevent negotiation. . . . Successful negotiations depend not only upon the status of the relations between siblings, but upon those between their spouses as well" (Pastner 1981:309).

The story of Pheroras, the brother of Herod the Great, is a telling one with regard to endogamy. Herod first arranged for Pheroras to marry his wife's sister (evidently the sister of Mariamme, the Hasmonean princess); thus, *ZHB = BWZ* (Josephus, *War* 1.483). After this wife died, Herod then betrothed Pheroras to his oldest daughter by Mariamme, Salampsio (*FB = BD*). But because of his affection for a slave, Pheroras reneged on the betrothal (*War* 1.484). After a period of time, Herod betrothed Pheroras to Salampsio's sister, Cypros, whom Pheroras promised to marry in thirty days. But he reneged again, and these refusals were interpreted as affronts to Herod's honor (Josephus, *Ant.* 16.197). Pheroras's dishonor lay in his reneging on two promises to his brother, as well as opting for a slave-concubine over endogamous marriages. By doing so, he went against both custom and the head of his family.

Exogamy

The marriage strategy of the Herodians also included exogamy (marriage outside the kin-group): twenty-seven exogamous marriages are specifically known. For the most part, these marriages were for the advancement of the family's honor and power by establishing network links with political and religious leaders throughout the eastern Mediterranean.

Of the twenty-seven exogamous marriages entered into by fourteen different Herodians (accounting for multiple marriages), only six were to spouses of non-elite or unknown status. The marriage between Archelaus, **ethnarch** [1.25] of Judea, and Mariamme may have been endogamous, but the record is unclear with regard to Mariamme's identity. All the others were wives of Herod the Great, some or all of whom may have been elites, but Josephus provides no clues (Hanson 1989b:144–46). While Pheroras had a child by a slave, she was most likely a concubine rather than a wife (*War* 1.483–84//*Ant.* 16.194–99).

What functions did these exogamous marriages serve beyond the obvious kinship functions? For many of them Josephus provides no information. But a few examples will demonstrate that more was at stake than home and hearth.

The political importance of the marriages between the Herodians and the Hasmoneans (the **Judean** [1.43] royal-priestly family who had ruled Palestine from 142 to 63 B.C.E.) can hardly be overestimated. The marriage of Herod the Great and Mariamme was of central importance; important also were those of Pheroras (Herod's brother) and Mariamme's sister (whose name is unknown), as well as Herod's oldest, most powerful son, Antipater, and the daughter of Antigonus the Hasmonean. The effects of these relationships were far-reaching. This strategy was an attempt at solidifying Judean legitimacy to Herod and his reign by marriage alliances to the previously reigning Hasmonean family, who were still very popular in Palestine. That this strategy was at least partially successful is spelled out by Josephus: "And Antigonus being banished, he [Herod] returned to Jerusalem where [his] success made him everyone's favorite. Even those who had not formerly been devoted, were now reconciled by his marriage into the family of Hyrcanus"

(*War* 1.240). This desire to marry into the preceding king's family seems to have been the motivation behind David's betrothal to Saul's daughter Merab, his marriage to Saul's daughter Michal, and his demand for Michal's return (1 Sam 18:17-29; 2 Sam 3:12-16).

A further consequence of these three Herodian family marriages was that they tied the two competing segments of the Hasmonean family together: Mariamme and her sister (the wives of Herod and Pheroras) were the granddaughters of both Aristobulus II (paternal) and Hyrcanus II (maternal); and Antipater's wife was the daughter of Antigonus, and her paternal grandfather was Aristobulus II. Smallwood also concludes that Pheroras's and Antipater's marriages functioned to neutralize the threat of a further Hasmonean revolt against Herodian power (1981:72).

The marriages to Roman **client-kings** [1.13] and their daughters served to secure Palestine's borders as well as provide political alliances among other Roman **clients** [3.8]. When Herod the Great died in 4 B.C.E., political chaos ensued. One of the leaders who aided the Roman **legate** [1.45] Varus in his suppression of the Judeans in revolt was King Aretas IV of Nabatea (of the Harith tribe). But later, Herod Antipas (**tetrarch** [1.83] of Galilee and Perea) married Aretas's daughter and thus secured his eastern and southern borders. The political character of this marriage is evident from their subsequent divorce to facilitate Antipas's marriage to his niece (and brother's wife), Herodias (c. 29–30 C.E.; Hoehner 1972:129–31). The consequence

of this divorce was that the alliance was broken, and Aretas eventually waged a successful war against Antipas in 36 C.E. Antipas was only rescued by Roman intervention (*Ant.* 18.109–26; Hoehner 1972:142–44; Smallwood 1981:185–87).

Liberty

Todd discusses the question of spouse selection in terms of "liberty" and "authority" (1985:26–32). He identifies each of the seven family types with one of four forms of selection. In the endogamous community family (Israelite), custom determines the choice (Todd 1985:28). In the endogamous community family of Hellenistic Israelites, one can see that the family patriarch played a vital role in spousal choice and negotiations and that custom was not the only operative force. This is necessarily the case, since all members do not marry endogamously, and multiple "customary" endogamous spouses might be available (Pastner 1981:309–11). This more complex perspective is affirmed by Hildred Geertz in analyzing modern Moroccan kinship: "Any study of the patterns of actual marriage choices must be centered not on the marrying couple, but on their parents and their parents' situations, concepts of their social world, and interests" (1979:374).

The powerful role of the family, and especially the head of the kin-group, is seen in the various betrothal arrangements of the Herodian family. Josephus specifically identifies Herod as the arranger of the marriages of ten couples (figure 2.3). The same is true in subsequent generations. The arrangements of Herod the Great for his sister Salome and

- Pheroras (Herod's brother) and Alexander's daughter (*War* 1.483)

- Salome (Herod's sister) and Costobarus (*Ant.* 15.254)

- Salome (Herod's sister) and Alexas (*War* 1.566)

- Aristobulus (Herod's son) and Berenice (Herod's niece; *Ant.* 16.11)

- Alexander (Herod's son) and Mariamme (Herod's granddaughter; *Ant.* 17.22)

- Cypros (Herod's daughter) and Antipater (Herod's nephew; *War* 1.566)

- Salampsio (Herod's daughter) and Phasaelus (Herod's nephew; *Ant.* 17.22)

- Salome's daughter (Herod's niece) and Alexas's son (*War* 1.566)

- Antipater's son (Herod's grandson) and Pheroras's daughter (*War* 1.565)

Figure 2.3 Marriages Arranged by Herod the Great

King Agrippa II for his sister Drusilla demonstrate patriarchal power of brothers over sisters when the former are the head of the kin-group. The women remain embedded in the status of males, even after their fathers or husbands have died. Negatively, Herod also prevented the marriage of his sister Salome to the Nabatean **governor** [1.33] Sylleus, because the latter refused to submit to circumcision (*War* 1.487//*Ant.* 16.220–25). Another significant aspect of this marital negotiation is that Herod is described as consulting Salome with regard to her interest in the marriage. This was presumably because she was a mature woman who had been twice married, in addition to having a close relationship with her brother (*Ant.* 16.225). But even her appeal for Livia's help (the **emperor's** [1.21] wife) did not sway Herod from following Israelite custom in this regard. He then forced her with threats to marry his friend Alexas (*War* 1.566//*Ant.* 17.10).

Endowment at Marriage

The economic aspects of marriage are complex arrangements in all societies. In the United States, prenuptial agreements have become more important as a way to protect assets accrued before marriage or the inheritance of children from earlier marriages. But ancient Mediterranean societies also had complex "prenuptial agreements" as a means of clarifying the flow of property from one family to another, to endow the new couple, and to protect the bride's rights in case of a divorce.

Dowry
Dowry is the property that a bride's family provides the bride or couple (usually under the control of her husband) at the time of marriage. This might be immovable property (land and buildings), movable property (such as animals, bedding, cooking utensils,

jewelry), cash, or a combination of these. Dowry is mentioned in the Bible in the context of the pre-Israelite period as well as the early Israelite monarchy (for example, Gen 30:20; 31:14-16; and 1 Kgs 9:16).

Three broadly based cross-cultural studies of preindustrial societies have appeared that inform our understanding of dowry (Goody; Harrell and Dickey; and Schlegel and Eloul). Jack Goody was the first to demonstrate that dowry has broader implications than just a gift to the bride or couple. It is, in fact, a payment of a daughter's share of the family inheritance (full or partial) given to the daughter at the time of marriage (Gen 31:14-16; Josh 15:18-19; *m. Ket.* 6.6). Since it is distributed before the death of the parents, Goody refers to it as "pre-mortem inheritance."

Women in traditional, patriarchal societies shift from being "embedded in" (under the authority, legal responsibility, and care of) their fathers to having a similar relationship to their husbands (*m. Ket.* 4.4–5). Thus the groom was given the woman's property to administer (the legal term is **usufruct** [3.55]), but it nonetheless belonged to her and was passed to her children, as distinct from the personal property of the husband, or his kin-group, or his children from other marriages.

Israelite evidence appears in a fifth-century B.C.E. document from the **Elephantine papyri** [2.4]: Mahseiah bar Yedoniah (the bride's father) and Yezaniah bar Uriah (the groom) contract Yezaniah's marriage to Mibtachiah (the bride). Mahseiah stipulates that Mibtachiah's dowry (a house) is for the couple's joint use; it was not for them to sell or give away (the "dowryhouse" mentioned in *m. B. Batra* 6.4). If Mibtachiah were to divorce Yezaniah, the property would be passed to their children. If Yezaniah were to divorce Mibtachiah, half the property would go to her, and half to Yezaniah (for his labor on it), until his death, when their children would inherit it (Ginsberg 1969:222).

In the Apocrypha, the story of Tobit (second century B.C.E.) illustrates what has been said with regard to the economic import of the dowry. The angel Raphael promised Tobias that he would marry Sarah, because the family's inheritance should stay within the family (Tob 6:12; Num 36:6-12). And Goody's identification of the dowry as "pre-mortem inheritance" is specifically confirmed in this marriage transaction:

> And Raguel swore to him [Tobias] before the completion of the feast-days that he should not leave until the fourteen days of the wedding feast were ended, and then he should take half of his [Raguel's] property and journey safely to his father, "and the remainder when I and my wife die." (Tob 8:20-21)

Raguel (the bride's father) and Tobias (the groom) had already secured the terms of the marriage in formal declarations, written contract, and betrothal feast:

> "I am not free to give her [Sarah] to any other man than yourself, because you are my closest kin. . . . But now, my child, eat and drink, and the Lord will act on behalf of you both."

But Tobias said, "I will neither eat nor drink anything until you settle the things that pertain to me."

So Raguel said, "I will do so. She is given to you in accordance with the decree in the book of Moses, and it has been decreed from heaven that she be given to you. Take your kinswoman; from now on you are her brother and she is your sister. She is given to you from today and forever. May the Lord of heaven, my child, guide and prosper you both this night and grant you mercy and peace." Then Raguel summoned his daughter Sarah. When she came to him, he took her by the hand and gave her to Tobias, saying, "Take her to be your wife in accordance with the law and decree written in the book of Moses. Take her and bring her safely to your father. And may the God of heaven prosper your journey with his peace."

Then he called her mother and told her to bring writing material; and he wrote out a copy of a marriage contract, to the effect that he gave her to him as wife according to the decree of the law of Moses. Then they began to eat and drink. (Tob 7:10-14)

The dowry is not only an economic transaction, but also an expression of the family's honor on the occasion of a daughter's wedding (Harrell and Dickey 1985). The size of the dowry demonstrates to the community how wealthy the family is and is one signal of their publicly displayed honor. This is not hoarded wealth but transmitted wealth, providing the daughter with her portion of the family's goods, money, and property.

A dowry may also be the means of acquiring honor or a client: a son-in-law of higher status increases the family's honor, or one of lower status may enlist him and his family as clients (Schlegel and Eloul 1988:301). Marriage transactions are also "a function of the kind of property relations within the society" (294) and are a means of adjusting "labor needs, the transmission of property, and status concerns" (305). Several characteristics should be noted about societies that utilize dowry and indirect dowry:

- They are "complex agricultural and commercial pastoralist societies," as opposed to foragers, horticulturalists, or subsistence pastoralists (294).
- They have substantial private property (294).
- They have three or more social classes (297).
- They are patrilocal, as opposed to matrilocal (living with the bride's family), avunculocal (living with the bride's uncle), ambilocal (living with the families of both the groom and the bride), or neolocal (living by themselves in a new residence) (298).

These characteristics generally fit first-century Palestinians and thus provide a social profile to accompany the marriage transactions one observes in the biblical and Herodian kinship arrangements.

Throughout the ancient Mediterranean, dowries varied, but over the centuries, families gave houses, land, and slaves (Gen 24:59-61; 29:24-29; Josh 15:18-19; *m. Yeb.* 7.1). The Mishnah stipulates that a **poor** [1.58] orphan should be given a minimum dowry of fifty zuz (twenty-five **shekels** [1.76]) from the community's poor-fund (*m. Ket.* 6.5b). In the hypothetical case of a dowry, the Mishnah uses the amount of one thousand *denars/zuz* (*m. Ket.* 6.3). For elites, dowries are mentioned in 1 Maccabees 10:54 and Josephus, *Ant.* 13.82.

Befitting their royal status, the Herodian dowries were considerably more than the aforementioned examples. Herod the Great betrothed his brother Pheroras to Salampsio with a dowry of three hundred talents, an enormous sum (Josephus, *War* 1.483). When Pheroras reneged on his promise to marry her, Herod added one hundred talents to Salampsio's dowry (*Ant.* 16.228). Salampsio's four-hundred-talent dowry amounted to two years of Galilean **tribute** [1.86] collected by Herod Antipas. This highlights the point made by Harrell and Dickey that the dowry functioned as a public display of the family's wealth, status, and honor.

After Herod's death, Augustus gave Herod's daughters Roxanne and Salome 250,000 **denarii** [1.18] (twenty-five talents) each for their dowries—not as large as the amount given for their older sister's, but still significant sums. That these were actually dowries (as opposed to simple gifts to the bride) is demonstrated by the mention of Augustus's arrangement of their marriages in the same sentence (Josephus *Ant.* 17.322). This further establishes the link between dowry and inheritance (Goody).

The cases of Sarah (Tobias's wife), Salampsio, Roxanne, and Cypros also make clear that dowries were paid even within the family (in endogamous marriages). Thus the wealth of the kin-group is circulated by gift to the next generation, but simultaneously concentrated (keeping it in the family), maintaining the economic strength of the family group. Dowry is also required in endogamous marriages among the twentieth-century Zikri Baluch, an Islamic tribe in Pakistan (Pastner 1981:309).

Bridewealth and Indirect Dowry

Bridewealth is a term employed by anthropologists to cover the transfer of goods and services from the groom's family to the bride's family. And, as Goody makes clear, these diverse transactions have very different implications for social structure (1973:2). Like dowry, bridewealth is also attested in the Old Testament (Heb. *môhar*, Gen 34:12) and the Mishnah (*m. Ket.* 1.2; 5.1), as well as in the literatures of Babylonia, Nuzi, Ugarit, and Greece, but not Rome.

"Indirect dowry" is property or cash given by the groom's kin either directly to the bride or indirectly through her kin; it may be all or part of the bridewealth. The story of Isaac's betrothal to Rebekah demonstrates both indirect dowry (in the form of silver and gold jewelry and clothing) and general bridewealth given to her mother and brother (Gen 24:53).

The mistranslation and misunderstanding of the ancient terminology (such as the Hebrew *môhar*) as "bride-price" misled some to conclude that dowry arrangements constituted the sale of the bride. The Hebrew and

Greek technical terms are all associated with "gift-giving" rather than "sale" (Finley 1981). Bridewealth was used in Israelite society to purchase furniture and household goods for the couple. This does not, however, lead us to conclude that a daughter was a "free-agent" in the marriage transaction in the ancient Near East, nor that her rights were the same as those of a son.

Dowries and indirect dowries, as already noted, originate in opposite families. On the other hand, they have the same (or similar) economic result by bestowing property on the new couple. This gives each family a vested interest in the new couple. Bridewealth that is not handed over to the bride is utilized in most societies to secure wives for the bride's brothers, if she has any: "Indeed it involves a kind of rationing system. What goes out for a bride has to come in for a sister" (Goody 1973:5).

The place of indirect dowry in combination with dowry in societies that compete for honor (such as those in the Mediterranean) is a procedure for balancing honor concerns. By these means, both contracting families avoid becoming too indebted to the other: becoming the client of the other (Schlegel and Eloul 1988:303).

In her excellent historical and anthropological synthesis on the roots of patriarchy, Gerda Lerner outlines the importance of taking **class** [3.7] and economics into any analysis of marriage arrangements. She makes it clear that dowries and bridewealth perpetuate the **social stratification** [3.52] of society: **homogamy** [3.24] (marriage within the group of one's own social level) maintained the circulation of property within a given social class (1986:108). Furthermore, concubinage and slavery served to keep a segment of the women disenfranchised and in a "power-down" position. The variables involved in bridewealth and dowries (direct

	DISTRIBUTIONS	
Transaction Elements	**Bridewealth**	**Dowry and Indirect Dowry**
Content of Gifts	Movable property	All property
Gift Recipients	Kin of bride	Bride
Gift Givers	Kin of groom	Dowry: bride's kin Indirect dowry: groom's kin
Returnability of Gifts	Usually	Always
Variability of Gifts	Sometimes	Always
Time of Gift-Giving	Over time	At marriage
Use of Gifts	Societal fund	Familial fund

(Adapted from Goody 1973:21)

Figure 2.4 Bridewealth and Dowry Distributions

and indirect) in preindustrial societies may be summarized as in figure 2.4. Most of these categories are self-explanatory, but a few should be clarified. By "returnability" Goody means the obligation to return the property or cash in the event of the dissolution of marriage (1973:12). By "variability" he refers to the variability or fixity of the amount within a given society (12–14). And the distinction between "societal fund" and "familial fund" is that bridewealth is most often used by the bride's brothers to acquire wives (it is thus circulated wealth), while dowries and indirect dowries are specifically for the use of the bride and her descendants (and thus are wealth concentrated and handed on to the next generation) (5–11).

The flow of property can thus be diagramed as in figure 2.5. The ways in which these marriage negotiations manifest conflict include (a) competing for the most honorable marriage for one's children, either in high status or in good prospects for clientage; (b) competing for the best deal from the other family in terms of their contributions to the couple or to the bride's family; (c) protecting one's child in the marriage contract; and (d) manifesting one's honor in the community by way of extravagant dowry and indirect dowry grants.

Divorce

Divorce is the severing of marital relations; it breaks the bonds of attachment and obligation instituted in marriage. Again, this is not just between two individuals but between two families. It also calls for returning dowries and other disentanglements of property, as witnessed in documents from the early second century (the **Babatha Archive** [2.2]).

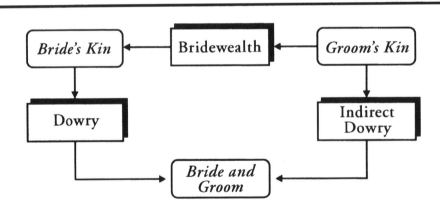

(Adapted from Hanson 1990:15)

<u>Figure 2.5 Flow of Property for Marital Endowment</u>

Israelite Divorce

While Mark 10:2-9 indicates that divorce and remarriage were allowed under no circumstance in the early Jesus **movement** [3.36], Matthew 5:31-32 and 19:3-9 parallel the rabbinic school of Shammai in specifically restricting divorce to cases of the wife's adultery (*m. Giṭ.* 9.10a). The rabbinic school of Hillel, on the other hand, seems to represent the dominant Israelite practice of allowing a man to divorce his wife for any displeasure with her (*m. Giṭ.* 9.10b; Deut 24:1; Sir 25:26).

> If a man marries a woman, but she does not please him because he finds something objectionable about her, and so he writes her a certificate of divorce, puts it in her hand, and sends her out of his house; she then leaves his house and goes off to become another man's wife. Then, if the second man dislikes her, writes her a bill of divorce, puts it in her hand, and sends her out of his house—or the second man who married her dies; her first husband, who sent her away, is not permitted to take her again to be his wife after she has been defiled. (Deut 24:1-4a)

Indeed, the Mishnah contains an entire tractate (book) on divorce regulations: *Giṭṭin.*

In the divorce laws of the Mishnah, an Israelite wife could obtain a divorce in several instances: the husband's persistent refusal to fulfill his conjugal duties (*m. Ket.* 7.1–5), the husband's physical impurity due to illness or vocation (*m. Ket.* 7.10), her own impu-

rity, her husband's impotence, her refusal to have intercourse (*m. Ned.* 11.12), or with her husband's consent (*m. 'Arak.* 5.6; Falk 1974:517–18). Josephus narrates his own divorces in *Life* 414–15, 426.

Herodian Divorces

Josephus mentions nine divorces among the Herodians. In four cases the husband divorced his wife, and in five the wife divorced her husband. These cases illustrate some of the basic values operating in the family, as well as the reasons that might arise to break the marriage bond. It becomes clear that divorce is as social an arrangement as marriage: it has immediate implications for the family and not merely the two individuals. Furthermore, it is always tied to the value of honor. These Herodian divorces inform our views on how divorce was practiced among Israelite elites.

Herod the Great divorced both Doris and Mariamme II for reasons of honor, but the circumstances were significantly different. He divorced Doris and banished her son Antipater in order to marry Mariamme (I) the Hasmonean. Not that he was averse to polygyny, but political considerations outweighed any devotion he had for Doris or the heir she had borne him. What was at stake, then, was an alliance with the Hasmonean royal-priestly family, and consequently an opportunity to increase his honor and power. In order to secure that alliance, Herod had to ensure Mariamme's honor as **"queen"** [1.67] and clear the path of inheritance and throne succession for any children she might bear him (Josephus, *War* 1.431–33). Doris was evidently reinstated at some point, since Herod divorced her again, stripping her of her expensive wardrobe (her indirect dowry?—see chapter 5), when a plot against Herod was exposed and she was implicated (Josephus, *Ant.* 17.68; Schalit 1969:634).

The issue at stake between Herod and Mariamme II was loyalty. Mariamme was accused (along with Doris) of being one of the conspirators who planned the death of Herod, instigated by Doris's son Antipater and others. The result of this accusation was that he divorced her. Moreover, he struck her son (Herod Philip) from his will and the throne succession and removed her father, Simon, from the **high priesthood** [1.38] (*Ant.* 17.78).

Herodias divorced one uncle, Herod Philip, in order to marry a second, Herod Antipas (*Ant.* 18.109–36; see chapter 3). The effects of this transaction were far-reaching for kinship and for politics. Antipas had stayed at the house of Philip and Herodias on his way to Rome, and during that visit proposed marriage to Herodias (c. 29 C.E.; Mark 6:14-28; Hoehner 1972:128–31). If this was against the wishes of Philip (Josephus does not say), it was a double breech of honor—intruding on the relationship of a husband and wife, and betraying a brother. Herodias accepted Antipas's offer with the stipulation that Antipas divorce his wife the daughter of Aretas IV, client-king of Nabatea.

It is clear that Herodias significantly enhanced her status by changing husbands. As noted above, Herod Philip had been disinherited because of his mother's indictment as a conspirator against the life of Herod

the Great. Thus Herodias advanced from the wife of a disinherited son (and private **citizen** [1.11]) to the wife of the tetrarch of Galilee. Antipas exchanged an exogamous, political marriage for an endogamous one. Josephus viewed this divorce, initiated by a wife, as a flouting of tradition (*Ant.* 18.136). As already mentioned, Antipas's consequent divorce from Aretas's daughter resulted in a border war between the two rulers (*Ant.* 18.113–15). It may, however, have been an attempt by Antipas to have a more traditional Israelite marriage. Another case of "arranged divorce" can be seen among the Romans: Augustus convinced Tiberius Claudius Nero to divorce his wife, Livia, so that Augustus himself could marry her (Purcell 1996).

Archelaus, the ethnarch of Judea, divorced his wife, Mariamme (whose descent is unknown), in order to marry Glaphyra, daughter of Archelaus, client-king of Cappadocia (*War* 2.115//*Ant.* 17.350). Josephus understands this to be the result of Archelaus's "overwhelming attraction [*eros*]" for Glaphyra. Whatever the immediate cause, the result was a suitably royal marriage for the man who was ethnarch of Judea; and Josephus connects Archelaus's marriage to Glaphyra with his accession to the throne (*Ant.* 17.339–41). Josephus also sees this marriage to be against tradition: Glaphyra had already borne the Herodian family children with her deceased husband, Alexander.

It is pertinent that Josephus takes every opportunity to assert that the women divorcing their husbands were acting shamefully and against Israelite tradition (*Ant.* 15.259–60; 17.341; 18.136; 20.143). In what social frame of reference can these women's actions then be placed? One might interpret their boldness in terms of their Hellenization; they did not feel bound to follow Israelite tradition in matters of kinship. But as we have pointed out, their marriage strategies and negotiations as well as their requirement that exogamous husbands be circumcised demonstrate that they were fully Israelite in their family system. And while the Herodians were granted Roman **citizenship** [1.11] in the time of Antipater, the grandfather of Herod the Great (47 B.C.E.; *Ant.* 14.137; Smallwood 1981:38–39), the same arguments speak against that citizenship as the necessary interpretative framework.

Nothing can be proven in this regard, but we conclude that their status as nonpriestly, urban elites gave them the social flexibility to act in their own (and their family's) interests in terms of honor. While they evidently acted shamelessly in the eyes of Josephus, John the Baptizer, and perhaps the general population, the shame of these women (evaluated positively or negatively) was determined by their own social circles—other (nonpriestly) urban elites—not by Pharisaic interpretation of tradition (Malina 1993:50–53).

The dissolution of marriage, like the contracting of marriage, is a social transaction that affects more than the divorcing couple. The divorces in the Herodian family demonstrate the competition for honor in marriage strategy. A spouse could be dropped when a better alliance became available, even exchanging one endogamous marriage for a superior one. Divorces may also demonstrate the expectations and breakdowns of family loyalty within the kin-group. Josephus's divorce of his third wife demonstrates that Hillel's liberal interpretation of divorce custom for men was actually practiced.

Inheritance

Inheritance is the distribution of the family's movable property (livestock, jewelry) and immovable property (fields, barns), most commonly at the death of the male head of the family (Sir 33:23). But, as discussed above, dowry is a means of inheritance given to the daughters at the time of their marriage.

The legal paragraph in Numbers 27:3-4 acknowledges that sons had priority in the claim to inheritance (other than dowry). The case of Zelophehad's daughters raises the issue of inheritance when the deceased left no sons. The precedent was set in this case, and the order of inheritance was designated as daughters, brothers, father's brothers, near kin. Each successive category of relatives was included only if there was no one in the preceding categories (Num 27:8-11). Note that the wife was not included in the Numbers list or in most ancient lists of successors. The reason is that her portion was her dowry and indirect dowry.

Deuteronomy 21:17 designates a double portion for the eldest son. This was also stipulated in the Mishnah (*m. B. Batra* 8.3–5), as well as in other ancient Near Eastern societies (for example, Nuzi and Babylonia). The Israelite distribution of inheritance thus followed the path in figure 2.6.

The Mishnah's laws of inheritance follow a similar sequence to the one articulated

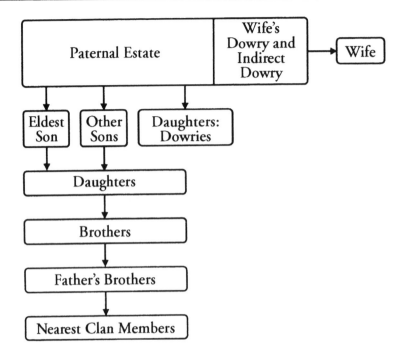

Note: After the first row, the lines and arrows represent the contingent sequence of inheritance. (Hanson 1990:16)

Figure 2.6 Israelite Law of Inheritance

in Numbers 27:8-11, but two new factors are added. First is the general rule: "Whosoever has precedence in inheritance, his offspring also have precedence" (*m. B.Batra* 8.2). In other words, if a son has died before his now deceased father, and that son had children, those children inherited ahead of the deceased's daughters, and so forth. Second, it provided for ascendant inheritance, stipulating that the father of the deceased would inherit ahead of brothers and sisters.

The Mishnah also notes regional diversity concerning the rights of the widow in Palestine. In Jerusalem and the Galilee, the tradition was that the widow had a legal right to stay in the family home and live off her husband's property, as directed in marriage contracts (*m. Ket.* 4.12a). But in Judea, the heirs were free to dispose of a widow by giving her the amount of her *kethubah* (that is, dowry plus indirect dowry; *m. Ket.* 4.12b; Falk 1974:520).

We possess no narrative information about Herodian inheritance except for that which followed Herod the Great's death. And it is at this point that Todd's point about "equality" (distribution among all the children) is demonstrated. One of the most striking things to note about Herod's distribution is that Augustus Caesar and his wife,

Livia, were included as major heirs. Herod willed Augustus ten million *denarii* (one thousand talents), silver and gold vessels, and expensive clothing (Josephus, *Ant.* 17.190). Augustus, moreover, was in charge of disposing and ratifying the terms of the will (Josephus, *War* 1.669). To Livia (along with other, unnamed, Roman friends) he gave five million silver coins (five hundred talents) (*Ant.* 17.190). These endowments given to the emperor and the imperial family were neither whimsical nor an affront to Herod's family, but were the **reciprocity** [3.46] of the client (Herod) to his patrons (Augustus and Livia). The Roman historian **Suetonius** [2.16] discusses the patron/client relationship between Augustus and client-kings (*Lives of Caesars*, "Augustus," 60). Furthermore, the relationship of patron and client was inherited from generation to generation (Saller 1982:186; John H. Elliott 1987). This explains the enduring relationship between the Herodians and the Julio-Claudians and then the Flavians over a 160-year period: Julius Caesar appointed Antipater, the father of Herod the Great, governor over all Judea in 47 B.C.E. (*War* 1.199//*Ant.* 14.143), and Trajan appointed Gaius Julius Alexander Berenicianus (a Roman senator and a great-great-great-grandson of Herod the Great) consul of Rome in 116 C.E. (Smallwood 1981:391n).

The major portion of Herod's kingdom was divided among three of his sons (all named Herod). Herod Antipas, Malthake's son, became tetrarch over Galilee and Perea (*Ant.* 17.188, 318), with an annual revenue of two hundred talents. Herod Philip,

Cleopatra's son, was made tetrarch over the northern territories: Trachonitis, Batanea, Gaulanitis, Peneas, Auranitis, and the domain of Zenodorus. This gave him an annual income of one hundred talents (*Ant.* 17.189, 319). And Herod appointed Herod Archelaus, Malthake's oldest son, client-king (*War* 1.668//*Ant.* 17.188), but this was reduced to ethnarch by Augustus (*Ant.* 17.317). Archelaus had jurisdiction over Judea, Samaria, Idumea, Jerusalem, Caesarea, Sebaste, and Joppa; and these gave him an annual income of six hundred talents (*Ant.* 17.319–20). This distribution, consequently, followed the Israelite tradition of giving the eldest son a larger portion but including everyone. Josephus also recounts the angry response to the will from Herod Antipas and Herod Philip (*War* 2.14–38, 80–100; Smallwood 1981:107–10).

It is significant that the standard textbooks omit Salome from the list of rulers who succeeded Herod and inherited from him (Kee 1983:40; Koester 1995:375–76; Duling 2003:15; but see Stern 1974a:278). While her jurisdiction was much smaller than that of Herod's sons, Josephus nonetheless identifies her as a ruler over a **toparchy** [1.84] (*War* 2.167), consisting of Jamnia and Azotus (both on the Mediterranean coast) and Phasaelis (in the Jordan valley), with the epithet *despoina* ("ruler" [feminine]; *War* 2.98). This provided an annual revenue of sixty talents, accompanied by a lump sum of 500,000 silver coins (fifty talents). Augustus added the royal residence in Ascalon to her holdings (*Ant.* 17.321), and later the city of Archelais (*Ant.* 18.31). She ruled over this territory until her death (c. 10 C.E.), when she willed it to her patron, Augustus's wife, Livia (*Ant.* 18.31). Herod also left unspecified monetary sums to the rest of his family (*Ant.* 17.189). To these sums, Augustus added either one thousand (*War* 2.100) or fifteen hundred talents (*Ant.* 17.323) from what Herod had willed him, thus perpetuating the patron/client relationship. As noted above, Augustus also gave Herod's daughters Roxanne and Salome dowries of 250,000 silver coins (twenty-five talents) each and arranged their marriages to the sons of Pheroras (*Ant.* 17.322). This division of property is adequate demonstration of Todd's principle of "equality" (1985:7–11). The Herodian inheritance was thus distributed as shown in figure 2.7.

Several family members are missing from figure 2.7. Antipater (Herod's son by Doris), Mariamme the Hasmonean, and her sons Aristobulus and Alexander were dead (all executed by Herod the Great). Herod had previously divorced Doris and Mariamme, the daughter of Simon the priest (and presumably already returned their dowries). And Herod Philip (the son of Mariamme, Simon's daughter) had been disinherited. How many of Herod's wives were actually still living is unknown. The only children unaccounted for are Herod (his son by Cleopatra) and Phasaelus (his son by Pallas); it is quite possible that they were also dead by this time.

That this equality of distribution is the rule rather than the exception can be seen in

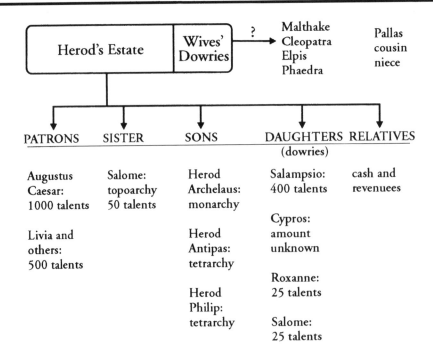

Figure 2.7 The Estate of Herod the Great

both Israelite documents and the Gospels: the division of Noah's legacy by lot, a Greek practice (*Jub.* 8:10-11); the request for Jesus to arbitrate a just division of two brothers' inheritance (Luke 12:13; *Gos. Thom.* 72); and the parable of the Prodigal Son (Luke 15:12). Abraham, however, is said to have given an undivided legacy to Isaac, giving Ishmael and his other sons "gifts" (*Jub.* 20:11). This would be due to the lower status of Ishmael as the son of a concubine.

Inheritance is the means of distributing the family's movable and immovable property after the death of the patriarch. It transfers the property from one generation to the next, providing the sustenance of the family, the possession of the land, and acknowledgment of patron/client obligations. The aspects often overlooked by historians have been the function of dowries as premortem inheritance, the return of the wife's dowry and indirect dowry, the contingencies of inheritance distribution, and the acknowledgment of patron/client relationships. Herod followed the Israelite tradition of inheritance distribution, while the inclusion of Salome as an heir remains unclear.

Jesus' Family in the Gospels

Matthew 1:1-17 and Elite Interests

The kinship models of genealogy and descent treated here are necessary to read biblical texts as products of the ancient Mediterranean world. To test these models it is necessary to address specific passages and family groups. We begin with Jesus' genealogy in Matthew 1:1-17, since this is perhaps the best known to readers of the New Testament.

The Gospel of Matthew begins with a provocative phrase: "The lineage record of Jesus Christ" (1:1). In order to tell the story of Jesus, the Gospel writer chose to begin with the issue of Jesus' kinship. A fundamental way for traditional societies to express kinship, as we have seen, is to establish an individual's lineage, his or her connections to a family group that defines the present, is rooted in the past, and expresses future potentialities. The genealogy expresses social relationships in terms of experienced, multidimensional time, which is an organically linked process (Malina 1989:31). A résumé or formal introduction for a contemporary U.S. leader would rarely be expected to mention kinship beyond "married" or "single," but would likely focus on education, work experience, and financial status.

Mediterranean cultures, however, place high value upon the kin-group to which one belongs, not only one's living family, but also the lineage of that family. That lineage may express the family's relative honor in contrast to other families, the trades that they have been handed, the stories out of which they live, the patron/client associations they have made, their religious purity, the potential marriage partners who are accessible to them, and much more.

Genealogies, then, provide one avenue of understanding the present—by appealing to the past in terms of one's lineage. Any individual listed in a genealogy is meant to be interpreted in light of the larger pattern of social relationships that the genealogy reflects.

Since Matthew 1:1-17 is a dominantly unilineal (though occasionally segmented) genealogy, a "tree" model of Jesus' lineage according to Matthew appears in figure 2.8.

In traditional Mediterranean societies throughout history, the fundamental and overarching social value has been honor. The type of honor that a genealogy communicates is ascribed honor (based upon who one is, especially in reference to one's group).

But precisely as a social value, ascribed honor, too, must continually be asserted and maintained, and it is always open to challenge. Like the priestly writers' materials in Genesis, which introduce a set of stories about a character with a genealogy (in the case of Abraham, Gen 11:10-26 introduces 12:1—25:11), Matthew introduces the story of Jesus with his genealogy. In their final redaction (both Genesis and Matthew), the stories are rooted in a preunderstanding of the kin-group from which the character comes and in the context of which he must be interpreted. That is, one must first situate the main character in terms of family honor, partially determined by descent expressed in a genealogy. Thus the literary sequence of genealogy followed by story symbolizes the social value placed on kinship and descent. If the Gospel of Mark was the primary narrative source of the Gospel of Matthew, then one can readily conclude what deficiency the gospel writer saw in Mark's introduction to the Jesus story: it failed to root his story in family honor.

One of the key ways that a genealogy expresses the claim to honor is by the choice of the apical ancestor—the one at the head (apex) of the list. That the gospel writer had choices is clear: Luke roots Jesus in "universal" history by tracing his genealogy to God by way of Adam (3:38), including (but placing no special emphasis on) David (3:31) and Abraham (3:34). And John introduces Jesus' story by declaring him to be the embodiment of the divine Logos (Word and Wisdom; John 1:1-18). Matthew could have chosen Jacob as Jesus' apical ancestor, the namesake of the people of Israel (John 4:12); or Judah, the head of his ancestral "tribe" (Heb 7:14); or Solomon, the archetypal sage-king (Matt 12:42). These all appear in Matthew's genealogy, but not at the head.

The importance of Abraham as apical ancestor is as the first patriarch to have received the divine promises of children, land, and reputation. But note that primacy of place is given to "son of David" in Matthew 1:1.

This prompts the audience to interpret "son of Abraham" in terms of "son of David," in other words, to interpret Abraham in royal terms. Two passages are relevant here. In the **Septuagint's** [2.15] rendering of Genesis 23:6, the Hittites say to Abraham, "You are a king from God among us." In the *Testaments of the Twelve Patriarchs* (in the Pseudepigrapha), Levi is promised that a Judean king will arise to create a new priesthood, and that king will be a descendant of Abraham (*T. Levi* 8:14-15). The relevance of these texts is to demonstrate that in pre-Christian Israelite literature, Abraham is associated

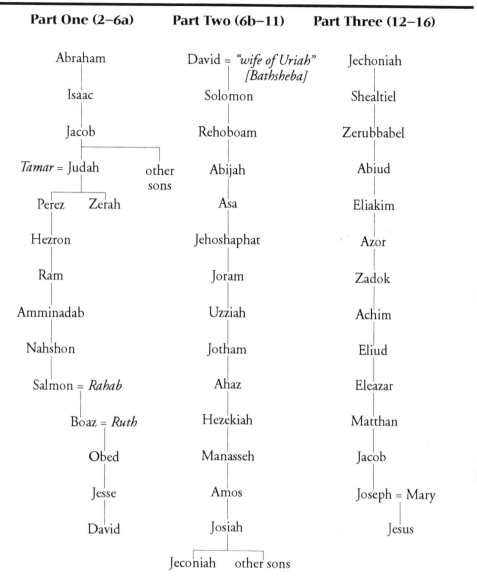

Part One (2–6a)	Part Two (6b–11)	Part Three (12–16)
Abraham	David = *"wife of Uriah"* [Bathsheba]	Jechoniah
Isaac	Solomon	Shealtiel
Jacob	Rehoboam	Zerubbabel
Tamar = Judah other sons	Abijah	Abiud
Perez Zerah	Asa	Eliakim
Hezron	Jehoshaphat	Azor
Ram	Joram	Zadok
Amminadab	Uzziah	Achim
Nahshon	Jotham	Eliud
Salmon = *Rahab*	Ahaz	Eleazar
Boaz = *Ruth*	Hezekiah	Matthan
Obed	Manasseh	Jacob
Jesse	Amos	Joseph = Mary
David	Josiah	Jesus
	Jeconiah other sons	

Figure 2.8 The Genealogy of Jesus: Forty-one Generations (Matt 1:2–16)

with kingship. As Gordon points out, it is not Jesus' identification as an Israelite that is open to question in Matthew, but the claim to kingship (1965:143).

Malina and Neyrey (1988) analyze the epithets (formulaic phrases characterizing individuals or groups) in Matthew in terms of labeling and deviance theory. As they make plain, Matthew's attestations of Jesus' honor as a "Davidic" king are set within the context of the Judean leaders' rejection of Jesus' kingship, and thus the conflict over whether

Jesus was a "prominent" or a "deviant." Jesus' Davidic lineage, then, is employed as one weapon in the gospel writer's arsenal for the agonistic struggle to establish Jesus' honor. This occurs both in the infancy narrative (Matt 2:7-8, 16-18) and in the passion narrative (21:15-16; 27:42). "But the treatment of the Christology in the Infancy Narrative is highly significant, since, as we have shown, Jesus is rejected as 'King of the Judeans' and is the 'Son of God' in exile and hiding. The Gospel writer would seem to be conditioning his audience to understand that the major labels of Jesus, while true, honorable and prominent, occur in contexts that are dishonorable" (Malina and Neyrey 1988:116). The genealogy thus promotes Jesus' claim to Judean royal lineage, and the subsequent birth story promotes his claim to divine parentage by means of miraculous birth.

The fact that Matthew wants both a genealogical connection to David and Abraham through Mary's husband, Joseph (1:16), and a virginal conception (1:18-25) does not constitute a conflict in terms of kinship. Biology is only one factor in establishing one's kin-group; the other is one's household. As Delaney makes plain, paternity is a social construct. Moreover, "dual paternity" was a well-established mode of expressing miraculous birth, royal authority, and divine power in the ancient Mediterranean.

Gordon points out that Odysseus was called "the Zeus-sired son of Laertes" (Homer, *Iliad* 10.144), and Queen Hatshepsut of Egypt was the daughter of both Pharaoh Thutmosis I and the god Amon (1977:101; 1978:26–27). Besides these examples from Gordon, stories

circulated to the effect that Alexander of Macedonia was the son not only of Philip II, but also of the god Zeus-Ammon (Plutarch, *Parallel Lives*, "Alexander" 2.1—3.2); Plato was the son of Ariston and the god Apollo (Diogenes Laertius, *Lives of Eminent Philosophers* 3.1–2), and Augustus was the son of Octavius as well as the god Apollo (Suetonius, *Lives of the Caesars* 2.4.1–7). The extraordinary character of these elites reputedly stemmed from both their divine origins and their kin-groups. Their kin-groups provided one form of legitimation—political right to the throne or social status (thus the importance of Joseph in Matthew's genealogy). Their divine procreation provided another: their honor was divinely ascribed, and their greatness as leaders derived from divine paternity.

Another issue involved in the composition of any genealogy is the form of descent employed. As we noted in reference to Mediterranean genealogies in general, patrilineal descent is the rule. This is clear in Matthew's genealogy of Jesus as well. The family's honor in blood and name is communicated from father to son. This must be understood in relationship to the fact that a woman was perceived as embedded in her father (or other male relatives) until she became embedded in her husband. Thus the woman became part of another family and was embedded in their honor. But as the Herodian genealogy also demonstrates, this patrilineal principle is occasionally supplemented with the cognatic principle: the tracing of heritage through maternal as well as paternal lines.

Matthew's inclusion of Tamar (1:3), Rahab (1:5a), Ruth (1:5b), Bathsheba (1:6), and Mary (1:16) calls for explanation. As Brown notes, Rahab is not connected to the Davidic lineage in the Old Testament; thus biblical genealogies were not Matthew's "direct source" for the women (1993:71 n. 21). He concludes that these particular women were chosen by the gospel writer for two reasons: "(a) There is something extraordinary or irregular in their union with their partners, a union which, though it may have been scandalous to outsiders, continued the blessed lineage of the Messiah; (b) the women showed initiative or played an important role in God's plan and so came to be considered the instrument of God's providence or of His Holy Spirit" (1993:73).

We agree with Brown's conclusions, but the underlying social values of these theological formulations must be probed further. Tamar was not Judah's "wife" but his daughter-in-law; she had to trick Judah into providing her with children when Judah failed to fulfill his "levirate" obligations (assigning one of his sons to give her dead husband an heir). Since her initiative, rather than his, resulted in a just solution, Judah pronounced her "more righteous than I" (Gen 38:26); in other words, "Tamar acted more honorably than I." Tamar was rewarded with protection within the kin-group, as well as with children (38:27-30). Thus Matthew emphasizes the honor of the line as based upon not only the promises of God to the patriarchs (ascribed honor), but also Tamar's acquired honor manifested in Judah's declaration.

Rahab's honor lay in her protection of the Israelite spies trying to capture Jericho, her own Canaanite city. Her service and loyalty (Josh 2:12) to Israel provide her with a grant of acquired honor, despite her occupation as a prostitute, which exposes the family to accusations of shame. The Israelites rewarded her with the deliverance of her whole kin-group and inclusion into "Israel" (Josh 6:25).

Ruth the Moabite acquired honor by virtue of her loyalty to Naomi and Naomi's kin-group. This is declared in two formal blessings on her: one by Naomi (Ruth 1:8) and one by Boaz (3:10). She left her own land to go, dwell, and remain embedded in Naomi's people and her God (Ruth 1:16-17). She was eventually rewarded with a new husband from Naomi's kin-group, Boaz, and a son, Obed (4:13-22). She was a foreigner from the land of one of Israel's traditional enemies, but she acted with honor to the benefit of an Israelite family. Bathsheba's relationship to David is potentially shameful for the Davidic line, since David acquired her through a sequence of adultery, conspiracy, and murder (2 Sam 11:1—12:25). But no guilt is imputed to Bathsheba, and she subsequently bore Solomon (also named Jedidiah, "Yah's beloved," 12:24-25). She also acquired honor by stepping into the dispute over David's succession and promoting her son Solomon over Adonijah (1 Kgs 1:11-21, 28-31; 2:13-25). Solomon accorded her special honor by bowing down to her and providing her a throne at his right hand (2:19). It is important that Solomon's obeisance directly follows the description of Bathsheba's actions on his behalf.

Finally, Mary acquired honor by submitting to the divine will and giving birth to Jesus (Matt 1:16) as a virgin (1:18, 23, 25). She is necessary for Matthew to include here in order to tie the genealogy to the following birth account that emphasizes Mary's impregnation by the Holy Spirit. Her shame was exposed in terms of a pregnancy before marriage.

Thus Brown is correct—these women "showed initiative." But this still leaves vague the fundamental issue, for all initiative is not honorable; all their initiatives specifically resulted in their acquisition of honor. For Tamar, Rahab, and Ruth this is specifically stated in the biblical stories by formal declarations and blessings; for Bathsheba and Mary it is implied. Jesus' ascribed honor, consequently, stems from the ascribed honor of his paternal lineage and the acquired honor of pivotal, exogamously related women in the lineage.

Jesus' Peasant Family

Matthew's genealogical concerns regarding Jesus, paralleled to a degree in Luke, are unknown in the other New Testament Gospels: neither Mark nor John has genealogies for Jesus. The New Testament Gospels also have different perspectives on Jesus' paternity: Mark refers to Jesus as "son of Mary" (Mark 6:3) and never once mentions Joseph; Matthew and Luke imply or refer to Jesus in passing as Joseph's son (Matt 13:55; Luke 4:22); and John consistently refers to Jesus as "son of Joseph" (John 1:45; 6:42). This is an important difference in view of the general acceptance of Mark as the earliest Gospel. Without a genealogy or clear statement about Joseph, Mark attests to uncertainty about Jesus' family background in the early Jesus movement. Paul's letters seem to confirm the Markan picture, likewise making relatively little of Jesus' genealogy (only Rom 1:3) or Joseph's paternity (Gal 4:4). Since later traditions are intent to show Jesus' divine origins (John 1:1-18; Hebrews 1–2), the general New Testament tendency is to obscure the factual origins of Jesus while "theologizing" them. Because of the historical uncertainty and the tendency to connect Jesus' origins with God, important contemporary scholarship has argued for Jesus' conception under less flattering circumstances. Schaberg, adopting a feminist viewpoint on both the New Testament traditions about Jesus' birth and later beliefs about his background, makes the case that Jesus' conception happened when Mary was raped (Schaberg 1987). Archaeological evidence offers some support for second-century claims of the (anti-Christian) Celsus and rabbinic traditions that Jesus was the offspring of a liaison between Mary and a Roman **soldier** [1.79] named Pantera. The tombstone for a Roman soldier from Sidon named Pantera, found in Germany and stemming from the time of the Roman emperor Tiberius, has been known since 1859. Pantera had served forty years in the Roman army at the time of his death, so he would have been a relatively new recruit in Roman Palestine when Jesus was conceived (Rousseau and Arav 1995:223). It is also possible that Celsus was making a hostile pun on the Greek word *parthenos*, "young woman, virgin," used of Mary in Matthew and Luke.

Similarly, the relationship of Jesus to presumed brothers and sisters is unclear

(Mark 6:3). The Gospel of Mark identifies four brothers of Jesus: James (Jacob), Joses (Joseph), Judas (Judah), and Simon (Shimon). These common Hebrew names perhaps reflect the great epic figures of ancient Israel (Jacob, Joseph, Judah) or one of the greatest of the Hasmonean leaders (Simon) of the second century B.C.E.; the sisters are not named. Later Christian tradition would identify them as either Assia and Lydia or Mary and Salome (*History of Joseph the Carpenter* 2; J. K. Elliott 1993:114). These "brothers" and "sisters" have been variously understood by critical scholars as blood relatives, stepsiblings, or cousins. Roman Catholic scholars especially have espoused the latter two understandings in view of the deeply held Catholic doctrine of "the perpetual virginity of Mary" (Jesus was the product of divine conception and Mary never had sexual relations after Jesus' birth). However this issue is decided, Jesus' identification by Mark as "Mary's son," the absence of Joseph throughout most of the Synoptic Gospels, and the information about Pantera leave many questions about his family situation unclear.

Neither are the Jesus traditions of one mind about the immediate relatives' attitude toward Jesus during his lifetime. On the one hand, the family seems hostile to Jesus in Mark's narrative (Mark 3:21, 31-35, which mention Jesus' mother, brothers, and sisters only). Jesus' brothers "do not believe in him," according to John (John 7:5-8). On the other hand, Jesus' mother sides with him in the later material of Luke-Acts and John (Luke 2:19, 51; John 2:4-5; 19:25-27). In Acts 1:14, Jesus' brothers are not said to

be hostile to his cause. Paul knows an early tradition about the "conversion" of James after Jesus' death (1 Cor 15:7), a story that is more elaborately recounted in the apocryphal *Gospel according to the Hebrews* 9 (Miller 1994:434).

How are these divergent reports to be understood? The reader should keep in mind that people of peasant origins like Jesus of Nazareth did not have their birthdates carefully recorded as part of an illustrious genealogy by professional **scribes** [1.72]. Such genealogies were the prerogative only of powerful families capable of, and with an important interest in, preserving documentary archives. Most peasants had to keep their ancestry through oral traditions. There were periodic censuses by Roman officials for the purposes of taxation (every fourteen years under the **Principate** [1.63]; Lewis and Reinhold 1983:156); but the family had an interest in keeping the head count low. Besides, it is unlikely that the gospel writers had access to such census information, and, as noted, the genealogies for Jesus in Matthew 1 and Luke 3 do not agree in important respects.

It would seem, then, that the genealogies for Jesus ascribe important origins to him based upon his achievements during his adult lifetime. This was standard procedure even for notables from powerful Mediterranean families, as we discussed above. Matthew, as has been seen, is intent to link Jesus to the glorious ancestors of Israel, especially Abraham and David. This accords with Matthew's interests in showing Jesus' importance in terms that Judeans everywhere could appreciate. Luke, by contrast, has a quite different list of people leading ultimately back to Adam, the progenitor of all peoples. Luke is particularly intent to show Jesus' significance for non-Israelites (Luke 2:32; Acts 1:8).

Summary

The Herodians can be traced for eight generations in four major regions: Idumea, Palestine, Armenia, and Rome. Their family system affected the politics, political religion, and political economy of Palestine for a period of roughly 150 years, and the larger Roman Empire for even longer. They were thoroughly Israelite in the structure of their kinship. But as the top level of urban elites, they employed some variations on what could be expected from urban and rural non-elites. Their family group exemplified the typical patriarchal family system of the eastern Mediterranean. They were patrilineal, patrilocal, and endogamous; they employed dowry, (probably) indirect dowry, and bridewealth, with the eldest son provided a larger share of the father's inheritance. We have clear, worked-out genealogies covering eight generations for the Herodian family recounted in Josephus. They were also accountable to their Roman patrons when it came to inheritance. Far from random or individually determined, the family system to which the Herodians conformed was both predictable and patterned.

On the other hand, a tension arises when viewing the different traditions about Jesus' family. The earliest sources (Q, Paul, *Gospel of Thomas*, Mark) make no claims for the ascribed honor of Jesus' family lineage. The Gospels of Matthew and Luke, from later in the first century, seem very interested in rooting Jesus' story in the honorable framework of great elites with highly developed genealogies. And the Gospel of John and the book of Hebrews have a thoroughly theologized view of Jesus' origins.

Because all ancient Mediterranean institutions and relationships were in one way or another related to kinship arrangements, it is vital for the reader of the New Testament to have a good grasp of how different these arrangements are from modern U.S. configurations. Kinship arrangements are so deeply embedded in the consciousness of the ancients that they are often left implicit.

Applying the Perspectives

1. Develop a "word-field" of kinship terminology (for example: mother, family, marry, inheritance), then check a concordance for where these terms occur in one of the Gospels. What images of the family recur? Which of them are used literally and which metaphorically? Which are missing that you expected?

2. What are the chances that Mary and Joseph were cousins or otherwise closely related? How does that affect the way you think about their family? What other countries in the twenty-first century world have a high percentage of endogamous marriages? What are the social implications of this different marriage strategy?

3. Compare and contrast Matthew 1:19; 5:31-32; 19:3-9; Mark 10:2-12; and Luke 16:18. What factors might account for

different traditions regarding the divorce sayings in the Jesus tradition?

4. Given the differences with regard to access to education, women's employment, child-care, family structure, and so on, how is divorce in contemporary U.S. culture different from how it would be experienced in first-century Palestine? In what ways are they similar?

5. How do the kinship structures (for example, eligible marriage partners) and practices (for example, wedding arrangements and gifts) of your own national and ethnic group differ from those found in the New Testament? From other groups in your own society? How does this affect your reading of the New Testament?

6. Can any kinship structures or practices be identified as "universals"? What are the implications of this for contemporary religious pronouncements on marriage, divorce, or homosexuality?

7. What sorts of problems would the apostle Paul have faced in preaching the gospel to groups with different kinship structures around the eastern Mediterranean? How might this have affected leadership and organization in house churches? How would kinship have affected the networking of these families?

Suggested Reading

For an overview of kinship analysis, see Keesing (1975), Todd (1985), and Barnard (1994). For an analysis of sex and gender, see Lerner (1986) and Moore (1994). For an introduction to the secondary literature on kinship and using it with biblical studies, see Hanson (1994). For analyses of women's roles and gender issues in the earliest Jesus groups and churches, see Corley (1993), Torjesen (1993), Kraemer and D'Angelo (1999), Stegemann and Stegemann (1999), Wire (2005), and Osiek and MacDonald (2006).

For a more detailed analysis of Herodian kinship, along with more biblical and ancient Near Eastern examples, see Hanson (1989a; 1989b; 1990) and Richardson (1996). For overviews of the Bible and kinship analysis in social-scientific perspective, see Patai (1959) and Malina (2001:134–60). For an analysis of fictive kinship and the redefinition of "household" and "family" in churches at the end of the first century C.E., see John H. Elliott (2005) and Hellerman (2001). And for the relationship of kinship to discipleship, see Destro and Pesce (1995).

For a discussion of the archaeology and social history of kinship in the earliest churches, see Osiek and Balch (1997), Balch and Osiek (2003), and Osiek (2005). A detailed commentary on the gospel infancy narratives is available in Brown (1993) and on the genealogies in Johnson (2002). For first-century burial practices, see Hachili (1983; 1997) and Evans (2003).

Herodium fortress

The fortress/palace at Herodium, built into a natural hill, is located approximately ten miles southeast of Jerusalem. "Subsequently, to commemorate his victory, [Herod] founded a city, adorned it with the most costly royal trappings, and crowned it with a very strong acropolis, and called it Herodium after his own name" (Josephus, *War* 1.265). (Photo by Douglas E. Oakman)

CHAPTER 3

Pyramids of Power

Politics and Patronage in Agrarian Roman Palestine

And King Herod [Antipas] heard of it [Jesus' exorcisms and healings], for his reputation had become known. They said, "John the Baptizer has been raised from the dead, and that is why these powers are active in him." But others said, "He is Elijah." But others said, "A prophet, like one of the prophets." But when Herod heard, he said, "The one whom I beheaded, John, has been raised."

For Herod had sent for and seized John and bound him in prison due to Herodias, Philip's wife, since he [Herod] married her. For John told Herod, "It is not lawful for you to have your brother's wife." But Herodias had a grudge against him, and she wanted to kill him, but she could not do it. For Herod feared John, knowing that he was an honorable and holy man, and he protected him. When he heard him he was greatly confused, and yet he gladly heard him. But an opportunity arose when Herod gave a banquet on his birthday for his power-elites, the chiliarchs, and the leaders of the Galilee.

And when Herodias's daughter entered and danced, she pleased Herod and his guests. The king said to the girl, "Request of me whatever you want, and I will grant it to you." And he vowed to her, "Whatever you request of me I will grant it to you, up to half my kingdom!" And she went out saying to her mother, "What shall I request?" And she said, "The head of John the Baptizer." And immediately she entered with haste into the king's presence; requesting she said, "I want you immediately to give me the head of John the Baptizer on a platter." And the king became deeply grieved. But due to his oaths and his guests, he did not want to invalidate it [his oath]. And immediately the king sent an executioner and ordered him to bring his head. And he left and beheaded him in the prison, and brought his head on a platter and gave it to the girl. And the girl gave it to her mother.

And when his disciples heard about it, they arrived and took his body and laid it in a tomb. (Mark 6:14-29//Matt 14:1-2)

But the chief priest stirred up the crowd to have him release Barabbas for them instead. And Pilate again said to them, "Then what shall I do with the man whom you call the King of the Judeans?" And they cried out again, "Crucify him!" . . . So Pilate, wishing to satisfy the crowd, released for them Barabbas; and, having scourged Jesus, he delivered him to be crucified. (Mark 15:11-13, 15//Matt 27:20-22, 26)

Introduction

Questions

The first passage quoted above is an important part of Mark's gospel for a number of reasons, not the least of which is the connection made between Jesus and John the Baptizer. Mark is keen for his audience to see Jesus' mission as both connected to and distinct from John's work (see Mark 1:2-11; 2:18; 8:27-28; 11:27-33). Some of the historical questions one might ask are: Who are these people, and in what time period did they live? What is the historical reliability of this report? Do any archaeological or nonbiblical sources confirm or disconfirm this report? Questions from a literary-critical standpoint might include: In what genre is this story written? What literary devices does it employ? What can be said about the "implied author"? How does the narration interact with the dialog? These are important questions; but the social-scientific questions also call for answers. In what social structures do these people operate, and who benefits from them? How does this story inform our view of first-century Palestinian society? What **values** [3.56] are at stake? And what **groups** [3.23] are involved? Some of the specific questions the stories about Herod Antipas and John the Baptizer and the execution of Jesus raise are:

- What was Herod's rank, authority, and jurisdiction (6:14)? And what form of government does this represent?
- Why did Herod give a banquet for others on his birthday (6:21a)?
- What was the relationship between Herod and the power-elites, chiliarchs, and leaders of Galilee (6:21b)? That is, what can we learn about the social hierarchy depicted in the story?
- What was John's "standing" to attack Herod and Herodias, and for what reason (6:17-18)?
- Why did Herod have John beheaded (6:25-28)?
- Why was Jesus crucified (15:11-15)?
- Why was Jesus' crucifixion associated with "**bandits**" [3.51] (15:27)?
- Who were ancient bandits, and where did Barabbas fit in this political scenario (15:15)?

Models

When imagining "**politics**" [3.42] in modern Western democracies, what come to mind are political parties and conventions; city, county, state, and national elections and offices; referendums; lobbyists and interest groups; political action committees (PACs); and grassroots **movements** [3.36] of vari-

ous types. One also may assume clearly defined divisions between executive, legislative, and judicial functions, with "checks and balances" between their **powers** [3.44] defined in a written constitution. In the wake of political scandals in the United States such as Watergate (1970s), Irangate (1980s), the Congressional bank scandal (1990s), and the invasion and occupation of Iraq (2000s), the public may become cynical about those who abuse their offices. But the public has recourse to elect alternative candidates; initiate recalls, referendums, and impeachments; and petition for corrective legislation. In other words, Western democracies may not be more "efficient" than other governmental forms, but they have the advantage of participation by the governed. Furthermore, critique of and dialog about politicians are an integral part of the social landscape, both by professional commentators in the media and in informal public discussion.

Research Tip 3

Access the following online index Web sites to search for the most up-to-date articles on the subject you are researching:

BiBIL: *https://www.dbunil.unil.ch/bibil//bi/en/bibilhome.html*

RAMBI: *http://aleph1.libnet.ac.il/F/?func=file&file_name=find-b&local_base=rmb01*

In addition, search the **ATLAS** database (available at most college, university, and seminary libraries), which contains both articles and book reviews.

The scholarly literature is full of accounts of first-century political events and people (Smallwood 1981; Mendels 1992; Horsley 1995b; Rhoads 2008). But virtually none of the factors that comprise Western democracies operated in the politics of ancient Palestine. Those living in Judea, Samaria, Idumea, Galilee, Perea, Gaza, and the northern territories (Gaulanitis, Auranitis, Bata- nea, Trachonitis, and Iturea) were governed as an independent state by a dynasty of hereditary rulers (the earlier **Hasmoneans** [1.34]); by **client-kings** [1.13] and **governors** [1.33] (the later Hasmoneans and the **Herodians** [1.37]); and by Roman **prefects** [1.61] and **procurators** [1.65] (for example, Pontius Pilate, Porcius Festus, and Felix), who served at the will of Roman

---

Galilee

The administrative region of Galilee was approximately 40 miles in length and 28 miles wide in the first century. Geographically it is made up of rolling, rocky hills and fertile valleys. Both **Josephus** *[2.7] (War 3.35-40) and the* **Mishnah** *[2.8] (m. Šebi. 9.2) note the division between Lower Galilee and Upper Galilee, while the Mishnah also adds "the valley" (the region around the Sea of Galilee). The division between Upper and Lower Galilee is marked by the great escarpment, running east and west, located just north of Kefar Hanania. Upper Galilee includes higher elevations and more rainfall. The Sea of Galilee (or Lake Gennesaret) has always played a vital role in terms of commerce and transportation and is approximately 13 miles in length and 8 miles wide.*

The population lived primarily in villages, but the administrative towns of Sepphoris and Tiberias (both of which have been excavated in recent years) played significant roles as well. According to the Gospels, Jesus grew up in Nazareth and conducted his ministry primarily in Lower Galilee in the fishing villages along the northern and western shores of the Sea of Galilee (especially Capernaum and Gennesaret) as well as the farming villages of Cana, Nain, and Chorazin. He also frequented the fishing town of Bethsaida, but that was administratively just over the boundary into Gaulanitis.

Agriculture was the dominant form of livelihood, but fishing played an important role as well. Wheat, barley, olives, grapes, figs, and pomegranates were among the most widely cultivated crops and fruits of the region.

Herod the Great had, early in his career, been appointed the ruler over Galilee, prior to becoming king over all of greater Palestine. During the period of 4 B.C.E. to 39 C.E., Galilee was ruled by Herod Antipas (one of the sons of Herod the Great), with his capital in Sepphoris. He ruled as a client of the Roman emperors with the status of **tetrarch** *[1.83] (lower than client-king). Thus he controlled not only the taxation but also much of the economy of Galilee.*

emperors [1.21] (Augustus, Tiberius, Caligula, Claudius, Nero, Vespasian, Titus). As a whole or in parts, they had been provinces of the **Hellenistic** [1.36] empires (the Seleucids in Syria and the Ptolemies in Egypt), the Parthians, and, finally, following 63 B.C.E., the Romans.

The people of first-century Palestine did not elect their rulers. From emperors to regional governors, their rulers were either hereditary monarchs or **elites** [3.14]

appointed to their posts by distant empires. Urban elites, whether Romans or **Judeans** [1.43], decided both domestic and foreign policies with little attention paid to the majority of the **peasants** [3.41] who lived in villages. Taxes, tolls, and **tribute** [1.86] were not open to referendum but were imposed from above; and they were not collected to benefit the populace, but only the elites (see chapter 4). And even the post of **high priest** [1.38] at the Jerusalem temple was a

Characteristics	Roman Empire	Palestine*	U.S.
Classification	Empire	A. Client-kingdom B. Imperial province	Nation-state
Form of Government	Monarchy	A. Client-monarchy B. Province	Democratic republic
Executive	Emperor (hereditary)	A. Client-king B. Governor prefect procurator (appointed)	President (elected)
Legislative Body	Senate (hereditary and appointed)	Sanhedrin (hereditary and appointed)	Congress: House and Senate (elected)
Judiciary	Magistrates (appointed)	Sanhedrin (hereditary and appointed)	Federal judges (appointed and confirmed)
Control of Army	Emperor	A. Client-king B. Legate of Syria	President and Congress
Tax Regulation	Senate	A. Client-king B. Emperor	Congress
Modes of Change: Primary and Secondary	Imperial edict Senate decision	Royal edict Revolt	Election Referendum

*A and B distinguish between territories under direct Herodian rule (A) and those under Roman prefects and procurators (B).

Figure 3.1 Comparative Governmental Forms

political appointment subject to the **patronage** [3.40] of the Herodians or Romans (see chapter 5). The chart in figure 3.1, which identifies the basic parts in relation to the roles they play, provides a contrast between ancient Roman, ancient Palestinian (in the broadest sense), and modern U.S. political structures.

It is useful also to ask about the organization and administration of provinces in the Roman Empire. Since Judea was a Roman province, what are the characteristics of such a **status** [3.53] in the first century? See figures 3.2 and 3.3.

These charts help to envision the structures of political power operating in first-century Palestine. It is important to keep the role of the Romans firmly in mind since they governed Judea as a minor imperial province. It is Rome that had controlled Palestine's politics and political economy, by the time of Jesus' ministry, for nearly one hundred years. Rome also influenced Israelite political religion through control and patronage of the Jerusalem high priesthood. Through prefects and procurators, the Romans directly exerted their power over Palestine (backed by the Roman auxiliary troops headquartered

PROVINCES IN THE ROMAN EMPIRE			
	Senatorial Provinces	**Imperial Provinces**	
		Major	*Minor*
Characteristics	(Achaea)*	(Syria)	(Judea)
Oversight	Senate	Emperor	Emperor
Delegated Administrator (Order)	Proconsul (senator)	Legate (senator)	Procurator (equestrian)
Financial Officer (Order)	Quaestor (senator)	Procurator (equestrian)	Procurator (equestrian)
Army Strength	Legion	Legion	Auxiliary troops**

*Achaea, Syria, and Judea are mentioned here as examples of the three types.

**The province of Egypt was an exception to this practice: while it was an equestrian province, the governing prefect was given a legion.

Figure 3.2 Administration of Roman Provinces

ROMAN PALESTINE

JUDEA	GALILEE and PEREA	NORTHERN TERRITORIES
(Judea, Samaria, Idumea)		(Iturea, Gaulanitis, Trachonitis, Batanea, Aurantis)

	Herod the Great client-king 37–4 B.C.E.	
Archelaus ethnarch 4 B.C.E.–6 C.E.	Herod Antipas tetrach 4 B.C.E.–39 C.E.	Herod Philip tetrach 4 B.C.E.–34 C.E.

Roman Prefects and Procurators		Herod Agrippa I 37–40 C.E.
Coponius	6–9 C.E.	
Marcus Ambibulus	9–12	
Annius Rufus	12–15	
Valerius Gratus	15–26	
Pontius Pilate	26–36	
Marcellus	36–37	
Marullus	37–40	

Herod Agrippa I
40–44 C.E.

Roman Procurators	
Fadus	44–46 C.E.
Tiberius Alexander	46–48
Ventidius Cumanus	48–52
Felix	52–60
Porcius Festus	60–62
Albinus	62–64
Gessius Florus	64–66

FIRST JUDEAN REVOLT
66–70 C.E.

Figure 3.3 One Hundred Years of Rule over Palestine

in Caesarea and the legions in Syria) and indirectly through the Herodian tetrarchs in Galilee and Perea (Herod Antipas) and the northern territories (Philip).

The relationship between the Herodian family in Palestine and the Julio-Claudian emperors in Rome is a superb example of what Kautsky (1982) identifies as an "aristo-cratic empire." We may define an aristocratic empire as a political form in which aristocrats (defined as a nonlaboring, privileged, ruling **class** [3.7]) **rule** [3.49] agrarian peasants and live from the peasants' labor. We can abstract and elaborate a **model** [3.35] of aristocratic empires from the works of social scientists (figure 3.4).

Composition

1. *Aristocratic families* (usually less than 2 percent of the population) and *agrarian peasant families* are the two necessary groups in this model. Aristocratic empires may also include townspeople and more primitive hunter-gatherers, but they are not necessary to this form of society.

2. Furthermore, the political institutions inaugurate and maintain the *social stratification*.

3. Such an empire can hold together *diverse peasant groups* who have different ethnic identities, languages, religions, and cultures.

4. The control by aristocratic families is *based on tradition and heredity*, and it is unaffected for the most part by commercialization or modernization.

5. Since most aristocratic empires are hereditary, *upward mobility* for lower elites and bureaucrats is possible only through proximity to an aristocratic family (patronage).

Governance

6. Governing tends to be *limited and decentralized*.

7. *Powers, civil abilities, and obligations* are not "constitutional" (or even rights) but are aspects of the exploitative relationship between aristocratic families and peasant families that operate by custom.

8. The primary concern of aristocratic families is not ownership of land, but *honor and the control of both land and peasant families, that is, the exercise of power*.

9. *The sale of office and judicial decisions* is a commonplace.

10. *Marriage to spouses from powerful families* (foreign or domestic) generates a network of powerful relationships for the monarch; this may be true to a lesser extent for other elites.

11. The monarch may increase control by *subjugating neighboring groups and territories* (clans, tribes, cities, smaller states) through conquest or by receiving these as gifts from another monarch.

Political Economy and Infrastructure

12. The primary functions exercised by aristocratic families are *tax collection* and *warfare* in support of "the noble life." This is institutionalized in a standing army, which enforces taxation and conscripted labor as well as carries out warfare.

13. The monarch may *conscript peasants* for building projects, the army, or "industries" (such as logging, stone quarrying, mining) that support the interests of the monarch.

14. While the small number of elites compete for honor and the right to control and tax peasant families, peasant families are kept at *subsistence level*.

15. These empires are *exploitative* in that peasants have little say in the control of production or taxation.

16. Since much of the peasant families' produce (the so-called surplus) is extracted by aristocratic families in the form of labor, produce, and money (through the instruments of tithes, taxes, tolls, rents, tribute, and confiscation), *technological progress is impeded*, minimizing change; the exception to this is the technology of warfare, since it is subsidized by the aristocratic families to protect their honor, power, privilege, holdings, and possessions.

17. *Improvements in the infrastructure* (for example, roads, aqueducts, harbors, sewers) are for the increased benefit of the aristocratic families, not to benefit the peasant families in return for their taxes.

Figure 3.4 Aristocratic Empires

It is helpful to keep in mind one of Kautsky's warnings with regard to terminology: "Nor do more old-fashioned but still commonly used concepts like 'state' or 'country,' let alone 'nation,' fit traditional aristocratic empires, and it is by no means clear that they have 'governments' in the modern sense of that word, though I shall use the word for lack of a better one" (1982:13). Indeed, the notion of "nation-states" does not emerge until the period following the Peace of Westphalia (1648) at the end of the Thirty Years' War in Europe.

Moreover, the power of rulers was exerted in very personal ways. The ancient Mediterranean was composed of "face-to-face" societies; that is, these societies operated at every level on the basis of personal contact. The emperor personally appointed prefects and procurators, and he held them accountable for honorably (and tenaciously) representing his and Rome's interests. The Herodian client-kings and tetrarchs depended upon their families, **clients** [3.8], and spies to keep them abreast of their realms' activities. **Honor** [3.25] and **shame** [3.50] were strong components in these ancient societies because one constantly dealt with others face-to-face.

In modern Western societies, social **institutions** [3.30] are most often perceived as impersonal. Social policies are administered as if by a faceless bureaucracy (for example, Internal Revenue Service, Social Security Administration, Veterans Administration). Television only provides the illusion that our government officials are close to us.

Elite Interests: Patronage

Personal Obligation

The people in the ancient Mediterranean world did not understand themselves in the individualistic model of modern Westerners, who can be described as "weak group" (see Malina 1991a; 1993:63–89). Persons (as individuals and as groups) were embedded in others: at the immediate **kinship** [3.31] level, in the head of their family; at a local geographical level, in their neighborhood or village; and interpersonally, perhaps in one or more powerful **patrons** [3.40]. Furthermore, one did not survive on one's own "merits" but by being connected to **networks** [3.37]: family, **friends** [3.20], **brokers** [3.6], and patrons. These were the means by which one dealt with the serious power differentials in the peasant world.

Patrons are elite persons (male or female) who can provide benefits to others on a personal basis because of a combination of superior power, influence, reputation, position, and wealth. In return for these benefits, patrons (who were both men and women in the ancient Mediterranean world) could expect to receive honor, information, and political support from clients. Clients, on the other hand, are persons of lesser status who are obligated and loyal to a patron over a period of time. In Roman society, patronage/clientage was a clearly defined relationship between individuals of different status for their mutual benefit. While this was most often an informal arrangement, Roman law mandated and regulated the duties and services between **freedmen/women** [1.29] and their former owners. A client could appeal to a patron for help with bureaucratic, legal, financial, or other social arrangements. Furthermore, "brokers" were often needed to act as go-betweens for patrons and clients, due to the disparity of their social status. De Ste. Croix observes about the early **Principate** [1.63]: "With the collapse of the Republic and the virtual elimination of the democratic features of the constitution in the last half-century B.C., patronage and clientship became as it were the mainspring of Roman public life" (1954:40). This situation has persisted over the centuries:

> Mediterranean societies are all undercap-italized agrarian civilizations. They are characterized by sharp social stratification and by a relative and absolute scarcity of natural resources. There is little social mobility. Power is highly concentrated in a few hands, and the bureaucratic functions of the state are poorly developed. These conditions are of course ideal for the development of patron-client ties and a dependency ideology. Patronage relations provide a consistent ideological support for social inequality and dependency throughout the Mediterranean area. (Gilmore 1987:192–93)

It is fundamental, then, to examine what patronage and clientage meant in first-century Palestine. The elements in figure 3.5 are basic for a model of ancient patronage.

On the last point of the model, the Romans categorized friends as "superior," "equal," and "inferior" (Pliny, *Epistles* 2.6.2; 7.3.2). In a letter from the Roman orator Cicero (*Epistles to Atticus* 1.20), a list of those who might bring him some books follows a descending social sequence: friends (Latin *amicos*), clients (*clientes*), guest-friends (*hospites*), freedmen (*libertos*), and slaves (*servos*) (Saller 1989). Depending upon the context, "friend" could be used synonymously with "client," especially if the client was also an elite.

Because of the hierarchical structure of power in the ancient world and the huge gap between "power-elites" and the rest of the population, patronage functioned as the means by which elites could increase honor and status, acquire and hold office, achieve power and influence, and increase wealth. Patronage facilitated the maintenance of power differentials and control by those with power (patrons), exchanging their exercise of it on behalf of others (clients) in return for their clients' support, honor, information, and loyalty. In other words, it kept the social hierarchy intact. By acting in this way, networks of clients were developed.

What patrons had to offer clients was a wide variety of "services." Patronage might take the form of physical protection against enemies, support in a legal case, food, money, **citizenship** [1.11], work, appointment to an official post, or freedom from taxes (John H. Elliott 1987:42–43). This system of patronage operated from the highest levels of society down to the lowest, so that the "making of friends" was an ongoing task for everyone in this world (Matt 5:25; Luke 7:6).

1. Patron/client relations are usually *particularistic* (exclusive) and *diffuse* (covering a wide range of issues).

2. Patron/client interaction involves *the exchange of a whole range of social interactions* (what Parsons called "generalized symbolic media"): power, influence, inducement, and commitment.

3. The exchange entails a *"package deal,"* so that power, influence, inducement, and commitment cannot be given separately (for example, concretely useful goods must go along with loyalty and solidarity).

4. Solidarity here entails a strong element of *unconditionality and long-range social credit*; that is, benefits and obligations are not usually exchanged simultaneously.

5. Hence, patron/client relations involve a strong element of *interpersonal obligation*, even if relations are often ambivalent.

6. These relations do not usually take on legal or contractual forms but are very strongly binding; that is, they are *informal* and often opposed to official laws of the country.

7. In principle, patron/client relations *entered into voluntarily can be abandoned voluntarily*, although always proclaimed to be lifelong, long-range, forever.

8. Patron/client relations are *vertical* (hierarchical) and *dyadic* (between individuals or networks of individuals), and thus they undermine the horizontal group organization and solidarity of clients and other patrons.

9. Patron/client relations are based on a strong element of *inequality and difference* between patrons and clients (social stratification). Patrons monopolize certain positions of crucial importance to clients, especially access to means of prosecution, major markets, and centers of society.

10. A client might easily have *more than one patron* (usually for different purposes).

11. The patron/client relationship was *on the same sliding scale with "friendship."*

For the elements of this model, see John H. Elliott (1987), Malina (1988:3–4), and Saller (1982; 1989).

Figure 3.5 Patronage/Clientage

What clients had to offer patrons was first and foremost honor, the primary "commodity" and value in the Mediterranean. By praising the benefits of one's patron in the community, the patron's honor and reputation increased, which might have the residual effect of their increased influence. But clients could also offer loyalty and support to their patrons, which might be expressed in performing tasks, collecting information, spreading rumors, backing the patron in a factional fight, or attending funerals. After Antipater (the father of Herod the Great) had provided military aid to Julius Caesar, Josephus describes the outcome: "He [Caesar] conferred on Antipater the privilege of Roman citizenship and tax-exemption, and by other honors and displays of friendship made him the object of jealousy" (Josephus, *War* 1.194).

In Roman society, patronage took on a very ritualized form. The clients of a Roman patron (especially his or her freedmen and freedwomen) were expected to appear every morning at the patron's home to salute the patron, pay deference, and find out if there was anything they could do for the patron. Thus, clients were often called "those who salute" (*salutatores*).

Patronage operated from the micro-level of relationships within a village to the macro-level of rulers and states. The Roman emperor was the most powerful patron in the empire: appointing to office, freeing slaves, raising status (from **equestrian** [1.23] to **senator** [1.73], for example), granting citizenship, endowing building projects, sponsoring athletic competitions, giving preference in legal cases, or granting exemptions from taxation. His freedmen became the most powerful network in the empire: "Caesar's family" (Latin *familia Caesaris;* Greek *Kaisaros oikia*; Phil 4:22). He depended upon his freedmen, **legates** [1.45], and closest advisors to keep him in contact with his provincial clients (especially client-kings such as the Herodians) and to protect his interests.

Josephus's accounts of his own relationship to the Roman imperial family indicate the variety of things a powerful patron like a general or an emperor might do for a client. Vespasian (ruled 69–79 C.E.) arranged a **marriage** [3.34] for him, granted him Roman citizenship, set him up in Rome with an apartment and a pension, protected him against false accusations, and gave him Judean lands. Titus (ruled 79–81 C.E.) also protected Josephus against false accusations;

freed his family, friends, and acquaintances who were prisoners of war; arranged for him to receive biblical scrolls; had three of his friends taken off crosses; and gave him land in the Judean plains. Domitian (ruled 81–96 C.E.) protected him from further false accusations and granted him freedom from taxes on his Judean estates. Domitia, Domitian's wife, also acted as Josephus's patron. As Titus's client, Josephus scouted out a campsite for the Roman troops in Tekoa (Josephus, *Life* 75–76). Furthermore, he protected Titus's honor, not only by his praise, but by defending his political and military actions during the **First Judean Revolt** [1.28] (his "Preface" to *War*).

Another way in which clients were expected to acknowledge elite patrons was to leave them bequests in their wills. The Roman historian **Suetonius** [2.16] notes that in the last twenty years of his reign Emperor Augustus (the ultimate Roman patron) received 1.4 billion **sesterces** [1.75] from his clients in wills (*Lives of the Caesars,* "Augustus," 101). As discussed in chapter 2, Herod the Great left great sums to Augustus and Livia, his royal patrons. This demonstrates Herod's sensitivity to the whole network of Romans to whom he was tied. The patronage system, therefore, continuously reinforced the honor, wealth, power, and influence of the elite.

One of the ways patrons maintained their networks of clients and fostered their loyalty was to invite them to meals. In a comical description from the first century, the Roman poet Juvenal pokes fun at patrons using dinner parties to repay debts to clients (*Satires* 5.12–25). Note the various dinner

The Parable of the Banquet

A certain man gave a great dinner and invited many. At the time for the dinner he sent his slave to say to those who had been invited, "Come, because it is now prepared." But they all alike demurred. The first said to him, "I have bought a farm, and I must go out and see it; I ask you to be excused." Another said, "I have bought five yoke of oxen, and I am going to try them out; I ask you to be excused." Another said, "I have just married a wife, and therefore I cannot attend." And arriving [back] the slave reported this to his master.

Then the householder became angry and said to his slave, "Go out quickly into the streets and lanes of the town and bring in the poor, the crippled, the blind, and the lame." And the slave said, "Master, what you ordered has been done, and there is still room." Then the master said to the slave, "Go out into the roads and lanes and compel people to come in, so that my house may be filled. For I tell you, none of the men who were invited will taste my dinner." (Luke 14:16-24)

arrangements portrayed in Luke 14:1-24. In 14:1-6 Jesus has been invited to dinner by one of the "ruling elite" (*archon*), who also belonged to the **faction** [3.19] of **Pharisees** [1.57]. In 14:7-11 Jesus describes a hypothetical situation about cultural expectations: Having been invited to a marriage feast, where does one sit? The lesson turns on the shame that one would experience if a later arrival with more status edges one into a less prestigious position.

The instructions Jesus gives to the powerful banquet-giver in Luke 14:12-14 speak to the importance of understanding ancient Mediterranean notions of patron/client networks. The banquet here serves as a metaphor of relationships in God's reign, and the ruler is admonished to invite a wider guest list than cultural expectations would allow. Jesus first lists those one would normally expect at the banquet: (a) friends, (b) brothers, (c) kin, (d) wealthy neighbors (14:12). Especially

when one understands that "friends" is part of the vocabulary of clientage, and that "brothers" (*adelphoi*) and "kin" (*syngeneis*) probably distinguish between blood kin and fictive kin, respectively, it becomes clear that what Jesus is describing here is the social network. These people would normally be invited because the banquet-giver can honor his wealthy patrons, repay his clients or put them in his debt, broker new relationships, and generally maintain contacts with his whole network. Jesus plays down this network precisely because it is the social norm. All persons invite their social network because they always have something to gain by entertaining such a group: invitations, favors, power, honor. If new members to one's network are sought, a patron would naturally recruit from the most influential, powerful, and well-connected people as possible. To highlight the distinctiveness of his approach to social relations in God's reign, Jesus instructs the ruler instead to invite the people at the bottom of the social scale: the **poor** [1.58], the maimed, the lame, the blind (14:13). These are the socially powerless who have nothing tangible to offer the network. But if God is willing to act toward humans in a gracious way, those who look to God for their cue should also include the outsiders, those too weak to be powerful network contributors. Rather than keeping low-class clients outside one's house (as expected in Greco-Roman society), Jesus' image of God's reign is that everyone is invited to the table.

Finally, in 14:16-24 Jesus tells a parable about a dinner party that exhibits the elements in the preceding instruction. The banquet-giver announces the readiness of the banquet, only to be shamed by the refusals of his friends. Note the indicators in the story that this is a story about elites: it is a large banquet to which many are invited (v. 16), the banquet-giver has a household servant (v. 17), and the friends buy fields (v. 18) and multiple yokes of oxen (v. 19). In the *Gospel of Thomas* [2.5], one of the refusals comes from someone going to buy a large estate (*Gos. Thom.* 64). At the parable's conclusion, it is the people on the periphery of society who are at the table: the urban non-elite (**artisans** [3.3] and traders) and those outside the city who are dependent on the city. (For further analysis of this parable, see especially Rohrbaugh 1991:137–47; but also Jeremias 1972:63–70, 176–80; Crossan 1973:70–73; and Scott 1989:161–74.)

In another mode of patronage, an individual might be the patron or benefactor of a large group or locale. By building the city of Caesarea, Herod the Great acted in his capacity both as client and as patron (Josephus, *War* 1.408–15//*Ant.* 15.331–41). As the client of Augustus, Herod did a number of things to honor Augustus:

- Named the city Caesarea (Latin for "Caesar's city")
- Named the harbor Sebaste (Greek for "imperial harbor")
- Named a harbor tower for Drusus, Augustus's dead stepson
- Built a temple to Augustus and Roma (the patron goddess of the city of Rome)
- Dedicated a musical and sports festival competition to be celebrated every fifth year

This musical and sports festival honored Augustus's victory over Antony at Actium (the Actian Games had become a traditional honor in many Mediterranean cities). But Herod also served as patron of the city and the games. The city was indebted to him for the temple, theater, amphitheater, hippodrome, and games, and his reputation increased in the empire. He also financed the parties connected with the festivals (*Ant.* 16.136–41).

Originally a small Hellenistic anchorage on the Mediterranean coast called Strato's Tower, Caesarea was greatly expanded c. 22–10 B.C.E. by Herod the Great. It was a gift of Caesar Augustus to Herod, who renamed the city after his **benefactor** [3.4]. When the Romans took direct control of Palestine in 6 C.E., Caesarea became their capital, and they renamed it *Colonia Prima Flavia Augusta*

Caesarea (the first colony of Flavius Augustus Caesar).

Several aspects of this city are significant for understanding the social dynamics of Herodian Palestine. Foremost is the well-designed harbor that Herod had built (Josephus, *War* 1.409–14//*Ant.* 15.331–38). A massive construction project called *Sebastos* (Greek) or *Portus Augusti* (Latin), the harbor provided safe haven for ships traveling up and down the eastern Mediterranean coast or from the West. It became a major port for exporting Palestinian goods and importing goods from the rest of the Mediterranean, as well as establishing a Hellenistic-Roman city with all the trappings of these cultures. The southern breakwater was a 600m arc, while the northern breakwater ran 250m, encircling a harbor of approximately 3.5 acres. These breakwaters were constructed of great wooden forms that were filled with rubble; the rubble was set with hydraulic concrete (then a fairly recent Roman invention). These installations also included siltation control with flushing channels. The harbor project demonstrates a high degree of technical skill as well as the need for a large number of construction workers.

The city was only habitable in its expanded form because of the major aqueduct (still partially visible), which supplied water from the hills approximately seven miles to the east. Also helpful for this expanded population was a sophisticated sewer system, continuously flushed out by its connection to the sea. The Herodian-era central sewer was approximately 1.8m deep and 1m wide, and Josephus notes that a sophisticated set of channels ran under each street toward the sea (Olami and Peleg 1977).

The temple that Herod built was dedicated to the emperor Augustus (his patron) and Roma (the patron goddess of Rome) with a colossus (oversized statue) for each (*War* 1.414). This provides insight into a number of important issues. First, Caesarea was outfitted with one of the most important monuments of a Roman city—a temple connecting it with the political religion of Rome. Second, any reservations Herod may have had as a Judean monotheist against such a move were overridden by his **role** [3.49] as a client of the Roman emperor. And third, it is a specific example that the cities were considered by the Palestinians as something separate from the land as a whole. The Herodians could get away with things in Caesarea, Sepphoris, or Tiberias that never would have been acceptable to the general population in the countryside of Galilee or Judea.

The **synagogue** [1.81] in Caesarea mentioned by Josephus has not been discovered by archaeologists (*War* 2.285–91). But Josephus's anecdote concerning the synagogue highlights the tensions between ethnic Israelites and the gentile population, the need for powerful patrons and brokers, the use of "gifts" for officials (bribes), and the fact that ethnic Israelites were in fact tax collectors. It also provides documentary evidence of first-century synagogue buildings used within Palestine.

A Latin inscription at the theater is Pilate's dedication to the emperor Tiberius (Pilate's patron), who ruled the empire 14–37 C.E. One reconstruction of it can be

The Pilate Inscription

(Photo © Erich Lessing / Art Resource, NY. Used by permission.)

[Dis Augusti]s Tiberieum	*To the honorable gods (this) Tiberieum*
[Po]ntius Pilatus	*Pontius Pilate,*
[Praef]ectus Iuda[ea]	*Prefect of Judaea,*
[fecit d]e[dicavit]	*had dedicated*

seen in the sidebar above. This inscription provides inscriptional evidence in support of the New Testament and Josephus's references to Pilate as governor over Judea. It also indicates the need for Pilate to act as a good client by constructing public monuments to honor his patron, the emperor. The fact that the theater was dedicated as a Tiberieum (a "religious" building) also indicates the embeddedness of Roman religion as political in nature since it bore the name of the emperor.

A hippodrome is an oval track for horse and chariot races, both popular throughout the Roman Empire. It was used in the Actian Games established and patronized by Herod the Great.

The Mithraeum, a temple dedicated to Mithras, lies just south of the Augustan temple near the water. Since Mithras (whose origins may have been Persian) was one of the traditional gods worshiped by the Roman army, this temple undoubtedly served the Roman troops **garrisoned** [1.31] at Caesarea after 6 C.E. But since Mithraism seems to have flourished later in the Roman Empire, the Mithraeum may originate in the late first or early second century C.E.

The construction of Caesarea is vital for understanding a variety of aspects of Palestinian society in the first century. Cities in the ancient world drew workers and resources away from the agrarian villages. On the one hand, this provided jobs for artisans; but on the other, it drew workers off the farms. The temples, theater, hippodrome, and other building projects all provided for the elites at the expense of the villagers. As Rohrbaugh summarizes:

The urbanization of antiquity was the result, at least in part, of the organization and appropriation by cities of an agricultural surplus produced in the hinterlands.

... Thus cities accumulated what was produced beyond the subsistence needs of the peasants. By bureaucratic, military, commercial, or fiduciary means, they became the centers of control, primarily over land use and raw materials, and thereby determined the conditions under which all other parts of the system operated. (1991:131)

We find the type of benefaction described above operating in the New Testament as well. Note that Joseph/Barnabas acted as patron to the early Jerusalem church by selling his field and allowing the apostles to distribute the proceeds among the group (Acts 4:36-37).

The Theodotus Inscription

(Photo courtesy Israel Antiquity Authority.)

Theodotus, son of Vettanos, priest and archisynagōgos, *son of an* archisynagōgos, *grandson of an* archisynagōgos, *built the synagogue for Torah-reading and for the teaching of the commandments. Furthermore, [he built] the hostel and the chambers, and the water installation for lodging needy strangers. Its foundation stone was laid by his ancestors, the elders, and Simonides.*

Immediately following this account, Acts relates that Ananias and Sapphira also wanted recognition as patrons of the group, yet lied to Peter about the sale price of their property and the donation of the whole amount. The judgment against them can be interpreted as punishment for treating their fictive kin-group with negative **reciprocity** [3.46]: they wanted their benefaction for a bargain price. One may lie to outsiders, but one owes the truth to one's family and social equals (Malina 2001a:41–42).

Another significant first-century inscription from Palestine illustrates benefaction. An inscription in Greek uncovered in Jerusalem identifies Theodotus, the **"head of the synagogue"** [1.35] (*archisynagōgos*), as the benefactor who built a synagogue and adjoining support-facilities (*CIJ* 2.1404; see Riesner 1995:192–200; and Kloppenborg 1996).

If a large social gap separates a patron and a client, intermediaries are often used (**brokers** [3.6]/mediators). These brokers make the connection between interested parties for their mutual benefit (note, for example, the recurring role of Tom Hagen, Vito Corleone's *consigliere* [counselor], in the movie *The Godfather*). If patrons have access to the primary resources of power, influence, and goods, brokers have access to the secondary resource of patrons. The broker would usually be in a position to accomplish this because he or she had worked at either developing a complex network, having an intermediate social status (age, reputation, occupation), or living in geographical proximity (neighborhood access). Furthermore, brokers build "capital" in the form of debt-

obligation and can use their friends as a network (see Boissevain 1974).

In the passage discussed above (Josephus, *Life* 75–76), Josephus acted as broker for his brother, 50 friends, 3 crucified friends, and his 190 Jerusalem acquaintances. All of these people would be in Josephus's debt, and it would be to his advantage to keep them there. This is how network-building operates (see also *Life* 244; Duling 1999; 2000; 2002).

What Malina has further demonstrated is that this model of patronage may be profitably applied to the Synoptic Gospels and especially Matthew (1988:2–32): God is father/patron, and the reign of God/heaven is "God's patronage and the clientele bound up in it" (9); Jesus is broker; and believers are clients.

In the Gospel of John, it is Andrew, among the Twelve, who is repeatedly described as a broker between Jesus and outsiders. After encountering Jesus for the first time, Andrew negotiates the meeting between Jesus and his brother Simon (John 1:35-42). Being followed by a huge crowd across the Sea of Galilee, Jesus ponders how to feed them. Philip is at a loss, but Andrew finds a young boy with meager provisions and brings him to Jesus (6:5-8). And finally, when a group of "Greeks" (presumably hellenized Israelites from outside Palestine) want to meet Jesus, they ask Philip to make the arrangements, and Philip asks Andrew (12:20-22). Andrew, consequently, is depicted as recruiting faction members (Simon) and people with resources needed by the group (the boy with food), as well as making formal introductions of outsiders (the "Greeks") to Jesus. These are all functions of an efficient broker.

The Political "Family"

The result of long-term patronage is the creation of a political "family." That is, the relationships and roles, obligations and responsibilities between the patron and his or her clients is shaped into what social scientists call "fictive kinship" or "pseudo-kinship" (Pitt-Rivers 1968; Malina 1988; 1996b). In 140 B.C.E., for example, the Seleucid **king** [1.13] Antiochus VII Sidetes "heard that the Judeans were addressed by the Romans as friends, allies, and brothers" (1 Macc 14:40). The political relationship between Rome and Judea was articulated, then, not simply as an abstract contract, but as kinship. "Politics," in the ancient world, as this illustrates, is not the rule of one individual over numerous other individuals (as in Western democracies), but a family (or group of families) exercising control over other families. Not the result of votes, policy decisions, or impersonal institutions, this political power is *personal* and the result of creating alliances and networks, reciprocity, debts, force, and taking advantage of **social stratification** [3.52].

A variation on this type of kinship is the political marriage. In 150 B.C.E., when the Seleucid ruler Alexander Balas (Alexander Epiphanes) took the throne and defeated his rival, Demetrius I Soter, an ancient Judean historian narrates how Alexander wrote to the Egyptian emperor, Ptolemy VI Philometor, petitioning him for peace: "And now let us establish a friendship with one another. And now give me your daughter for a wife,

and I will become your son-in-law, and I will send gifts to you and her as befits your dignity" (1 Macc 10:54). The marriage (real kinship) became the seal of their political alliance (fictive kinship). This type of political marriage is evidenced in ancient Israel and Judah beginning with David (2 Sam 3:3) and Solomon (1 Kgs 1:3), and it continued with virtually all of the Herodian family's **exogamous** [3.17] marriages (see chapter 2).

Elites with political power also appointed their family members to offices. In modern democracies this would be considered nepotism, a charge that can cause scandal or outrage (as when President Kennedy appointed his brother Robert to be attorney general). In the ancient Mediterranean, preference given family members was not only allowed, but expected; a more neutral term for this type of family networking is *familism*. That is, as **"strong group"** [3.54] people, the primary allegiance was not to the state with weight given to the value of efficiency. Rather, one strategized to maximize the benefits to one's family. Antipater (Herod the Great's father) appointed his two sons Herod and Phasaelus as tetrarchs over Galilee and Judea (Josephus, *War* 1.203). Herod the Great appointed his brother-in-law, Costobarus, governor over Idumea and Gaza (Josephus, *Ant.* 15.253).

The negative reciprocal of this is that families could bear the brunt of political intrigue. When ten men conspired to assassinate Herod the Great and were then discovered, their families were punished along with them (*Ant.* 15.290). In a strong group society, the assumption would be that the conspirators never would have proceeded without the complicity of their families. In modern Western societies, the family of a political conspirator could not be held liable by the authorities. The value of "individual responsibility" is that it rules out blaming the larger group for an individual's actions.

The Herodians' Political Family: Mark 6:14-29

The rising power of the Herodian family was due to two interactive factors: their ability to secure the help of powerful patrons and their adaptability in shifting alliances. Because of Octavian's patronage, Antipater (the father of Herod the Great) was able to appoint his sons as tetrarchs: Herod over Galilee, and Phasaelus over Jerusalem and Judea (Josephus, *War* 1.203//*Ant.* 14.158). Josephus says of Antipater during this period that he was treated as if he were king and "lord of the realm" by the Judeans (*War* 1.207). Herod the Great (along with his brothers Phasaelus and Joseph) was a military envoy for the Romans, but Herod repeatedly found himself in the position of quickly having to find a new Roman patron. After Caesar's assassination, Herod sided with Cassius and Brutus against Octavian, and Cassius made him governor of Syria (probably the district of Coele-Syria, part of modern-day Lebanon) in 43 B.C.E., with the promise of the Judean kingship after the Romans were done with their civil war (*War* 1.225//*Ant.* 14.280). But within a year, Cassius was captured at Philippi and committed suicide (*War* 1.242). Mark Antony then confirmed Herod and Phasaelus as tetrarchs (*War* 1.244). And when Antipater was

assassinated and Hyrcanus was captured by Parthian invaders (40 B.C.E.), Julius Caesar and Mark Antony got the Roman Senate to confirm Herod as king over Palestine: Judea, Samaria, Galilee, Perea, and Idumea (*War* 1.282–85). But it took three years to secure his throne with Roman military backing (*War* 1.286–353).

After the death of Herod the Great in 4 B.C.E., Palestine was segmented again, with three of his sons and his sister Salome ruling each part, and each owing allegiance to their Roman patrons: Augustus and his wife, Livia (*War* 2.93–100//*Ant.* 17.317–21). Archelaus was named client-king of Judea, Samaria, and Idumea by his father (Matt 2:22) but was only confirmed in the lower status of **"ethnarch"** [1.25] by Augustus (*Ant.* 17.317). Herod Antipas was tetrarch over Galilee and Perea (Luke 3:1) but had contested his share when he compared it with Archelaus's (*War* 2.94). Herod Philip was tetrarch over the territories in the northeast (Gaulanitis, Batanea, Iturea, Trachonitis, and Auranitis; Luke 3:1). And Salome was ruler (*despoina*) over a number of independent Palestinian cities (although subject to Archelaus's ethnarchy): Ashdod, Jamnia, and Phasaelis, with a palace in Ascalon. (Salome's status and role, while repeatedly mentioned by Josephus, is often overlooked by modern scholars.)

We now turn to addressing the questions raised above concerning Mark 6 and Herod Antipas. What was Herod's rank, authority, and jurisdiction (6:14)? His place in society needs to be interpreted in light of client-kingship and the development of the

Herodian family as clients of the Roman emperors. Beginning with his paternal great-grandfather, Antipater, the Herodian family had worked in cooperation with Roman interests. Antipater was an Idumean general who became the military governor of Idumea under the Judean king Alexander Jannaeus (the Hasmonean who ruled 103–76 B.C.E.; see Josephus, *Ant.* 14.10), and presumably also during Alexandra Salome's reign (76–67 B.C.E.). Under Hyrcanus II (the Hasmonean who had limited rule as ethnarch under the Romans, 67–40 B.C.E.), his grandfather, Antipater, was the governor of Judea (actually encompassing all of Palestine). And his father, Herod the Great, ruled over all Palestine as the client of Mark Antony and then Augustus. Furthermore, for providing military support to Julius Caesar, his grandfather, Antipater, was given Roman citizenship in 47 B.C.E. (see Josephus, *War* 1.194//*Ant.* 14.143). This citizenship was shared, therefore, by the rest of the succeeding Herodian family members.

While Mark calls him "King Herod" (6:14), Herod Antipas ruled Galilee and Perea as tetrarch (a status below that of client-king) from 4 B.C.E. until 39 C.E. The evangelist's failure to distinguish between tetrarch and client-king may be due to the evangelist (or the people of Galilee?) not caring to make the distinction between the two terms, since Herod was from an acknowledged "royal" family (but compare Matt 14:1 and Luke 9:7, where he is identified as tetrarch). Or, since Herod the Great (Matt 2:1), Herod Agrippa I (see Acts 12:1), and Herod Agrippa II (see Acts 25:13) were all client-kings, Mark may have mistakenly assumed that Herod Antipas also held that rank. Another possibility is that Mark got the different Herods confused. In any event, Herod Antipas was deposed and banished to Lyons in Gaul (modern France) by the emperor Gaius Caligula for ambitiously seeking the status of client-king in 39 C.E.; Josephus attributes the instigation of this ambition to Herodias, Herod's wife (see *War* 2.181–83//*Ant.* 18.240–55), who also figures prominently here in Mark's narrative.

Herod Antipas, like his relatives, was a client of the Julio-Claudian emperors: of Augustus, Tiberius, and Caligula. After Caesar had assigned additional territory to the rule of Herod the Great, for example, Josephus describes the relationship: "But what Herod valued more was that in Caesar's affection he stood next after [M. Vipsanius] Agrippa, and in Agrippa's [affection] next after Caesar" (*War* 1.400). In other words, Herod the Great was in the inner circle of Roman clients and "friends."

What is the relationship between Herod Antipas and the power-elites (*megistanoi*), chiliarchs (*chiliarchoi*), and leaders (*prōtoi*) of Galilee (Mark 6:21b)? This list leads us to conclude that those attending Herod's party are his clients and retainers, since he is not only the head of the government but also the most powerful patron of the region. His role as patron stems from two interconnected sources: his family and the Roman government. By the time of this incident with John the Baptizer (c. 29 C.E.), Herod's family had been developing networks and exercising military and political control in Palestine for more than a century.

The terms *power-elites* and *leaders* are both somewhat vague and overlap in meaning; they refer to those who exercised political and economic control of the region. The New Testament books and Josephus have a large vocabulary to cover these elites: powerful ones, great ones, leaders, aristocrats, illustrious ones, leading men, nobles, notables, distinguished ones. All of these stand over against the general population: the peasants. These elites have some combination of superior honor, power, office, influence, networks, and wealth. And these terms speak to the social hierarchy of a highly stratified society in which power and wealth are held by a small percentage of the population, probably 2 percent or less (Lenski 1984:219–30). Furthermore, the same small group would comprise absentee landlords (Mark 12:1-12), land speculators (*Gos. Thom.* 64), bureaucrats, and retainers (Luke 14:1).

Why did Herod give a banquet for others on his birthday (Mark 6:21a)? One of the key attributes of patronage/clientage in the ancient Mediterranean was banqueting. By having banquets for one's "friends," patrons reinforced their connections to their network and could honor those to whom they were also indebted (D'Arms 1984). It was a time to display one's honor by how grand a feast could be offered. The seating arrangements symbolized the relative status within the group. Being invited indicated one's membership in the in-group. And banquets were opportunities not only to socialize but to share information, make deals, and cement attachments (see the discussion of Luke 14, above, and Crossan 1991:341–44). Herod's

birthday seems to have been just such an occasion to entertain his circle of elite clients. In return, these clients and friends showed up to honor their powerful patron.

But what can we deduce from the fact that it is specifically a birthday celebration? Birthdays were rarely celebrated except for elites in the Roman world. Moreover, no birthday celebrations are known in the Semitic world; this was a Hellenistic phenomenon. In the Bible, the only birthday celebrations mentioned are for rulers: the Egyptian pharaoh (Gen 40:20), Antiochus IV Epiphanes of Syria (2 Macc 6:7; see also 1 Macc 1:58-59), and Herod Antipas of Galilee (Mark 6:21//Matt 14:6). Keep in mind that Herod Antipas was educated and socialized in Rome (Josephus, *Ant.* 17.20), and in Roman circles the "genius" of the male head of the household (Latin *pater familias*) was celebrated on his birthday. The genius was the life-force of the family residing in the father and passed on to the next generation (Scheid 1996:630). But the genius of a king or emperor was especially significant because of his representative status; that is, his genius affected his whole kingdom. (Note Tertullian's ironic comments about perjury based on swearing to the Romans' gods versus the emperor's genius in *Apology* 28.3.)

Finally, what is John's "standing" to criticize Herod and Herodias, and for what reason (Mark 6:17-18)? Why is John beheaded (vv. 25-28)? John is characterized in the Gospels as a prophet. A "prophet" is a type of shaman who has socially acknowledged forms of "altered states of consciousness": visions and auditory messages from the divine realm

Josephus on the Death of John

When others also joined the crowds surrounding him, because they were highly affected by hearing his [John's] words, Herod became alarmed. Eloquence that had such a great affect on people might lead to some form of sedition, for it looked as if they might be led by him in everything they did. Herod, therefore, decided that it would be preferable to strike first and be rid of him before his work led to a rebellion. . . . Because of Herod's suspicions, he brought him [John] in chains to Machaerus, the fortress we have previously mentioned, and there executed him to death. The verdict of the Judeans, however, was that the losses to Herod's army were a vindication of him [John], since God inflicted such a blow on Herod. (Ant. 18.118-19; LCL revised)

(see Craffert 2008). In Israelite tradition, prophets were understood to communicate messages from Yahweh, Israel's patron God, to the society as a whole, but especially to the rulers. This sets up an inherently tenuous relationship between prophets and the structures of power: rulers, **priests** [1.62], and other elites. The prophet Nathan delivered the message of Yahweh's contract/covenant with David (2 Sam 7:4-17), but also accused David of adultery (2 Sam 12:1-15). The **Old Testament** [2.10] narratives about Elijah and King Ahab (1 Kings 21), Micaiah ben Imlah and King Jehoshaphat (1 Kings 22), and Jeremiah and the Jerusalem elite (Jeremiah 26) provide especially good examples of how dangerous this relationship was.

In this Markan passage, John publicly criticizes Herod Antipas and his wife, Herodias, for their marriage relationship. Once the modern reader learns that the spouses are actually uncle and niece, it is easy to jump to the conclusion that John's critique is aimed at incest. But, as pointed out in chapter 2, **endogamous** [3.15] marriages between

two cousins or uncle and niece were perfectly acceptable throughout the eastern Mediterranean. In fact, what John is exposing for public shame is that Herod and Herodias precipitated divorces in order to get married. Beyond that, Herod virtually "stole" this new wife from his half brother, Philip, who was still alive. Herodias's motivation for pursuing the relationship may well have been increased honor and prestige: Herod the Great had disinherited her first husband, and her new husband was the ruling tetrarch over Galilee and Perea.

Theissen (1991:81–97) prefers Josephus's version of this story as more historical, because Josephus emphasizes that John posed a *political* threat (*Ant.* 18.116–19). Josephus recounts that the reason Herod executed John was that John was becoming more popular with the public, and he therefore feared John might start a rebellion. Theissen is undoubtedly correct that Mark's version has more of the elements of popular storytelling. But the basis for his preference of Josephus's political explanation over the gospel's focus on shame and kinship is not well founded. There is no reason Josephus and Mark could not both be identifying fundamental issues involved, emphasizing the rationales that made the most sense for themselves or their audiences.

But, as the stories of other Israelite and Judean prophets make clear, challenging rulers could quickly lead to imprisonment or death. In Josephus's account, John posed a potential threat of public rebellion as leader of an anti-elite movement group. In Mark's account, John posed a threat to the honor of Herod and Herodias, because he was an acknowledged prophet holding their marriage up to public ridicule and shame. Either way (or both), the uneasy relationship between elites and peasants is laid bare in these accounts. Because ruling elites had access to troops and prisons, they could use force against those who voiced public criticism and threats to their honor or who posed potential threats to their "peaceful" rule—challenging the social hierarchy.

Peasant Interests: Rebellion and Social Banditry

Palestine's geographical location always placed it in a precarious position politically. In the pre-Roman era it lay as a buffer between the Seleucids in Syria and the Ptolemies in Egypt. (Compare this phenomenon to Alsace-Lorraine's turbulent history, positioned between France and Germany, or East Prussia's position between Germany, Russia, and Poland.) In the Roman era, Palestine lay between the Roman Empire and Rome's eastern enemies in Parthia and Nabatea. During the period following Alexander the Great's subjugation of Palestine in 332 B.C.E., the political allegiances of the Jerusalem elite factions swayed back and forth: from the Seleucids (rulers of Syria) to Ptolemies (rulers of Egypt), and later from Parthians to Romans.

The urban elites of Judea sought out the backing of a series of imperial states because

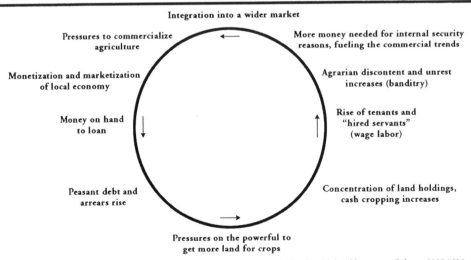

(Based on H. Landsberger; see Oakman 2008:168.)

Figure 3.6 A Dynamic Model of the Causes of Agrarian Conflict

Prepolitical				Political	
common thievery	social banditry	haidukry	frontier raiding	rebellion (sporadic)	revolution (sustained)
individuals	*small groups*			*large groups*	

Figure 3.7 Forms of Stealing, Attack, and Rebellion

the patronage of these foreign states provided protection (coercion of external and internal enemies), access to power (political offices), religious control (influence), and inducement (control of land and economic resources). If one faction of elites was backed by the Seleucids, then another faction would seek the backing of the Ptolemies. If Herod's enemy (Antigonus) was backed by the Parthians, he looked for help from the Romans (Josephus, *Ant.* 14.324–467). In the twentieth century, one can compare how the United States, the U.S.S.R., and China repeatedly backed opposing factions in smaller countries following World War II (Korea, Vietnam, Yemen, Angola, and Nicaragua, to name a few).

The peasantry, on the other hand, had little or nothing to gain from these shifting alliances. Their perspective was that the elites continually bartered with foreign powers at the peasants' expense. The peasants' lot did not change if their grain and produce were extracted by Roman clients instead of Seleucid clients. Eric Hobsbawm has described peasant rebellion as "pre-political" (1981; figure 3.7), meaning that peasants do not attempt "programs" of political reforms or focus on the larger political picture. They react against economic, military, or **ideological** [3.27]

pressures manifested in new or increased taxes; occupation by foreign troops; disruption of temple functions; or the imposition of new gods, temples, and priesthoods.

One of the recurring ways disaffected peasants react is through "social banditry." **Social bandits** [3.51] are peasants who have been repressed and separated from their land and village. This is usually the result if they have been excessively taxed and forced to sell their land, have had their land confiscated by elites, or have broken a law enforced by the elites. They lash out by organizing into bands that raid and steal to survive, usually from the local and imperial elites (like Robin Hood of English legend; figure 3.6).

We see this phenomenon in biblical narratives as far back as those about Jephthah (in the book of Judges), when he was cut off from his inheritance, and David, when he was labeled a threat to, and was on the run from, the Israelite king Saul:

Then Jephthah fled from his brothers, and settled in the land of Tob. And worthless men gathered around Jephthah and went raiding with him. (Judg 11:3)

And everyone who was oppressed, and everyone who was in debt, and everyone

Context

1. Social banditry is a *rural phenomenon* appearing in peasant/agrarian societies.
2. Social banditry may appear when *the social equilibrium is upset* in drastic ways; peasants are under increased pressure due to
   a. ecological factors—drought, famine, plague—or
   b. political-economy factors—increased taxation, land confiscation, political disruption, inequitable exercise of authority.
3. The *state administration is too inefficient* to deal adequately with the bandits swiftly.
4. *Rule by a foreign power* ("colonialism") is often at the root of the bandits' disaffection with the political elites.

Operation

5. The bandits are *labeled deviants* by political authorities (often for minor infractions), isolated, and hunted down as a threat to the state and economic stability; but they are considered honorable by the peasant population.
6. The bandits are often *supported by the local peasants* because of general peasant disaffection and the sense that the bandits stand against injustice.
7. While hiding from authorities, bandits usually *stay close to their home villages*.
8. Besides providing *an outlet for peasant disaffection*, bandits often provide tangible goods, protection, or redress of injustices for their villages.

Organization

9. They are held together by the *prestige of the leader*.
10. They are primarily *composed of young, unmarried males* (but whole families may be included).
11. They are *limited to groups of fifteen to forty members* due to organizational difficulties; but, in unusual circumstances, bands may be larger.

Outcomes

12. They are usually limited in duration to *less than two years*, either because they get caught and are punished or the authorities lose interest.
13. Social banditry is usually *an ineffective strategy* for bringing about long-lasting change because
    a. they do not originally form for political purposes;
    b. they lack the size and organization to pressure the authorities; and
    c. old and new oppressions coalesce to keep them isolated.
14. Social bandits often *look for opportunities to be reintegrated* into the mainstream of their peasant society.
15. The bandit bands may be *utilized (or co-opted) by local elites* for their own purposes (mercenaries).
16. The social bandit bands may become *haiduks* ("institutionalized" outlaw bands).
17. In unusual circumstances, the social bandit phenomenon may accompany or be integrated into *a full-scale peasant revolt* (like the First Judean Revolt).

For the elements of this model, see especially Hobsbawn 1959:13–29; 1974; 1981; Koliopoulos 1979; Horsley and J. S. Hanson 1985:48–87; Freyne 1988a; Horsley 1979; 1986; 1988; 1995b; and K. C. Hanson 2002.

Figure 3.8 Social Banditry

who was embittered rallied to him [David]; and he became their chieftain. And there were about four hundred men with him. (1 Sam 22:2)

As an author who represents the perspective of the Judean elite, Josephus is repeatedly disparaging of social bandits, characterizing them as dishonorable, violent, and surrounded by "rabble" (*War* 2.588). As John Dominic Crossan so clearly puts it:

They rob the monopoly of violence from the rich and distribute it to the poor, and, more significantly, they rob aristocratic and structural violence of the veneer of morality under which it operates. They force the question: what is the moral difference between a gang and an army, a peasant bandit on the make and an imperial entrepreneur on the throne? (1991:304–5)

Gospel traditions link Jesus to the issue of social banditry in several ways. Jesus inquired whether the temple guards thought him to be a bandit (Mark 14:48); he was crucified between two such bandits (Mark 15:27); and just such a bandit, Barabbas, was released by Pilate at Jesus' trial (Mark 15:6-15). While Jesus was not a social bandit himself, several factors linked him with these issues. Like the social bandits, Jesus was from the villages (Mark 2:1). He associated with a variety of people who were "disreputable" by urban elite standards (Luke 7:36-38). And he was known to have uttered sayings about Roman

taxation (see chapter 4) and the Jerusalem temple (see chapter 5) that were potentially inflammatory issues with regard to the peasants (Mark 12:13-17). Based on the cross-cultural analyses of several scholars, we can summarize the basic characteristics of social banditry (figure 3.8).

Josephus recounts the exploits of several bandit leaders and their groups from the first century B.C.E. to the first century C.E. In the wake of civil strife and upheaval when Herod the Great was coming to power and ringing in a new era of Roman-backed Herodian control of Palestine, Hezekiah raised a band of bandits in the borderlands between Galilee and Syria, now called the Golan Heights (47–38 B.C.E.; *War* 1.204// *Ant.* 14.159). Later, in the early 30s B.C.E., during the power vacuum of shifting Roman and Hasmonean power, Herod had to subdue a major threat from bandits living in Galilean caves, and engaged them in battle near Arbela, just west of the Sea of Galilee. After some success in battle, the rebels retreated to the caves, where Herod eventually burned them out (*War* 1.304–14//*Ant.* 14.420–30). Figure 3.9 lists the social bandits mentioned in the Gospels, Josephus's works, the Babylonian **Talmud** [2.18], and Dio's *Roman History*. This gives a sense of how pervasive this "institution" was in ancient Palestine.

Note also Josephus's summary comments about widespread social banditry during the procuratorships of Albinus (62–64 C.E.; *Ant.* 20.215) and Festus (64–66 C.E.; *Ant.* 20.255).

Bandits	Region	Dates	Ruler	References
Hezekiah	Syrian Frontier	47–38 B.C.E.	Herod the Great	*War* 1.204 *Ant.* 14.159-60
cave bandits	Galilee	38–37 B.C.E.	Herod the Great	*War* 1.304-13 *Ant.* 14.413-30
unnamed bandits	Galilee	37 B.C.E.	Herod the Great	*War* 1.314-16 *Ant.* 14.431-33
unnamed bandits	Trachonitis	24 B.C.E.	Herod the Great	*War* 1.398-400 *Ant.* 15.344-48
Judah ben Hezekiah	Galilee	4 B.C.E.	Herod the Great	*War* 2.56 *Ant.* 17.271-72
Asinaios and Anilais	Mesopotamian Marshlands	20–35 C.E.	Artabanos III	*Ant.* 18.310-73
Jesus Barabbas	Judea	29 C.E.	Pontius Pilate	Matt 27:15-26 John 18:38b-40
Tholomaeus	Idumea	44–46 C.E.	Fadus	*Ant.* 20.5
unnamed bandits	Judea	48 C.E.	Cumanus	*War* 2.228-29 *Ant.* 20.113-14
Eleazar ben Danai and Alexander	Judea and Samaria	35–55 C.E.	Cumanus and Felix	*War* 2.235 *Ant.* 20.121
unnamed bandits	Galilee	66 C.E.	?	*War* 2.595-98 *Life* 126–31
Jesus ben Shaphat	Ptolemais	65–67 C.E.	Vespasian	*War* 3.449-52 *Life* 104–11
bandits hired by Josephus	Galilee	66 C.E.		*War* 2.581-82 *Life* 77–79
bandit coalition of "Zealots"	Jerusalem	67–70 C.E.	Vespasian and Titus	*War* 4.135-39 *War* 4.160-61
unnamed bandits	Galilee	135 C.E.	?	*b. Ned.* 61a
Claudius	Judea and Syria	195 C.E.	Severus	Dio, *Roman History* 75

Figure 3.9 Social Bandits in Palestine and Environs (47 B.C.E.–195 C.E.)

In describing the Galilean "cave bandits," Josephus provides a good overview of the problem rulers had in dealing with them:

> For it was really not easy to restrain people who had made banditry a habit and had no other means of livelihood. For they were living neither in the city nor on the agricultural estate, but resided only in underground shelters and caves with their animals. They had also managed to accumulate supplies of water and food beforehand, and so they were able to hold out for a very long time in their hideout. (*Ant.* 15.346)

They were not common thieves; their targets were primarily the urban elites and the large estate holders. Consider, for example, the report by Josephus about bandits attacking Caesar's slave Stephanus outside the village of Beth-horon and stealing his baggage. The Roman governor Cumanus took this incident as a particularly grievous assault on the Roman administration, and he arrested the leaders of the surrounding villages for doing nothing to stop the bandits (Josephus, *War* 2.228–29//*Ant.* 20.113–14).

Crucifixion: Elite Force in Action

Anthropologists who study peasants note that peasants do not often revolt or even voice their feelings of hostility and oppression against elites. They usually find covert ways of protesting: keeping secrets or lying to elites, hiding taxable goods, practicing sabotage (Scott 1985). But if peasants occasionally responded by forming bandit groups when the situation became intolerable, then crucifixion was the ruling elites' way of responding to banditry and other forms of rebellion

Augustine on Social Bandits and the Empire

And thus justice having been removed, what are kingdoms but large-scale bandit bands? And what are bandit bands but small-scale kingdoms? [A bandit band] is composed of men, ruled by the authority of a leader, bound together by a social contract; the booty is divided by an agreed-upon principle. If this evil increases, by the admittance of destructive men—to such a degree that it controls regions, sets up home-bases, occupies cities, subjugates peoples—it more obviously takes on the name "kingdom," because it is now openly conferred upon it—not by the absence of ambition, but by adding impunity. Indeed, it was an elegant and accurate response given to Alexander the Great by a pirate who had been seized. For when the king asked the man what he meant by his hostile control of the sea, he insolently answered, "The same as you by seizing the whole earth, but because I do it with a small ship, I am called a 'bandit'; when you do it with a great fleet, [you are called] 'Emperor.'" (Augustine, *The City of God*, 4:4; our translation) (along with other means of execution). Crucifixion was an institution of humiliation, torture, and execution designed to deal with the people considered most threatening to the establishment and its interests (Neyrey 1996). It was public, demeaning, and painful; and it was designed to strike fear into the hearts of any who would dare pose a threat to the status quo. "Whenever we crucify the condemned, the most crowded roads are chosen, where the most people can see and be moved by this terror. For penalties relate not so much to retribution as to their exemplary effect" (Pseudo-Quintilian, *Declamations* 274; also Josephus, *War* 5.450–51). Both Cicero (*Ag. Verr.* 2.5.168) and Josephus (*War* 7.203) refer to it as the worst form of death.

The condemned were often tortured by whipping, burning, or stabbing. They were marched to their deaths carrying the crossbeam, paraded in humiliation through the streets. They were then nailed to the cross, although sometimes the arms were tied rather than nailed. And sometimes signs designating their crimes were placed on or near the cross (John 19:19). Death could be slow or swift, depending upon a variety of factors: the victim's physical constitution, prior sleep deprivation, degree of torture, and whether the arms were nailed rather than tied. The exact cause or causes of death in the crucifixion process have been disputed over the past century, and the exact form of crucifixion could vary (*War* 5.460). Le Bee and Barbet both concluded that the immediate cause would have been asphyxiation when the diaphragm

and intercostal muscles weakened. Zugibe argued that hypovolemic shock was more likely. (For a discussion of these theories, see Zias and Charlesworth 1992:281–82.)

The origins of crucifixion cannot be pinpointed, but Greco-Roman sources mention different forms of nailing to a cross, a tree, or a board as widespread in the ancient world among the Persians, Scythians, Taurians, Celts, Britons, Germans, Carthaginians, Greeks, Judeans, and Romans. Alexander the Great crucified two thousand Tyrians who had refused to surrender (Curtius Rufus, *History of Alexander* 4.4.17, cited in Hengel 1977:73). The Syrian king Antiochus IV crucified Judeans unwilling to give up traditional practices in 167 B.C.E. (Josephus, *Ant.* 12.256). Alexander Jannaeus, the Judean high priest, crucified eight hundred Judeans who had rebelled against him in 88 B.C.E. (*War* 1.97–98//*Ant.* 13.380–83; see also the Qumran commentary [4QpNah] on Nah 2:13). The revolt in the wake of Herod the Great's death in 4 B.C.E. prompted Varus, the Roman legate in Syria, to execute two thousand of the rebels (*War* 2.75). **Philo** [2.12] recounts a story of how the governor Flaccus crucified ethnic Israelites in the theater in Alexandria, Egypt, in the early first century (*Ag. Flacc.* 82–85). Prisoners of war were crucified by Titus's troops throughout the Roman siege of Jerusalem at the end of the First Judean Revolt (66–70 C.E.; *War* 5.449–51; *Life* 420; see Hengel 1977). And the Temple Scroll from the **Dead Sea Scrolls** [2.3] lists "hanging from a tree" (perhaps indicating crucifixion) as the punishment for

Josephus on Releasing Prisoners

But when Albinus heard that Gessius Florus was coming to succeed him, he wanted to be known to do something that might be gratifying to the people of Jerusalem. So he brought out all those prisoners who clearly deserved death, and he ordered them to be put to death accordingly. But those who had been put into prison on some minor offense, he took money from them, and released them. This resulted in the prisons being emptied, but the country was filled with bandits. (Ant. 20.215; LCL revised)

an offender who betrays the group to a foreign power (11QTemple Scroll 64.6–10).

For all the literary reports of crucifixion under the Romans, the body of only one victim of crucifixion has ever been recovered. It is the body of a young adult male named Yehochanan, whose remains were found in an **ossuary** [1.54] (bone box) with his name on it, buried in the Giv'at ha-Mivtar area of Jerusalem. He was apparently twenty-four to twenty-eight years old, 5 feet, 5¾ inches tall, and was executed early in the first century. The reason it is certain that he was crucified is that his executioners were not able to extract the nail from his heel bones (see Strange 1976; Zias and Charlesworth 1992; and Rousseau and Arav 1995:74–78; on first-century ossuaries, see Evans 2003).

Normally, the Romans and Judeans reserved crucifixion for the most heinous crimes: rebellion (including social banditry), treason, military desertion, and murder. And since it was associated with slaves, the Romans would, under most circumstances, not crucify a Roman citizen, considering it too shameful. This explains where Barabbas

fits into the social landscape of first-century Palestine. The Gospels indicate that he was being held for crucifixion by the Romans because he was a bandit chieftain, a social bandit. When Pilate, the Roman prefect of Judea, offered the crowd a choice between releasing Jesus or Barabbas (Mark 15:6-15), the Gospels say the crowd chose Barabbas. (On Roman governors releasing prisoners [including bandits] in Jerusalem, see Josephus, *Ant.* 20.215 in the sidebar above.) This may sound like a perfectly idiotic decision to a modern reader; after all, what sensible people would call for the release of a convicted bandit and murderer rather than a peaceful prophet and healer?

But this reaction fails to take into account both the popularity of social bandits like Barabbas and the potential danger posed by Jesus. If Barabbas was a threat to the social order because he led a violent band of bandits, at least these bandits usually concentrated on attacking country estates, Roman garrisons, and Roman supply lines. Jesus posed a different sort of threat to the urban elites. He gathered large crowds wherever he went, and he was recruiting members for a new group.

Rumors had begun to spread about his healings and exorcisms and his radical statements about Roman taxation, the Jerusalem temple, and Herod Antipas. He was known to flaunt the **scribes'** [1.72] conservative interpretations of the Sabbath and **purity** [3.45] laws. And, pivotal to the Gospel passion narratives, Jesus was accused of actually being a pretender to the royal throne of Judea (a **"messiah"** [1.51]), meaning he was a threat to both the Roman rule of Palestine and the leadership role of the high priestly families.

Notice that when Jesus was interrogated by the Jerusalem high priest (Joseph Caiaphas), he was asked, "Are you the Christ, the son of the Blessed?" (Mark 14:61). This is parallel to Pilate's question: "Are you the king of the Judeans?" (15:2a). Pilate uses the common term *king*, and Caiaphas uses traditional Judean designations. "Christ" (Greek *christos*) is the equivalent of "messiah" (Hebrew *mašîaḥ*), both meaning "anointed one," referring to the traditional anointing as part of the Judean royal ritual (1 Kgs 1:33-35). And "son of the Blessed" is a phrase acknowledging the Judean king's "adoption" as son of Yahweh (2 Sam 7:7; Pss 2:7; 89:26-27). What both Caiaphas and Pilate want to know is this: Was Jesus intentionally a threat to the political status quo by reinaugurating popular Judean kingship? The Gospels, in fact, differ in their accounts of how Jesus answered these questions. In Mark, Jesus seems to answer Caiaphas affirmatively (14:62) and Pilate vaguely (15:2b). In Matthew, Jesus is evasive to Pilate and silent before the Jerusalem leaders (27:11-14). In Luke's account, Jesus gives the evasive "You say that I am" to the Jerusalem leaders (22:70) and "You have said so" to Pilate (23:3). And in John, Jesus answers the Jerusalem leaders evasively (18:19-23) while telling Pilate, "My royal power does not come from this world [Palestinian politics or the Roman Empire]; otherwise, my adherents would have fought to keep me from being handed over to the Judeans" (18:36). The difference between these accusations is not between religious and political deviance, but political deviance in Judean and Roman terms (Belo 1981:223–24).

What Jesus actually said or did not say to the accusations made against him cannot be assuredly recovered by comparing these accounts. It does appear that Jesus' ambiguous answer, which plays a role in all of the accounts, fits both his way of dealing with direct challenges (as seen in many of the Gospel dialogs) and his skepticism that any sort of straight answer would satisfy these authorities. But all the passion narratives agree that Jesus was not crucified for being a teacher or healer or for making personal claims. He was crucified as a perceived enemy of the Romans and the Jerusalem priestly elite. Jesus was not a messiah in a traditional sense—a reigning king—but he led a faction under the banner of "the reign of God." How do authorities usually deal with someone who refuses to conform and who fails to fit widely accepted categories? Execution usually works well when the political establishment wants to ensure that a leader not upset the status quo and that a group gets derailed. Public crucifixion was usually a great damper on popular movements. Little did they know that this execution would not be the last word.

Summary

The politics of first-century Palestine must be interpreted in light of its domination by Roman interests. The different parts of Palestine were successively ruled by Roman client-rulers (first the Hasmoneans and then the Herodians), prefects, and procurators. Unlike politics in modern Western nation-states, ancient Mediterranean politics were run solely in the interests of the urban elite rulers and their retainers: rule was hierarchical, aristocratic, and **extractive** [3.18], with the peasants having virtually no say in the process. For the maintenance of status and protection of interests, patronage was of vital importance, with lower-status people needing to attach themselves to more powerful patrons, creating networks of interest. These networks provided patrons with increased honor and influence, and the clients with access to goods and services.

When the pressures of rents, taxation, tolls, duties, and confiscation became too heavy for peasants to bear, one means of extreme resistance to the imperial powers and wealthy elites was banditry. Groups of bandits raided country estates and Roman garrisons for both survival and revenge against those who had forced them from their lands or into poverty. The Roman means of dealing with rebels and bandits was public execution by crucifixion—humiliating, torturing, and killing the "deviants" in a manner that would warn others about attempting similar strategies against the state. Jesus was considered a dangerous deviant by both the Jerusalem elites and the Roman prefect. They feared his recruitment of a large group, and the crowds spoke of him in terms of traditional Judean kingship.

Applying the Perspectives

1. After reading Luke 7:1-10, explain how the patron/client relations are at work. Who are the patrons, clients, and brokers? What does it mean that the **centurion** [1.10] sends his "friends" with a message? To what characteristics of Mediterranean societies does the whole discussion about "commands" relate?

2. Choose one of the Gospels and chart Jesus' network of relationships. Categorize these people in terms of their gender, social status, basis of relationship (such as shared meal, healing, discipleship), closeness, endurance (momentary or enduring), and location. What conclusions can you make about whom Jesus comes in contact with? Who is helping him? Whom does he help? What is the geographical pattern of these relationships (cities, towns, villages; fishing or farming villages)?

3. Read Matthew 27:38, 44; Luke 10:30, 36; Mark 11:17; 14:48; and John 10:1; 18:39-40. What do these passages reveal about the importance of social banditry in the first century? What characteristics of Jesus might make the Jerusalem and Roman

authorities identify Jesus as sympathetic with social bandits?

4. Choose one (or more) of the social bandits from figure 3.9. Look up the ancient references and discuss the specifics that are identified in those ancient texts (time period, location, identity of the leader, size of the group, aims of the group). How do these specifics comport with the model of social banditry in figure 3.8? Can you see any ways to improve or adjust the model?

5. How would an understanding of patrons, clients, and brokers inform one's understanding of the social dynamics operating in the instructions of 1 Timothy 2:1-7? What are "supplications, prayers, intercessions, and thanksgivings" (v. 1)? Why the emphasis on God as "Deliverer" (v. 3)? What is Jesus' role in this network (v. 5)? What would an apostle's function be in such a network (v. 7)? What benefits do clients expect to receive?

6. What is the significance of Mark's note that Jesus went to the "villages of Caesarea Philippi" (Mark 8:27) rather than to the city itself? Note that this Caesarea (also known as Paneas) was a different location from Caesarea on the Mediterranean coast discussed above. What might be the significance of the fact that the Gospels never mention Sepphoris and Tiberias (the only real cities in Galilee) as part of Jesus' itinerary?

Suggested Reading

For treatments of Palestine's political history, see Sullivan (1977), Smallwood (1981),

Mendels (1992), Koester (1995), and Rhoads (2008). On structural elements, consult Stern (1974a; 1974b) and Applebaum (1977). On the political history of Galilee, see Horsley (1995:19–107).

On patronage and biblical texts, see Malina (1980; 1988; 1996b), Pilch (1980), Danker (1982), and Winter (1994). For an overview of the secondary literature and key issues, one should consult John H. Elliott's "reading guide" (1987). De Ste. Croix (1954), Saller (1982; 1989), Garnsey and Saller (1987:148–59), and the collection edited by Wallace-Hadrill (1989) provide important analyses of patronage in the Roman Empire. For a cross-cultural analysis of networks and brokers, the study of Boissevain (1974) and the collections of essays in Boissevain and Mitchell (1973), Gellner and Waterbury (1977), and Eisenstadt and Roniger (1984) are indispensable. On the networks and the New Testament, see the collection edited by White (1988) and the important articles by Duling (1999; 2000; and 2002).

On social banditry in Palestine, see Isaac (1984), Horsley and J. S. Hanson (1985:48–87), Horsley (1979; 1988; 1995b:258–68), Freyne (1988a), Schwartz (1994), and K. C. Hanson (2002). Shaw treats banditry throughout the Roman Empire (1984; 1990; 1993). Most of these treatments are rooted in the theoretical work of Hobsbawm (1959, 1974, 1981). On crucifixion, see Strange (1976), Hengel (1977), O'Collins (1992), and Zias and Charlesworth (1992). Neyrey (1996:113–37) carries out a social analysis of Jesus' crucifixion and the gospel passion narratives, emphasizing the aspects of shame. Sanders sorts through the historical evidence (1985:294–318). For brief overviews of Caesarea Maritima, see Finegan (1992:128–42) and Hohlfelder (1992). For a fuller treatment with fine photographs, see Holum (1988). See also Levine (1975a; 1975b).

Boat from the Sea of Galilee

"And going a bit farther, he [Jesus] saw James, Zebedee's son, and John, his brother, who were in their boat repairing the nets. And immediately he called them, and they left their father Zebedee in the boat with the hired hands and they followed him" (Mark 1:19-20). This boat was discovered in the shallow waters of the Sea of Galilee near Migdal (ancient Magdala) in 1986; see pp. 102–3 below for details. (Photo © Erich Lessing / Art Resource, NY. Used by permission.)

CHAPTER 4

The Denarius Stops Here

Political Economy in Roman Palestine

"Bring me a denarius to look at." So they brought it. And he asked them, "Whose image is this, and whose inscription?" They said, "Caesar's." Jesus said to them, "Repay Caesar's things to Caesar and God's to God." (Mark 12:15-17)

"I tell you that to everyone who has it shall be given, but from the one who has not, even what he has will be taken away." (Luke 19:26; see Mark 4:25; Matt 25:29)

"Do they not sell five sparrows for two assaria?" (Luke 12:6//Matt 10:29, Q)

"No household slave can serve two masters. For either he will hate the one and love the other, or he will be devoted to the one and despise the other. You cannot serve God and Mammon." (Luke 16:13//Matt 6:24, Q)

Then the other came, saying, "Master, here is your mina, which I kept concealed in a napkin; for I was afraid of you, because you are an austere man; you take away what you did not lay down, and harvest what you did not sow." He said to him, "Out of your own mouth I condemn you, evil slave! Did you know that I was an austere man,

*taking up what I did not lay down and harvesting what I did not sow? So why didn't
you deposit my silver money in the bank, and upon my arrival I should have collected
it with interest?"* (Luke 19:20-23//Matt 25:24-27, Q?)

*Remembering the words of the Lord Jesus, how he said, "It is more honorable to give
than to receive."* (Acts 20:35)

Introduction

These quotations reflect social features of
Roman Palestinian society that modern
people undoubtedly would identify as "economic." (See chapter 5 for economic issues
related to **religion** [3.48] and temple.) Yet
understanding these features is complicated
for us precisely because of the assumptions
we bring out of modern economic experience. For example, the use of money, **banks**
[1.6], and interest is familiar to us, so that we
may not think to investigate whether money,
banks, and interest functioned socially in the
same way in first-century Palestine.

Questions

The difference between the U.S. **economy**
[3.13] and that of first-century Palestine is a
major subject of this chapter. Exploring the
passages will raise a number of other interesting questions and generate important new
insights as well:

- How was the economy organized in
  antiquity? Why claim it was so different
  from modern **institutions** [3.30]?
- How was production organized? What
  were the basic commodities of antiquity? What were luxuries?
- How were goods distributed? Who got
  what, and why?

- What kinds of money were first-
  century people familiar with? How did
  money function? How extensively did
  money circulate? Who had access to it?
- What were ancient banks like? What
  did debt imply?
- What is "Mammon"? What does it
  mean to "serve" Mammon?
- Why did the sentiment "more honorable to give than to receive" assume
  such a central place in the Jesus
  movement [3.36]?

Models

As stressed in previous chapters, the society
of early Roman Palestine, within which Jesus
of Nazareth lived and worked, was a variant
of what Gerhard Lenski has called "advanced
agrarian society [3.1]" (Lenski 1984;
Nolan and Lenski 2006). Certain technological developments and settled ecological-
adaptive strategies played a profound role in
shaping such societies. The most useful indicator of this macrosociological type has been
the availability of iron for common tools,
especially the use of the iron plow. As will be
seen, not only technology but also social organization shaped by specific cultural **values**
[3.56] in such societies seriously limited
their productive capabilities and distributive
patterns.

Approaching "economic" phenomena in ancient societies from the standpoint of the adaptive arrangements and cultural values that shaped social organization and institutions lends important insight into how dif-

---

Research Tip 4

To research a particular location in ancient Palestine (such as Nazareth or Bethsaida), assemble information from a variety of sources: (a) a Bible concordance, (b) Bible dictionaries, (c) an archaeological encyclopedia, (d) journal articles, (e) commentaries, (f) monographs, and (g) Web resources (such as Josephus's works online).

Pay close attention to the dates of publication, the author's expertise, and the importance of the data for biblical interpretation.

---

ferently from our experience the economy and society operated in first-century Palestine. The modern word "economy" itself comes from two Greek words, *oikos* and *nomia,* meaning "household management." The modern word indicates the core concern of the ancients with provisioning and sustaining the family and household. In agrarian societies, though, no family was an island to itself. Such societies always had **elites** [3.14] who dominated other families; hence the larger economy was a political economy. Figure 4.1, "Political Economy in Agrarian Roman Palestine," aids and focuses further discussion in this chapter.

Political Economy in Agrarian Roman Palestine

The agrarian economic institutions in Jesus' day can be further examined under several broad rubrics: production, distribution, and mechanisms of control.

Production

Production refers to the interactions with the natural environment humans regularly require in order to transform raw materials into food, clothing, shelter, and other things considered essential for life. Generally, the productive forces of all ancient agrarian societies had serious technological restraints relative to modern industrial situations and standards, while distribution of goods was significantly distorted by **power** [3.44] relationships within society. The following topics help us to better appreciate the agrarian productive arrangements of Roman Palestine: technology, agriculture, organization of production, fishing, manufacture, and trade and commerce.

Technology placed definite limits upon ancient forces of production. Most labor-energy came from animals (especially oxen, asses, and camels) and humans. Agriculture involved manual operations supplemented by ox-drawn plow.

Besides human or animal power, attempts were made to harness the forces of gravity and wind for channeling water or other purposes. Aqueducts, for instance, depended for their operation upon a minuscule slope over many miles to bring water to the Greco-Roman city. Enormous human labor was needed to

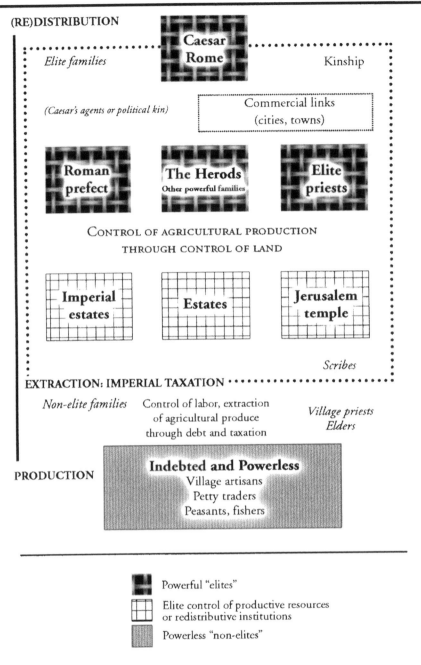

(RE)DISTRIBUTION

Caesar
Rome

Elite families

Kinship

(Caesar's agents or political kin)

Commercial links
(cities, towns)

Roman
prefect

The Herods
Other powerful families

Elite
priests

CONTROL OF AGRICULTURAL PRODUCTION
THROUGH CONTROL OF LAND

Imperial
estates

Estates

Jerusalem
temple

Scribes

EXTRACTION: IMPERIAL TAXATION

Non-elite families

Control of labor, extraction
of agricultural produce
through debt and taxation

*Village priests
Elders*

PRODUCTION

Indebted and Powerless
Village artisans
Petty traders
Peasants, fishers

Powerful "elites"

Elite control of productive resources
or redistributive institutions

Powerless "non-elites"

Figure 4.1 Political Economy in Agrarian Roman Palestine

Elite families controlled the mainly agricultural economy as well as the interurban commercial networks of the Roman Empire. Caesar and his "family" (agents, political kin) had an interest in everything; Caesar's estate was overseen in Palestine at the time of Jesus by prefects (Roman "governors"). Local elites like the Herods or Judean high priests controlled land and organized agricultural production by means of large estates. They kept liens on the labor power of peasants and artisans in towns through debt mechanisms.

construct an aqueduct. Boats were powered by oars or sails. Modern sources of energy—electricity, steam power, and gasoline—were unknown. Poor-quality roads and inefficient wagons (without ball bearings) made land transport extremely expensive (Lenski 1984:204; Malina and Rohrbaugh 2003:8). For this reason, local regions had to be largely self-sufficient in the staples of life.

Agriculture was the primary focus of production in Roman Palestine. The high incidence of agrarian motifs in Jesus' parables corresponds with this. The Gospels are rich with allusion to crops and agricultural operations. Parables like the Planted Weeds (Matt 13:24-30), the Mustard Seed (Mark 4:30-32), or Harvesttime (Mark 4:26-29) indicate Jesus' careful observation of Galilean agriculture. Nazareth was about four miles from Herod Antipas's capital city, Sepphoris. Immediately to the north of both is the Bet Netofa Valley, the rich agricultural land that is the likely locale for many of Jesus' stories.

Josephus [2.7] explicitly says **Judeans** [1.43] in Palestine were primarily agricultural (*Ag. Ap.* 1.60). Comparative studies suggest that 80 to 90 percent of the populace in Jesus' day regularly engaged in agricultural work (Lenski 1984:199–200, 266–78, 284; Malina and Rohrbaugh 2003:6–7). The elite 5 percent of the population—rulers, **soldiers** [1.79], **scribes** [1.72], administrators, and so on—did not regularly do agricultural work. These had to be fed from the labors of those who did and needed to defend or justify such arrangements. (On the social structure of agrarian societies, see Lenski 1984:243–85.) Elite, Greco-Roman culture disdained work

but exalted leisure as the goal of the best life. Aristotle (fourth century B.C.E.) expressed a general attitude and indicated reasons why slavery or servile relations were so prevalent in Greco-Roman antiquity:

> In some states the artisans . . . were once upon a time excluded from office, in the days before the institution of the extreme form of democracy. The occupations pursued by men who are subjected to rule of the sort just mentioned need never be studied by the good man, or by the statesman, or by the good citizen—except occasionally and in order to satisfy some personal need, in which case the distinction between master and servant would disappear. (*Politics* 3, 1277b 1–7; quoted in Austin and Vidal-Naquet 1977:171)

Kautsky situates such attitudes within aristocratic imperial values generally: "Another component of the **ideology** [3.27] of aristocrats, their contempt for productive labor, rationalizes their role as rulers" (1982:178). The Roman rhetorician Cicero (first century B.C.E.) makes clear the chief political interest of elites: "This is what is most excellent and maximally desirable for all who are healthy, good, and happy: honorable tranquility!" (*Sestius* 98). "Tranquility" (Latin *otium*) here means both time free for pursuing elite interests and an uncontested political order. Cicero attributes the causes of political strife to elite factionalism (*Sestius* 99), though he indirectly indicates the role played by deep-seated social and economic problems (100–101).

Compared with modern industrial agriculture, ancient agriculture was not very productive. Ancients could expect at best a yield of 10 to 15 times the grain seed sown; modern grain production, with aid of tractors and chemical fertilizers, often yields forty times or better (Oakman 1986:63). Basic agricultural operations were undertaken by families of **peasants** [3.41] living in villages. Standard operations were plowing, sowing, weeding by hand, and reaping with scythes (Jeremias 1972:11–12; Dalman 1964; Turkowski 1968; 1969). Deuteronomy 8:8 succinctly indicates the staples of Palestinian agriculture (called the "Seven Kinds" in the Mishnah): "a land of wheat and barley, of vines and fig trees and pomegranates, a land of olive trees and honey." The land of Roman Palestine was extensively cultivated. Broshi estimates that ancient utilization of land for agriculture was 65–70 percent, compared to 40 percent in Israel today (1987:32). Josephus confirms this for Galilee when he says, "It is entirely under cultivation and produces crops from one end to the other" (*War* 3.4; LCL). But again we need to keep in mind that the land typically produced a lot less with peasant farming techniques than modern methods.

It is not sufficient, however, simply to speak of technical strictures or to enumerate the crops grown. It is also important to ask who could grow what. How was production organized? The society in which Jesus lived was structured in such a way that essential decisions about agricultural production (what could be grown) were often not in the hands of those who actually worked the land. The Jesus traditions attest to such

limitations in a number of places. Especially important is the excerpted quote above, in which the general social situation is evident in the slave's frightened comment about the estate owner: "You take away what you did not lay down, and harvest what you did not sow" (Luke 19:20). This situation is reflected as well in the Johannine tradition (though applied there metaphorically to the experiences of the evangelist's community): "One sows and another harvests" (John 4:37).

The story about the languishing fig tree (Mark 11:13-14, 20-24) symbolizes the elite stranglehold under which Jesus' society has fallen. While the story quite evidently bears the marks of editorial work by Christian scribes, its essential truth applies throughout the early first century up until the destruction of the Jerusalem temple. Since the time of Solomon (tenth century B.C.E.), the fig and the vine had been symbols of Israelite welfare (1 Kgs 4:25). When Simon established the **Hasmonean** [1.34] kingdom (second century B.C.E.), the expression of welfare was "Each man sat under his vine and fig tree, and there was none to make them afraid" (1 Macc 14:12). When Jesus calls Nathaniel a true Israelite, saying, "I saw you under the fig tree" (John 1:47-48), John's gospel indicates the aspirations of many common people in Jesus' time: to be traditional peasants with some control of agricultural production rather than laborers on an estate (see below, pp. 104–20).

The ill health of the fig tree, therefore, represents the generally bad state of agrarian affairs from the standpoint of Jesus and the Jesus tradition. The organization of

The Parable of the Great Fish

The man is like a wise fisher who, having cast his net into the sea, pulled the net up from the sea full of small fish. The wise fisher, upon finding among them a fine large fish, threw all the little fish back into the sea, choosing the big fish without difficulty. (Gos. Thom. 8)

production is increasingly affected by the way land is held and by the way productive decisions are made (and by whom). As more and more land is controlled by the elites and, conversely, more and more Palestinians within Judean-controlled areas come under tenancy arrangements (and grow what the landlord demands), production no longer reflects what the ordinary person wants or needs. Most want to produce for household consumption, but power relations prevent realization of this subsistence economy. Elites favor production of crops that replenish the estate storehouse (Luke 12:18) or have commercial value. Olives and grapes are more important than figs (Luke 13:6). Elite decisions have led to social sickness, and fig trees languish. Fig wood even comes to be used for the temple sacrifices when law forbids the use of olive-wood and grapevines! (The case for this understanding of the fig tree episode is stated more fully in Oakman 1993:261; 2008:190.)

Parables of Jesus also attest to Jesus' association with fishing towns and villages of the Sea of Galilee (Lake Gennesaret). Capernaum was an important center for Jesus' activity (Mark 2:1). Jesus occasionally used a fishing image (Matt 13:47-48). Fishing was an important part of the Palestinian economy in the first century C.E. But it was not the "free enterprise" that most modern readers of the New Testament imagine. Even fishers who owned their own boats were part of a state-run enterprise and a complex web of financial relationships (Hanson 1997b).

Fishing was controlled by the ruling elites. The local rulers (**king** [1.13], **tetrarch** [1.83], **prefect** [1.61]) sold fishing rights to **brokers** [3.6] (*telōnai*, commonly translated "tax collectors" or "publicans"), who in turn contracted with fishers. The fishers received capitalization along with fishing rights and were therefore indebted to the brokers (Wuellner 1967:23–24). The location of Matthew's (or Levi's) toll office in Capernaum—an important fishing locale—probably identifies him as just such a contractor of royal fishing rights (Matt 9:9; Mark 2:14).

Furthermore, Luke 5:1-11 indicates that fishers might contract as partners, forming a cooperative (or syndicate), presumably both for labor reasons and to meet their contract obligations to the brokers. At the bottom of the industry were the hired laborers who contracted with the fishers. In Mark 1:19-20 we find Zebedee as a net-fisher who has not only two working sons in the business but hired laborers as well. This number corresponds to the crew needed for the larger boats (see below, pp. 102–3).

The fishers could hardly be classed as "entrepreneurs" in such a highly regulated,

- The *Roman emperors* (Augustus, Tiberius, Caligula) were the main beneficiaries of the port taxes (Mediterranean and interregional roads), as well as tribute from Herod Antipas.

- *Herod Antipas* as tetrarch controlled the sea, the harbors, and fishing rights as well as the local roads. He (or his father?) also may have been responsible for building the harbors and breakwaters.

- *Brokers* (*telōnai*; "tax collectors" or "publicans") contracted to collect the leases and control the harbors. They were responsible to tax and toll administrators (*architelōnai*).

- *Fishing families* were the primary laborers who caught the fish; they formed collectives or *cooperatives* in order to bid for fishing contracts or leases.

- If there were not sufficient family members of laboring age in the cooperative, the fishermen had to hire *laborers* to help with all the activities: manning the oars and sails, mending and washing nets, and so on.

- The fishermen needed resources for their endeavors from *farmers and artisans,* including flax for nets, cut-stone for anchors, wood for boat building and repairs, baskets for transporting.

- *Fish-processors* produced fish sauces and other preserved fish products that could be taken to market. Their "workshops" were also taxed.

- The materials for fish processing had to be supplied by *merchants, farmers, and artisans,* including salt, wine, and oil for processing, and amphorae for shipment. These were also taxable goods and services.

- The preserved fish and fish sauces could be distributed to *merchants* throughout Galilee and the rest of Palestine, as well as around the Mediterranean. But the fish had to be hauled by *carters and shippers.* The merchants were required to collect sales taxes, and the carters and shippers could be taxed for use of roads, bridges, and ports and the crossing of Roman customs boundaries.

Figure 4.2 Galilean Fishing Economy

taxed, and hierarchical economy. While the boat-owner/fishers may or may not have also been involved in fish processing, this would not have made them wealthy and certainly not "middle class," as many authors have contended. The "surplus" went to the brokers and the rulers. This accounts for the hostility of the general population in both Judean and early Christian sources against the "tax collectors."

The fishing industry was also concerned with the preparation and distribution of the fish. During the **Hellenistic** [1.36] era, processed fish had become a food staple throughout the Mediterranean, in city and village alike. The result was the development of trade distinctions between those who caught fish, those who processed fish, and those who marketed fish. The distribution of the catch was also controlled by government-approved wholesalers. While fish processors are not explicitly referred to in the New Testament, processed fish is (John 6:9-11; see also Tob 2:2).

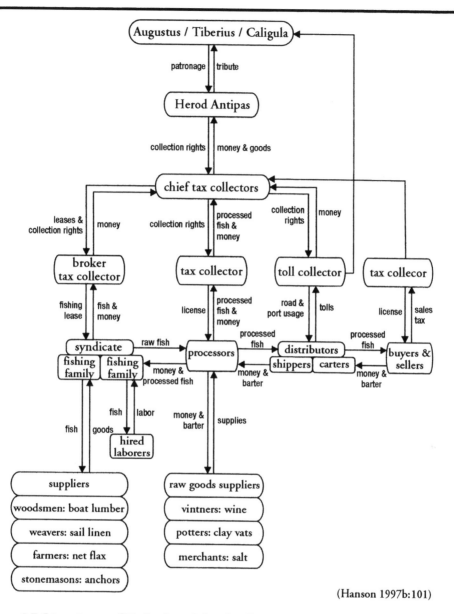

(Hanson 1997b:101)

Figure 4.3 Structure of Relationships in the Galilean Fishing Economy

Fish were processed for preservation and transportation as cured, pickled, salted, or dried (*m. Ned.* 6.4); and wine could be mixed in with fish-brine (*m. Ter.* 11.1). The New Testament and the Mishnah also men-tion eating fish in a variety of ways: broiled or roasted (Luke 24:42; John 21:9; Tob 6:5); minced (*m. ʾAbod. Zar.* 2.6); or cooked with leeks (*m. Maʿaś. Š.* 2.1); with an egg (*m. Beṣ.* 2.1), or in milk (*m. Ḥul.* 8.1). Fish oil could also be used as fuel for lamps (*m. Šabb.* 2.2) and as a medicine.

Fishing techniques in the Hellenistic era were of four basic types: (1) angling, using a rod with hooks on flaxen line; (2) casting with flaxen nets; (3) trapping; and (4) spearing with pronged tridents. While angling is mentioned in the New Testament (Matt 17:27), the most common mode of fishing in Galilee seems to have been with nets. Besides the generic word for "net" (Mark 1:18-19), two different types are mentioned in the New Testament: the casting net, used either from a boat or along the shoreline (Matt 4:18), and the much larger dragnet, used from a boat (Matt 13:47). Greek authors, such as Oppian, mention as many as ten different types of nets, but we are no longer able to distinguish between all of them. Nets required a great deal of attention: fishers and their hired laborers not only made the nets, but after each outing the nets had to be mended, washed, dried, and folded (see Mark 1:19).

The importance of fish in Palestinian culture is signaled by several geographical names: Jerusalem had a "fish gate" (Neh 3:3); the capital of Gaulanitis was Bethsaida (which means "Fishing Village"), located on the northern shore of the Lake of Galilee (see Mark 6:45); and the Greek name for the town of Magdala (the home of Mary Magdalene) on the western shore of Galilee was Tarichaeae, which means "Processed Fishville."

This importance is further highlighted by the references in the Gospels to people who eat fish and carry fish with them. That some of these references appear as metaphors or in nonhistorical stories does not diminish their importance as believable scenarios in a Palestinian context. A son asks a father for a fish (Matt 7:10//Luke 11:11). In the stories of Jesus miraculously feeding the crowds, the disciples gather bread and fish from among the crowd following Jesus (Mark 6:35-44; 8:1-10; Matt 14:15-21; 15:32-39; Luke 9:12-17; John 6:1-14). And in the post-resurrection stories, Jesus eats fish with his disciples, either broiled fish (Luke 24:42) or processed fish (John 21:13).

Besides supplying the Palestinian population, Galilean fish were exported to other sale-points. The distributors' route would most likely take them from Bethsaida in the north, to Tarichaeae on the western shore, through Cana, and finally to Ptolemais/Akko, the port city on the Mediterranean (Wuellner 1967:32–33).

Both the New Testament and Josephus mention boats on the Sea of Galilee for fishing and transportation. In 1986 an ancient fishing boat was discovered in the mud along the northwest shore of the Sea of Galilee, just north of Migdal (ancient Magdala). Its dimensions were 26.5 feet long, 7.5 feet wide, and 4.5 feet deep; various woods were used in its construction, but it is primarily of cedar and oak. The boat was built between 40 B.C.E. and 70 C.E., based upon the type of construction, carbon-14 testing, and adjacent pottery (Wachsman 1988; 1995; Wachsman et al. 1990). This means that it was the type most likely used by the Jonah-Zebedee cooperative (including their sons, Peter, Andrew, James, and John). The boat originally had a sail and places for four oarsmen and a tillerman. Boats of this size could accommodate a load in excess of one ton, which means the five crew members and their catch or cargo, or the crew and about ten passengers (see Mark 6:45).

Other goods besides foods had to be produced as well. Peasant villagers ordinarily made their own clothing and processed basic foods. Pottery, metal working, cloth weaving, leather working (sandals), wood working, and oil and wine making, however, all eventually required specialists. Specialties tended to be the monopolies of families, who nurtured trade secrets (we shall see this in the next chapter in relation to the temple). Powerful families controlled the production and distribution of specialized goods. Some of these were traded at some distance, particularly balsam and a dye-making material called henna (Broshi 1987:33).

Trade and commerce were always controlled by elites or their agents. In the **Old Testament** [2.10] period, for instance, Solomon's fantastic wealth was due in part to his control of trade (1 Kgs 9:26-28; 10:14-22). Herod the Great had taken steps to enhance Palestinian trade through building Caesarea on the coast, in the absence of a natural port (Josephus, *Ant.* 15.333–34). Even the **high priests** [1.38] were involved in commerce. Eleazar apparently had contacts with Phoenician glass-makers and controlled the Jerusalem distribution to pilgrims of glass vessels embossed with temple images (Engle 1977).

Long-range trade favored portable luxuries, carried overland by caravans of pack animals (see Matt 2:11). Bulk goods, like grain, were moved by water routes whenever possible. In the first century, Rome had organized the regular movement of grain along the Nile in Egypt to Rome via the Mediterranean. Egypt supplied one-third of Rome's annual grain consumption (Lewis 1983:165). Acts 12:20 indicates that grain was moved out of Galilee to the Phoenician coast. During the earlier Hellenistic period, this had been accomplished by pack animals, as shown in the **Zenon Papyri** [2.20].

Because of the limitations in technology and organization of production, the ancients tended to see the goods of life as in limited supply. If someone's wealth "increased," it therefore had to be at the expense of others (**limited good** [3.32]; Malina 2001a:81–107). Conversely, honorable people like Herod Antipas gave away their wealth in public displays of magnanimity (see chapter 3); such **benefactors** [3.4] are well known to modern historians through literally thousands of inscriptions on stone (Danker 1982). The Herods, for instance, built and adorned many cities in honor of their Roman **patrons** [3.40] (Herod the Great: Caesarea; Herod Antipas: Tiberias; Herod Philip: Caesarea Philippi).

Yet if anyone got ahead in the village or in society at large, this could be perceived as at someone else's expense. With life a zero-sum game—the increase of one means decrease of another—the quest for goods of life tended to become very competitive and full of conflict (Foster 1965; 1967; Malina 2001a:89). Rich and powerful people could be looked upon as robbers and thieves as much as benefactors. As the fig tree episode shows, villagers at the time of Jesus were not blind to their own circumstances. Feelings or perceptions of injustice could arise. Productive arrangements represent only one side of the social story. Distributive arrangements, and the accompanying picture of **social stratification** [3.52], need also to be examined carefully.

Distribution

Historically and comparatively speaking, social stratification in agrarian societies has been extremely pronounced; such societies typically have had enormous gaps between rich and **poor** [1.58]. In fact, power relations have tended to impress themselves remarkably upon the overall shape of society. Ancient societies were like many "Third World" societies today (Horsley 1989a). Under the Somozas prior to the 1970s, seventeen families controlled 85 percent of the land and resources of Nicaragua; fourteen families controlled El Salvador (Horsley 1989a:185). As typical of agrarian societies, Roman Palestine in Jesus' day was under the thumb of only a few major families (Caesar, Pilate and other prefects, Herods, high priests). Recognizing this important fact helps us to understand why economic transactions and the distribution of goods were as they were in Jesus' society. Social institutions that modern people take for granted, especially those that establish power balances or equilibriums, were largely absent.

Land and labor were not readily available for sale in the ancient world. Land, as the primary productive factor and requirement for survival, was held by families as hereditary patrimony (inherited) or taken by conquest (Hellenistic documents refer to land "won by the spear," Rostovtzeff 1941:267). Labor was ordinarily coerced rather than purchased in a free market by willing participants. We have spoken previously of "political kin" (fictive families) who worked for patrons under personal obligation (see chapter 3). Together with patronage, slavery or personal bondage was a regular feature of ancient societies, although Palestinian agriculture in the time of Jesus was not conducted primarily by slave labor. "Day laborers" were needed on large estates at labor-intensive times like the harvest (Matt 20:1-10); but estate payments for such labor should not be seen as wages, since very often these laborers were indebted to tax collectors or landlords and needed currency to repay the debts. Egyptian papyri show that a peasant named Kronion (c. 100 C.E.) "and his likes were chronically short of cash and constantly going into short-term debt. It is thus no accident that nineteen of the sixty-nine documents of the Kronion archive relate to loans" (Lewis 1983:71). Again, compulsion was a greater feature of such societies than free choice.

Likewise, markets and banks as institutions of capital (money used to "make money") were present only in ways severely circumscribed socially and culturally: The Roman Empire encouraged extensive trade **networks** [3.37], but these were controlled by small numbers of powerful family interests (with the "family" of Caesar chief among them). Widespread barter markets functioned in villages and towns for trading everyday goods and staples, but not land, labor, or capital markets as today. Money, as we shall see, was not available as a universal exchange medium. Without markets genuinely free of social constraint (**"politics"** [3.42]), or money with universal exchange value, ancient societies could not develop the kind of economy that we know today.

Elite honor concerns and the power relations that support them make economy in agrarian-aristocratic societies essentially **"extractive"** [3.18], "redistributive," or "tributary." Where peasants value self-sufficiency and consider working for others degrading (just as elites in agrarian societies), elites need to control and remove any agricultural surpluses (leaving peasants at a survival level) in order to live their valued leisure lives. Elites impose **tributes** [1.86], extract agricultural goods, and remove them for ends other than peasants want (**redistribution** [3.47]; Kautsky 1982:150–55; Oakman 1986:78).

Exchange of goods within families is ordinarily on a reciprocal basis. General **reciprocity** [3.46] means that exchanges are handled as gifts, without expectation of immediate repayment: "You get what you need." Balanced reciprocity means that exchanges happen on a *quid pro quo* basis: "You get what you pay for." Redistribution, by contrast, means that exchanges are under central control, that goods and services are collected to a central distribution point (a bank, storehouse, treasury) and distributed to whomever the controlling party wishes: "You get what the elites allow."

Taxation

Comparative studies indicate that the level of taxation in preindustrial societies has been steep. Lenski argues that the top 5 percent of any agrarian society (the governing class) might control 50 to 65 percent of their territory's goods and services:

> On the basis of the available data, it appears that *the governing classes of agrarian societies probably received at least a quarter of the national income of most agrarian states, and that the governing class and ruler together usually received not less than half.* In some instances their combined income may have approached two-thirds of the total. (Lenski 1984:228, his emphasis)

This picture is corroborated in the limited explicit information we have about taxation in Hellenistic-Roman Palestine. First Maccabees 10:30 suggests that prior to the **Hasmoneans** [1.34] (mid-second century B.C.E.), the Syrians regularly took 33 percent of the grain and 50 percent of the fruit. Roman imperial arrangements in the first century usually adopted Hellenistic taxation structures in the eastern Mediterranean. Herod the Great claimed 25 to 33 percent of Palestinian grain within his realm and 50 percent of the fruit from trees. Direct taxation also included poll (head) taxes in money. In addition, Herod imposed indirect taxes on transit trade and market exchanges (Broshi 1987:31–32). The temple establishment claimed "taxes" in kind (sacrificial goods) and money (the half-**shekel** [1.76]) on top of the rest, as we shall see in the next chapter. While it only gives a very general and static picture, figure 4.4 will help the reader to imagine the total impact of taxation.

Rome and Herod	Tax (if known)
Soil tax	1/4–1/2 (grain, orchards)
Head tax	1 denarius per year
Market taxes (cities)	
Transit tolls	
Port taxes (shipping)	
Access rents, city-controlled resources	
Labor for state projects (roads, aqueducts, etc.)	

Jerusalem temple	Tax (if known)
(see chapter 5 for discussion)	
Soil tax	Tithe (support for priests)
Head tax	1/2 shekel per year
Sacrifice	Animals, agricultural products
Vows	Dedicated material goods

Figure 4.4 Taxation in Early Roman Palestine

Udoh claims that we cannot know whether this situation was oppressive, but he does not incorporate comparative or social systems perspectives into such a judgment (1996:332, 336). The taxation structures that supported the elites of Jesus' day were elaborate, numerous, and often conflicting. Rents paid to large landowners only compounded state and religious tax burdens. After the death of Herod the Great, a Judean delegation was sent to Rome to complain to Caesar Augustus. Josephus is candid about the results of the tax situation:

> To be precise, [Herod] had not ceased to adorn neighboring cities that were inhabited by foreigners although this led to the ruin and disappearance of cities located in his own kingdom. He had indeed reduced the entire country to helpless poverty after taking it over in as flourishing a condition as few ever know, and he was wont to kill members of the nobility upon absurd pretexts and then take their property for himself; and if he did permit any of them to have the doubtful pleasure of living, he would condemn them to be stripped of their possessions. In addition to the collecting of the tribute that was imposed on everyone each year, lavish extra contributions had to be made to him and his household and **friends** [3.20] and those of his slaves who were sent out to collect the tribute because there was no immunity at all from outrage unless bribes were paid. (*Ant.* 17.306–8; LCL revised)

This is a powerful indictment of economic pressure put upon the whole land. The very people complaining, however, along with the Roman prefects, would inherit Herod's taxation structures! Regarding the latter, Josephus has a telling story

---

Roman Taxation of Judea

Coponius, a man of equestrian rank, was sent along with him to rule over the Judeans with full authority. Quirinius also visited Judea, which had been annexed to Syria, in order to make an assessment of the property of the Judeans and to liquidate the estate of Archelaus. Although the Judeans were at first shocked to hear of the registration of property, they gradually condescended, yielding to the arguments of the high priest Joazar, the son of Boethus, to go no further in opposition. So those who were convinced by him declared, without any delay, the value of their property. But a certain Judas, a Gaulanite from a city named Gamala, who had enlisted the aid of Zaddok, a Pharisee, threw himself into the cause of rebellion. They said that the assessment carried with it a status amounting to downright slavery, no less, and appealed to the nation to make a bid for independence. (Josephus, *Ant.* 18.2–4; LCL revised)

---

about Tiberius's policy to lengthen the tenure of prefects (Valerius Gratus, 15–26 C.E.; Pontius Pilate, 26–36 C.E.):

> [He did not dispatch] **governors** [1.33] continually to the subject peoples who had been brought to ruin by so many thieves; for the governors would harass them utterly like flies. Their natural appetite for plunder would be reinforced by their expectation of being speedily deprived of that pleasure. (*Ant.* 18.176; LCL revised)

Under the prefects, the Romans identified a hierarchy of people responsible for tax collection. What Josephus describes as the "buying of the high priestly office" likely included elements of the Hellenistic tax-lease system (*Ant.* 20.213; Evans 1989b:525). The office aspirant was promising to guarantee so much revenue for Rome. "Ten chief men" (the *deka prōtoi*) seem to have guaranteed the Roman tribute from their own resources (Jeremias 1969:228–30). But the powerful Jerusalem elite made sure others did the dirty work, compelling heads of Judean villages and families (elders) to participate as agents for tax collection. Josephus relates how such elders ("rulers and councilors") were made responsible just before the Judean Revolt for the collection of back-taxes (*War* 2.405, 407). According to the **Talmud** [2.18], the villagers of Bethar blamed the **fall of Jerusalem** [1.26] (70 C.E.) on extortionate practices of the Jerusalem elite. Bethar had been deprived of its ancestral lands when heads of the village were persuaded to bear liability for the Roman tribute (*j. Ta'an.* 4.8; Jeremias 1969:228; Applebaum 1976:663). Later, Bethar served as the hub of **Bar Kokhba's rebellion** [1.7] against Rome in 132 C.E. Agents of the leading **priests** [1.62] also collected tithes (*Ant.* 20.181, 206) and the temple poll tax (Matt 17:24).

Taxation in Roman Palestine was extractive, that is, designed to assert elite control

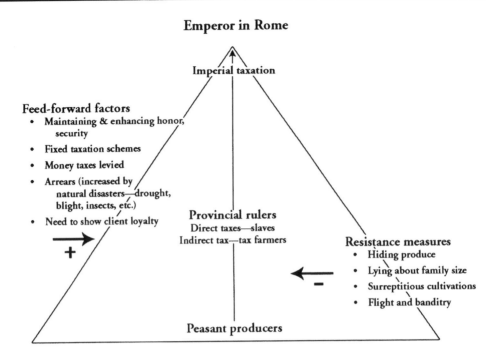

Emperor in Rome

Imperial taxation

Feed-forward factors
- Maintaining & enhancing honor, security
- Fixed taxation schemes
- Money taxes levied
- Arrears (increased by natural disasters—drought, blight, insects, etc.)
- Need to show client loyalty

+

Provincial rulers
Direct taxes—slaves
Indirect tax—tax farmers

Resistance measures
- Hiding produce
- Lying about family size
- Surreptitious cultivations
- Flight and banditry

−

Peasant producers

Figure 4.5 System of Taxation in Roman Palestine

over agrarian production. In the society of early Roman Palestine, villagers preferred to conduct business along the lines of reciprocity; but since elites controlled taxation (land products), labor, and commerce, redistributive arrangements tended to prevail. Caesar's agents collected taxes and redistributed them to **clients** [3.8]. The priests and the Jerusalem temple collected offerings and redistributed them. Redistribution exchanges were replicated throughout society. Their major impact was to remove most goods from the control and enjoyment of most people. The terms *extraction, redistribution*, and *tribute* reflect the political nature of these distributive mechanisms. All of these terms emphasize that the benefits

in ancient economy flowed "upward" to the advantage of the elites.

Control of Land: Cities and Estates

Cities, as the dwelling places of elites, dominated the social and geographical landscape of Greco-Roman antiquity. Elites built, controlled, and inhabited the cities. Caesarea and Jerusalem, of course, were major urban centers in Judea. Herod the Great constructed Caesarea to provide a port on the coast of Palestine and a monumental statement of loyalty to Caesar Augustus. Major cities in the Galilee of Jesus included Sepphoris and Tiberias. These cities were founded by Herod Antipas and were the headquarters for **Herodian** [1.37] officials. Not surprisingly, in view of the interests of the Jesus movement, they are never mentioned in the Gospels. Capernaum, Tarichaeae (Magdala), and Cana were administrative towns for fishing and agriculture. Peasants of the Galilean countryside lived in small villages like Nazareth or Nain (Oakman 1991b; 1994; Rohrbaugh 1991).

Peasants formed the productive basis of the city system. They were viewed as providers for the powerful, who could coerce or extract agricultural surplus from the peasantry. "Towns" were the collection and processing points for the various taxations in kind. Quite naturally, peasants resented these extractive policies. The elites, however, controlled the armed forces, and most of the time peasants simply grumbled. Only under rare circumstances did peasant villagers revolt (Horsley and J. S. Hanson 1985; Horsley 1987). Otherwise, they endured and dreamed of better times. Banditry was a constant phenomenon in antiquity, as some peasants dropped out of ordinary village life and took to the hills to live off plunder. Sometimes these bandits advocated notions of social justice (**"social bandits"** [3.51]; see chapter 3).

The control of land by the elite was also focused in the "estate." An estate was a political, and in Roman law a legal, entity referring to land and product controlled by the elite. The estate lord or owner (*kyrios*) was entitled to agricultural produce by written agreement or (more often) by custom. Labor on estates would be supplied by tenants living in neighboring villages (Mark 12:1) or for labor-intensive seasonal operations by hired workers (Matt 20:1-15).

Palestinian archaeology has shed some light on estates of the first century. A first-century *villa* (standard Latin word for estate) was excavated in the 1980s near Caesarea at Mansur el-'Aqab, uncovering remains of domestic quarters, storage rooms, and pressing installations for oil and wine (Hirschfeld and Birger-Calderon 1991). Like cities (Jerusalem), towns (Jotapata), and **garrisons** [1.31] (Herodium) of the period, this estate was walled for security reasons. The recurring problem of banditry made security a continuing issue even under Rome. A much later estate near Jerusalem shows a very sumptuous lifestyle, with beautiful mosaic "carpets" in the residential rooms, including a gorgeous Shield of David (Edelstein 1990:33). Elites loved luxurious accommodations!

Archaeology has shed much light on the technology of estate installations. Many instances of olive presses and winepresses have been discovered. Olive pressing, for instance, proceeded in two stages. First, the fresh olives were crushed in a circular, channeled stone basin under a rolling topstone. The crushed olives were placed in sacks, and a first skimming of the collected seepage yielded the purest oil. Next, the pulp went into a second basin. A large beam, suspended out from a wall socket over the basin, pressed down upon the pulp-sacks. As donut-shaped stones were tied by rope to the beam's end, the oil flowed through channels and was collected in stone or ceramic vats. Winepresses worked similarly, though human laborers might climb into a vat with fresh grapes and tread them until the juices flowed out through channels into collection basins. The juice was first fermented in the holding basins, then stored in pottery jars sealed with clay tops. A side vent initially allowed fermentation gases to escape before it was sealed. Wine jars had to be kept in cool buildings or caves (Rousseau and Arav 1995:221, 329). Such installations required substantial labor to build and maintain and are regularly associated with the dwellings of the powerful elites. It may be socially significant, therefore, that such installations and associated operations do not play a role in the parables and sayings of Jesus.

Near the presses of Mansur el-'Aqab, the excavators discovered stepped baths, which they identified as *miqva'ôth* ("ritual baths" related to Judean **purity** [3.45] laws). If this interpretation is correct, it may indicate that the pressed oil and wine were processed under ritually pure conditions and intended for use in the temple.

A significant body of elite Roman literature was devoted to the management of estates. Cato (second century B.C.E.), Varro (first century B.C.E.), and Columella (first century C.E.) wrote such treatises. Since members of the Roman elite often lived in major cities, trustworthy estate "managers" or "stewards" (*oikonomoi,* another Greek word related to "economy") were important to the success of landed estates. Columella says of the choosing of an estate manager:

A man should be chosen who has been hardened by farm work from his infancy, one who has been tested by experience. . . . He should be of middle age and of strong physique, skilled in farm operations or at least very painstaking, so that he may learn the more readily. . . . Even an illiterate person, if only he have a retentive mind, can manage affairs well enough. Cornelius Celsus says that an overseer of this sort brings money to his master oftener than he does his book, because, being illiterate, he is either less able to falsify accounts or is afraid to do so through a second party, because that would make another aware of the deception. (*On Agriculture* 1.8; quoted from Lewis and Reinhold 1990:80; see K. D. White 1977:50–62)

Significantly, the parables of Jesus include numerous reflections of estate life and comments on *oikonomoi.* Luke 16:1-8 has to do precisely with Columella's problem at the end of the preceding quote: a literate *oikonomos* takes advantage of his master through receipt manipulations. Matthew 24:47-51 envisions another quite typical estate situation: malfeasance of the slave overseer. In the master's absence the slave beats other slaves and gets drunk on estate wine.

The estate was meant to provide for the elite all of the goods of life, as far as this was possible in any given locale. Estate land was usually not clumped together in one place, but scattered in numerous places so as to control as many goods as possible and to "spread the risk" in areas where rainfall was unpredictable year by year. Estates were worked by tenants. Tenancy implies the transfer of primary productive decisions to the landlord/creditor. In terms of production, *what*

Debt Relief in Fifth–Century B.C.E. Judah

*And there were those who said, "We are having to borrow money to pay the king's tax. . . ."
[Nehemiah said,] "Let us stop this taking of interest. Restore to them today their fields, their
vineyards, their olive orchards, and their houses, and interest on money, grain, wine, and oil
that you have been extracting from them."* (Neh 5:4, 10b-11)

will be grown is no longer determined by the peasant household's food needs. Landlords, especially if they are interested in commerce, are tempted to plant cash crops (olives, vines, wheat) rather than subsistence crops (barley, beans, figs). Further, rental or share contracts deprive the peasant family of additional portions of the harvest. Tenancy affects and complicates distributive and consumption decisions as well.

Control of Labor: Indebtedness

Control of peasant labor was effected in ancient agrarian societies by heavy demands for taxes, rents, and debt repayments. Peasants did not voluntarily supply labor for elites, nor did they work willingly for wages. Most traditional peasants are as devoted to self-sufficient household economy as elites are to the welfare of their estates. Since elites need to control the labor of peasants without frequent recourse to military force, exorbitant taxation and debt contracts backed up by judicial authority come into play.

Peasant concerns for debt forgiveness and redistribution of land are well represented in the legal traditions of the Old Testament. Deuteronomy 15 and Leviticus 25 show how such concerns were prevalent in the legal thinking of the ancient Israelites. Alleviating the problem of debt is the object of Deuteronomy 15:2. Leviticus 25:10 demonstrates Israelite interest in permanent provisions for land redistribution. Nehemiah 5:1-13 shows the continuation of such concerns among Judeans after the Babylonian exile. Very often in the Greco-Roman period, land and debt were rallying cries for revolt (Oakman 1985:59; 2008:13). The Gospels also show these persistent scourges of agrarian societies: land division disputes (Luke 12:13) and peasant indebtedness (Luke 12:58-59). The **Q** [2.14] saying about going before the judge (Matt 5:25-26//Luke 12:58-59) reflects a situation in Roman Palestine in which it is at least perceived that informal justice is better than official justice. It is better to have a patron in the creditor ("make friends") than to face the courts controlled by the landlord class. The situation of the debtor seems abysmal. To have a patron in the creditor implies tenancy. Otherwise, debt prison is certain. The Lord's Prayer, too, shows Jesus' concern for release from persistent debt (Matt 6:12// Luke 11:4).

Thus, the powerful kept peasants and villages under a constant barrage of demands and obligations—perennially in debt, if possible.

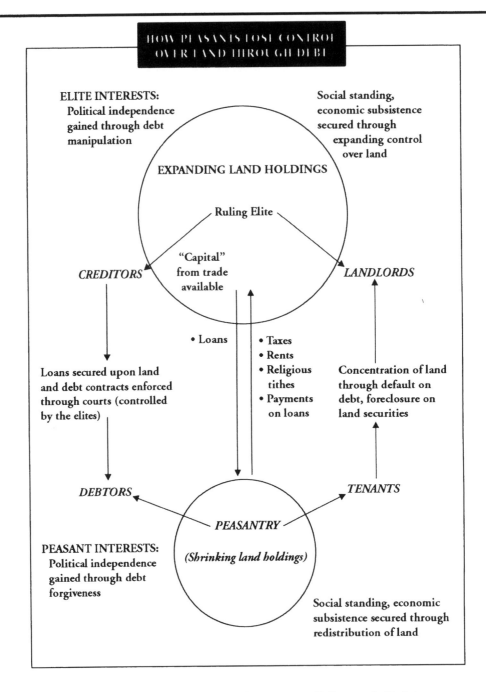

HOW PEASANTS LOSE CONTROL OVER LAND THROUGH DEBT

ELITE INTERESTS:
Political independence gained through debt manipulation

Social standing, economic subsistence secured through expanding control over land

EXPANDING LAND HOLDINGS

Ruling Elite

"Capital" from trade available

CREDITORS

LANDLORDS

• Loans

• Taxes
• Rents
• Religious tithes
• Payments on loans

Loans secured upon land and debt contracts enforced through courts (controlled by the elites)

Concentration of land through default on debt, foreclosure on land securities

DEBTORS

TENANTS

PEASANTRY

(Shrinking land holdings)

PEASANT INTERESTS:
Political independence gained through debt forgiveness

Social standing, economic subsistence secured through redistribution of land

Figure 4.6 How Peasants Lose Control over Land through Debt

Metal Basis	Function (F)	Examples
Gold and Silver	F1. Storage (hoards or bullion)	Matt 23:16-17 (gold)
		Luke 15:8-9 (silver)
Silver	F2. Measurement	Mark 6:37 (bread)
		Rev 6:6 (wheat and barley)
	F3. Standard of payment	
	a. Taxation (non-elite > elite)	Mark 12:15 (Caesar's tax)
	b. Debt (non-elite > elite)	Luke 7:41 (creditor/debtors)
	c. Elite or estate payment	Matt 20:9 (laborers' wages)
	(elite > non-elite)	
	F4. Exchange value: M-C-M'	Luke 19:23 (bankers, interest)
Bronze	F5. Use value, "money barter": C-M-C	Luke 12:6 (food)
		Matt 27:10 (land)
		Mark 14:5 (perfumes)
(Barter)	Barter in kind: C-C	Luke 11:5 (loaves)

C = Commodity; M = Money medium; M' = Money increase or profit; > = direction of exchange

Money originated historically in the need to make reliable state payments, but the storage function shows the household orientation of ancient economy. The relations of functions in our model are not historical; rather, money's political-functional logic is displayed. Elite functions are traced in the vertical extension of the model. Generally in antiquity, gold and silver were controlled always by elite hands. Non-elites usually saw only bronze coinage (in the provinces) and preferred exchanges of real goods (barter) or trading of coins for real goods ("money barter").

Figure 4.7 A Functional Model for Understanding Ancient Money

When peasants eventually got too far behind, they lost direct access to their traditionally held land. Long-distance commerce exacerbated these tensions and dynamics, because it made available to the elites wealth that fueled indebtedness. As Polanyi once noted, medieval European elites were reluctant to allow long-distance commerce to interfere with local political economy. The stability of the manor was a paramount concern (Polanyi et al. 1957:63). Apparently, first-century Judean elites were not so scrupulous. As Kreissig (1969) and Goodman (1982) both have argued, commerce played a significant role in the social developments leading to the **First Judean Revolt** [1.28].

Control of Capital: Money

The depth of the political nature of economy in Jesus' society is profoundly illustrated by an examination of money: a social phenomenon that in our modern context indicates freedom of choice was a symbol of domination and exploitation in ancient times.

Money is ubiquitous in modern experience and functions in manifold ways. Today, money is a universal medium of exchange, coming in many forms (coins, paper, credit cards, electronic transfers). Money buys things at the store (food, clothing, tools), purchases cars and houses, gets invested in life insurance and retirement funds, is saved at the bank, is put into stocks and bonds, and so on. Not only are land and labor available for purchase (in the "real estate market" or the "job market"), but money itself is bought and sold (arbitrage).

Circumstances were rather different in the first century. Whereas in our experience money controls everything else, in the first century money and the economy generally were subject to elite control. Figure 4.7 helps to develop a more elaborate analysis.

Classical scholars are quite familiar with the two-metal (silver, bronze) or three-metal (gold, silver, bronze) money systems of antiquity. So, for example, imperial Roman coinage existed in a gold denomination (the aureus), in silver (the **denarius** [1.18]), and in bronze (the **sestertius** [1.75] and others). Twenty-five denarii made up the aureus; four sesterces made up the denarius. There were other important denominations as well (for helpful tables, see Schmidt 1992:805; Rousseau and Arav 1995:57). Prior to the institution of this imperial coinage system, Rome's conquests of the eastern Mediterranean lands had incorporated a number of older money systems. These continued in use into the time of Jesus. The need to convert between the various systems led to the prominence of money changers, whose "tables" (the Greek word *trapezai* is often translated misleadingly as "bank") offered only rudimentary banking functions by our standards.

What is less appreciated is that money, especially coined money, has not always played the same role or function within social relations. Standard dictionary articles on ancient money continue to be content with descriptions of images on coins or with inappropriate assumptions about the role of money in ancient society. Figure 4.7, representing an analysis of first-century money functions (middle column), will help to show why these views are only partially helpful.

Gold and silver were employed regularly as media for storing "value" (F1 in the model) by those who had precious metals to hoard. The Mediterranean peoples of the eastern Roman Empire would tend to consider money value in the light of the core cultural values of Mediterranean societies: **honor** [3.25] and **shame** [3.50]. Wealth, the Aramaic term for which is *mamona*, would be the storage of resource values for creating, preserving, displaying, or recovering public reputation ("honor") and for protecting the economic integrity of family and household.

As previously mentioned, ancient value perceptions differed markedly from ours in believing that overall wealth did not increase. Wealth today is thought to increase indefinitely, with plenty enough to go around, and wealth's major purpose is to "make money" (capitalism) for the increasing well-being of the individual and society.

Archaeologists have recovered numerous hoards of silver coins from all over the ancient world. Perhaps the best-known silver hoards from first-century Palestine were discovered at Qumran and **Masada** [1.50] (Sussmann and Peled 1993; Yadin 1966). Of all the evangelists, only Matthew refers to gold, and always as a medium for storing value (Matt 2:11; 10:9). The tradition behind Matthew 10:9 is particularly interesting. Mark 6:8 states that the disciples are not to take along "bronze" (coins); both Matthew and Luke, probably reflecting a Q tradition variant to Mark, forbid the taking of "silver" (Luke 9:3). Only Matthew reads "not gold, nor silver, nor bronze." The changes in the tradition likely reflect differences in regional experience as well as the social **status** [3.53] of the evangelists: Mark writes from a non-elite perspective; Q reflects views of scribes who regularly handle silver coins; Matthew reflects a community familiar with gold as a banking medium. The **Babatha archives** [2.2], containing legal documents of the widow Babatha from En-Gedi near the Dead Sea, have a number of receipts for money "on deposit," for example:

> . . . thirteenth of Daisios, in the **consul-ship** [1.15] of Marcus Salvidienus Orfitus and Quintus Peducaeus Priscinus [110 C.E.], and of the foundation of the province year the fifth, in Maoza of the Zoara district, I, Joseph son of Joseph surnamed Zaboudos, inhabitant of Maoza, acknowledge to Jesus son of my brother Jesus, of the same place, that you have with me a thousand and a hundred twenty "blacks" of silver as a deposit. (*p. Yadin* 5; quoted in Lewis et al. 1989:39)

The editors speculate that due to a letter change in the original Greek, "black coins" are to be understood as silver minas. (Greek *m-l-n*, "black," could quite plausibly be a corruption from *m-n*, "mina.") The mina was an ancient Near Eastern measure of weight, equal to 60 shekels (Lewis et al. 1989:36; Powell 1992:897). Of the four New Testa-

ment Gospels, only Luke ever mentions silver minas (Luke 19:13). Matthew's parallel (25:15) speaks of the talent (a Greek measure of weight).

Denominations of precious metals had long provided a standard by which the value of goods could be measured (F2 in the model). The Gospels know of the "pricing" of bread and perfume in terms of the Roman denarius (Mark 6:37; 14:5). Note that in these cases, the "price" is for bulk—and a rather large sum. A major question is the extent to which such measurement implies the actual exchange of money for goods (F4 or F5). Luke 12:6 suggests that sparrows are actually exchanged for money in the Galilean markets. But it is surprising to us, given our familiarity with money as a universal medium of exchange, how infrequently in the Gospels money fulfills the function of an exchange medium. Out of twenty-one mentions of money in the Gospels, only three actually refer to money purchase of some item (Luke 10:35; 12:6; Matt 27:10).

The use of money as a standard of payment (F3 in the model) was one of its major social functions in Roman times. First and foremost, money was needed to pay taxes. The Romans demanded their tribute in official imperial coin (Mark 12:15). Likewise, the priests demanded that the temple tax be paid in an official medium; the Tyrian shekel served this purpose during the first century partly because of its high purity of silver content. Debt contracts were regularly written in Roman Palestine in terms of denarii; penalties were specified in denarii as well:

In the consulship of Manius Acilius Glabrio and Torquatus Tebanianus one day before the nones of May [124 C.E.], in Engedi village of lord Caesar, Judah son of Elazar Khthousion, Engedian, to Magonius Valens, centurion of *Cohors I Miliaria Thracum,* greeting. I acknowledge that I have received and owe to you in loan sixty denarii of Tyrian silver, which are fifteen staters, upon hypothec [security] of the courtyard in En-gedi. (*p. Yadin* 11; quoted in Lewis et al. 1989:44)

The Gospels are quite familiar with debts in denarii (Luke 7:41 or Matt 18:28). It has often been assumed that the standard wage in Jesus' day was one denarius; but such a standard appears only in connection with large landed estates (Matt 20:9-10). Estate laborers might be paid with the denarius, but most peasants would be unfamiliar with the coin (a point at issue in Mark 12:16), and it will soon return to Caesar's agents anyway (Mark 12:17).

Exchange and use value, F4 and F5 in the model, are the most rarely attested. Luke 19:23 is the clearest instance in gospel material of money used to "make money" through debt manipulations (F4). Rohrbaugh has argued that such a story would be experienced by peasants as a "text of terror" (1993). The Gospels do not seem to be aware of money "making money" through commercial transactions.

Matthew 13:45-46; 27:10; and Luke 10:35; 12:6 are the only instances in which money is explicitly stated to be exchanged for some other goods (F5). Merchants could use money as a middle term between two types of goods (Matt 13:45). Notable in Matthew 27:10 is that the priests (that is, members of the elite) are in control of the means to buy. Luke 10:35 shows a commercial figure (under elite control), the Samaritan, able to pay two denarii. Only Luke 12:6 reflects the experience of ordinary people. The rarity of this function, in view of its modern importance, is notable.

The analysis shows that storage (F1), payment (F3), and exchange (F4) are really available only to the elites and their agents. The accounting function (F2) might be used by ordinary people to estimate values of real goods (Mark 6:37), but the majority could afford at most an extension of barter in terms of small change (Luke 12:6). Only elites had large sums at their disposal and real monetary functionality.

Reflections about "money barter" (F5) show what is at stake politically with money: Peasants, concerned as they are about provisioning the household, prefer to exchange real goods (ordinary barter). Within the household or village, exchanges are either general (borrow now, repay sometime) or balanced reciprocity (borrow now, repay shortly). Political realities now impose a bronze currency and enforce its use (especially through debt or by requiring taxes paid in money; Carney 1975:145). Peasant families are forced to get money by selling or borrowing. They now have to hold a token in place of real goods but cannot eat a token. Village exchanges are now "converted" into the form of balanced reciprocity accountable in money. Peasant villagers can no longer routinely trade real goods in an informal barter economy. Thus the political authority can better assess agricultural production and maximize tax income.

Money systems in the Palestine of Jesus, like institutions of agricultural production and organization, reflect a political economy. Modern assumptions about money's general accessibility (people earn money to buy) or general utility (everyone can use money to buy anything) mislead as to money's functions in the Gospels.

Jesus and the Palestinian Political Economy

While the theological interests of the evangelists and the early church have obscured it to some extent, Jesus and the early Jesus tradition offered a potent critique of political economy and an alternative vision for ordering material human relationships. Jesus' alternative is first and foremost an expression of non-elite interests and aspirations.

Jesus himself came from a small village and was the son of an **artisan** [3.3] (*tektōn*). Those he recruited for his earliest network were peasants, fishers, and artisans from Galilean villages and towns. Central to Jesus' activity and message was his proclamation of God's reign. For well more than a century, scholars have been trying to understand what Jesus meant or intended by this conception (see Willis 1987). Much earlier work embraced individualist and purely religious assumptions that prevented recognition of Jesus' message in terms of social meaning.

Jesus was not an individualist, despite some recent attempts to make him so (recent proposals for a Cynic Jesus: Downing 1988; Crossan 1991; Mack 1993; Vaage 1994). Considerations of cultural anthropology make it more highly probable that Jesus shared in the **strong-group orientation** [3.54] of his general Mediterranean world and that any vision he articulated was a strongly social vision (Horsley 1987; Malina 2001). Furthermore, Jesus' vision emerged from an appreciation of non-elite experience in his social world. This fact makes sense of remarkable statements in early Jesus traditions about wealth's dangers (Mark 10:25; Luke 16:13//Matt 7:24), of hostility toward Jerusalem purity concerns (Mark 7:15, 18-23; Luke 11:39-41//Matt 23:25-26), and of conflict with the Herodian and Judean elites that eventuate in Jesus' death (Mark 3:6; Luke 13:31). It also makes sense of the constructive social concerns evident in the Jesus traditions.

To be more precise, Jesus' vision offered an alternative to the political society in his time (Mark 10:42-45). Elite families and their interests controlled the lives of the many in the first century. Jesus' vision needed to address this central fact, but his vision did so in socially predictable ways. When Jesus imagined an alternative to political economy, based upon Israelite traditions and proclaimed in the name of God's rule, he invariably returned to ordering society around **kinship** [3.31] (note the domestic values in Luke 6:29-36; 12:22-31).

The parable of the Entrusted Money, noted at the beginning of this chapter, exposes the implications of political economy for Jesus and his audience. Though without the benefit of modern social-scientific analysis, Jesus is intent to show that in political economy the many are always losers. Powerful interests, reaping where they have not sown, have established institutions like the banks and money that aid in the extraction of product and control of labor energy. Jesus opens the eyes of his contemporaries to the way the system is working against them. The proverb rings true: "I tell you that to everyone who has, it shall be given, but from the one who has not, even what he has will be taken away" (Luke 19:26; see Mark 4:25). There are "haves" and "have-nots," and the "haves" are winning at the political expense, and to the shame, of the rest. Jesus' proclamation announces the time for demonstrating loyalty to God. Concern for Mammon has become a constraint on the well-being of the many. When God's reign and purposes are established, that well-being will be established.

Jesus hopes to see the mechanisms for political economy dismantled. In their place, he sees economy reembedded within a broadened kinship organization. In place of redistributive mechanisms and balanced reciprocity, Jesus sees exchanges of goods and services based upon general reciprocity (Acts 20:35). "Reign of God" for Jesus means removal of the non-elite many from the domains of human politics; it means God alone will wield such power. In place of Herodian society, Jesus envisions "God's

household"; within it are many "brothers" and "sisters" (Mark 10:30). God's household is not based upon blood kinship, but on what anthropologists call "fictive" kinship (see chapter 2). Members of the Jesus movement, even though unrelated by blood, will still refer to one another by "brother" or "sister." Instead of being nominal members of Caesar's family (subject to taxation and labor demands), Jesus and followers belong to God's "family" (Mark 12:17).

These reflections help us to recognize the difficulties modern readers face in translating Jesus' core values into terms we can understand. A question like "Do they not sell five sparrows for two assaria?" (Luke 12:6) is not intended as a comment on better consumer practices, as we might misconstrue (especially when Matthew implies two sparrows an assarion). Jesus contrasts the present order with God's and expresses sorrow over the deplorable state of affairs when something as insignificant as sparrows are up for sale! The point belongs to a larger argumentative passage intent on convincing the audience that God's power to establish right relationships and the household economy of God's reign is real. In the Q context of Luke 12:2-9, the general theme is loyalty to a patron (whom to fear). Those who have no power to create life are not to be feared (v. 5), but "fear" (proper respect for a patron) belongs to the one who notices even sparrows falling to the ground. Just as God does not forget that they have died to be sold in the market, so he does not forget loyal humans (clients) who are even more important entities.

An interesting passage in this connection is Luke 11:9-13. The modern reader might wonder at the connection between "prayer," which for us is generally "spiritual" and private, and verses 11-13. Luke 11:13 might reinforce a modern prejudice with a reference to a gift of the Holy Spirit. To many of us, it seems crass to ask God for success in business or love. Notice, though, that the Matthean parallel "good things" (7:11) is more in line with the overall theme preceding. Matthew's text probably gives a version of Q closer to the original (hence to Jesus' intent) than Luke's.

This passage also depends upon a knowledge of the institution of patronage. God as divine patron can be asked for things, even material things. Now comes the most interesting part: Why the negative comparisons to fathers giving stones (Matthew), snakes (Matthew, Luke), or scorpions (Luke)? What is the point of the comparison? It makes sense as a commentary on the prevailing political economy, to which God's rule is posed as an alternative. Even more to the point, this passage is a commentary on money (as Luke's tradition realizes with the antecedent passage Luke 11:5-8). If a son asks a father for bread, will the father give him a stone? Rhetorically, Jesus provokes his audience to reflect upon the function of money. A peasant needing money for taxes, but with very little food in reserve, cannot give bronze coins to his children to eat! God's patronage, by contrast, is characterized by reciprocal exchanges; those seeking God's rule seek a kin-group relationship wherein stones, snakes, and scorpions are not the media of exchange, but real goods satisfying real need.

Summary

Social stratification within agrarian societies like that of early Roman Palestine was well defined and generally straightforward. Society was layered—elite above non-elite. In the Roman Empire, elites (rulers, military **commanders** [1.32], priests) inhabited the cities and large estates; non-elites (peasants, artisans, fishers, laborers, and "expendable" people of various kinds) populated outskirts of cities, towns, and country villages.

The society of early Roman Palestine, like almost all ancient societies, had an extractive economy wherein goods were taken from the agrarian producers and redistributed by the powerful. The fundamental flow was in a "vertical" social direction. For the non-elite family or individual, proportionately fewer goods and services flowed in a "horizontal" direction; horizontal flow would have involved very basic and locally available commodities only. The elite controlled the product of most land and the labor of most people.

Jesus offers a potent critique of political arrangements and through the symbol of God's reign speaks of a reorganization of society through fictive kinship patterns. Exchanges based upon general reciprocity will decentralize distribution and not be strictly accounted for by money mechanisms. We can now understand not only why "the Lord Jesus . . . said, 'It is more honorable to give than to receive'" (Acts 20:35), but how this might become a general economic principle in the inauguration of God's reign.

Applying the Perspectives

1. Household organization, and corresponding household economy, was a prominent theme in the early church. Consider the importance of this and its relationship to the concerns of Jesus and the Jesus movement in the light of Mark 2:15; 14:4-7; and Acts 2:44.

2. Jesus' attitudes toward political economy are implicit in a number of places in the Gospels. How might Mark 10:28-30 provide insight into his views on control of land?

3. In Jesus' parables, he mentions day laborers waiting in the marketplace for work. In many U.S. cities immigrant laborers wait on corners or in the parking lots of home improvement stores. Compare and contrast these two situations.

4. Debt and taxes were significant manifestations of political economy in Palestine at the time of Jesus. Study the Lord's Prayer in Matt 6:9-13 (and v. 14) and Luke 11:2-4. How does such Jesus material respond to the political realities?

5. The extent of family responsibility for debts, and the sometimes brutal means for collecting them, is shown in the following text from **Philo** [2.12]:

> Recently [early first century] a certain collector of taxes was appointed in our area [Alexandria, Egypt]. When some of the men who apparently were in arrears because of poverty fled in fear of unbearable punishment, he laid violent hands on their wives, children, parents, and other relatives, beating and trampling and visiting every outrage upon them to get them either to betray their fugitive or to pay up on his behalf. (*Laws* 3.159; quoted in Lewis 1983:161–62)

Consider similar procedures in Matt 18:23-30, 32-34. Why does Jesus utilize such an image? How does it perhaps point to alternative social relations?

6. Read Columella's treatise *On Agriculture* and identify what the issues are for accurately depicting a first-century agrarian society. What crops are planted, and who decides this? Whom does this crop choice benefit? How are estates run? Who is in charge? How are workers treated? How do estates and small landholders fit into the larger political economy?

Suggested Reading

Finley (1985) provides a useful overview of the economy of the Roman Empire. Archaeological information from the wider Roman world relevant to understanding the economy can be found in Greene (1986). Applebaum (1976) and Broshi (1987) summarize many issues relevant to Palestinian economics.

The present authors each have supplied more detailed treatments of matters discussed in this chapter: Hanson (1990) gives a focused treatment of economic issues related to the family of Herod (dowry systems and inheritance) and also analyzes the economics of Galilean fishing (1997b). Oakman (1986) relates a study of Palestinian agrarian economics to selected features of the Jesus tradition. For general orientation to ancient economics and detailed analysis of specific New Testament passages, the reader might profitably consult Oakman (2008).

Temple warning inscription

"It was at this time, in the eighteenth year of his reign . . . , that Herod began an extraordinary task: the reconstruction of God's temple at his own expense, enlarging its precincts and raising it to an imposing height" (Josephus, *Ant.* 15.380). Two copies of this warning inscription, presumably placed at the barriers between the Court of Gentiles and the Court of Israelites, have been discovered; one, discovered in 1871, is in the Istanbul Archaeology Museum (CIJ 2.1400), and the other, discovered in 1935, is in the Rockefeller Museum (OGIS II.598). See p. 131 for a translation. (Photo © Erich Lessing / Art Resosurce, NY. Used by permission.)

CHAPTER 5

Was Bigger Better?

Political Religion in Roman Palestine

[Herod] surpassed the [temple] expenditures of his predecessors, so that it was thought that no one else had adorned the temple so splendidly. (Josephus, *Ant.* 15.396)

He who has not seen the temple of Herod, has never in his life seen a beautiful structure. (*b. B. Bat.* 4a; quoted in Safrai 1976b:2.869–70)

When they came to Capernaum, the collectors of the didrachma approached Peter and asked, "Doesn't your teacher pay the tax?" He said, "Yes." And Jesus spoke to him as he entered the house, saying, "How does it seem to you, Simon? From whom do kings of the earth take toll or tribute? From their sons or from others?" But when he responded, "From others," Jesus said to him, "Well then, the sons are free." (Matt 17:24-26)

And [Jesus] taught and said to them, "Is it not written, 'My house shall be called a house of prayer for all the peoples?' But you have made it a cave of bandits." (Mark 11:17)

And as he came out of the temple, one of his disciples said to him, "Teacher, what wonderful stones and what wonderful buildings!" And Jesus said, "Do you see these great buildings? Not a single stone will be left here upon another that will not be thrown down." (Mark 13:1-2)

Introduction

The contrasts in the attitudes of **Josephus** [2.7], the **rabbis** [1.68] (**Talmud** [2.18]), and Jesus toward the temple in Jerusalem are striking. It was one of the greatest temples of antiquity and the key **institution** [3.30] of **Judean** [1.43] political **religion** [3.48]. In this chapter, we examine the constitution and construction of the Jerusalem temple, as well as its operations and social functions and effects.

Questions

The modern reader of the Gospels might be puzzled about Jesus' words. Why does royal taxation become an analogy for consideration of the temple tax (the two didrachma or half-**shekel** [1.76])? How does a "house of prayer" possibly become a "cave of bandits"? What were the grounds for the prediction of the temple's destruction? This leads us to a series of questions about the operation of the temple and whom it benefited:

- What was the temple like at the time of Jesus? Why was it important historically?
- How did the temple operate? Who were its basic personnel? If its central role was to support animal sacrifice, what did those operations require and mean?
- How should we think of the religious functions of the Jerusalem temple?
- Who controlled it? Who benefited from it, and how?
- What was the political and economic

impact of the temple upon Israelite society? How was the half-shekel tax used? What were other temple dues and obligations? Who was responsible to collect these?

- How did the temple system touch the lives of ordinary people? What were people's attitudes to the temple? Why would Jesus the Galilean concern himself with the Judean temple?

Models

The above epigraphs emphasize that religion appears with multiple social connections in ancient **agrarian societies** [3.1]. We will stress in this chapter that not only were "church and state" not separated in such societies, but religious institutions as a rule were routinely brought into alignment with political realities and served to justify and sustain those realities. Conversely, religious protest **movements** [3.36] tended to seek legitimation by appeal to higher religious principles and needed therefore to become "political" by contesting elite control of religious institutions. Moreover, matters that we would consider familial and economic were integrally involved in ancient religion. This "fusion" of social systems (religious and political) may confuse twenty-first-century Americans, who are accustomed to religious institutions unencumbered by or detached from **kinship** [3.31] or political associations. Religion for moderns is primarily individual, voluntary, and "spiritual." We will not understand the realities that made Herod's temple a "cave of bandits," nor will we be attuned to the visceral anger in Jesus' words about the temple's destruction or his defiant affirmation of freedom for "God's sons," without a clear grasp of the political nature of first-century religion.

Modern Americans are used to religious institutions that are explicit. "Attend the church of your choice" expresses a good American attitude; voluntary associations with religious institutions are the rule here. Membership is freely chosen, although family traditions play a role as well. Support is likewise subject to the discretion of the members. Religious institutions in America are divided into formal denominations. Individual participation is at a local congregational level, with representatives participating in the larger denominational polity. In line with the larger culture, people expect representative democracy in their churches. Leadership in religious bodies is achieved based upon voluntary choice and a formal course of education. Because of the overarching voluntary nature of modern religious institutions, frequent (often weekly) meetings are needed to sustain ties. The focus of modern American religious institutions tends to revolve around the individual and individual decisions. Worship, for instance, is centered upon actions that keep the individual involved and favorably disposed (preaching, prayer, congregational song). Since more people now than in the past are literate, in modern life, theological beliefs become discriminating and dividing criteria.

By contrast, ancient societies were used to religious institutions embedded in other frameworks. The two routine places for religious expression were at home (domestic,

kinship religion) or in elite-controlled temples (public, political religion). It is this latter **domain** [3.11] that we focus on in this chapter. "Attend the church of your choice"

Research Tip 5

Access the online versions of Josephus's works at:

http://www.ccel.org/ccel/josephus/works/files/works.html or *http://wesley.nnu.edu/biblical_studies/josephus/*

You can search the text for key terms (such as "honor" and "taxes"), historical persons and groups (Antipas, Pharisees), and locations (Cana, Tiberias). The same is true for the works of Philo, located at:

http://www.earlychristianwritings.com/yonge/ or *http://www.earlyjewishwritings.com/philo.html*

would have made no sense to most ancient persons; elective associations with religious institutions were the exception. "Religious associations" were found mainly in large cities of the first-century Roman Empire, and it may be doubted whether these were entirely voluntary for all members. Membership in domestic or political religious institutions was culturally and historically conditioned. Support for religious institutions outside the family was obtained through taxation compelled by political authorities. Religious institutions, as all political life generally, were divided by personal **factions** [3.19] striving to occupy the key positions of benefit from the religious system; participation happened through the **group** [3.23] and was relatively impersonal. Ancient religious institutions were hierarchical, on the model of the patriarchal family; any shared decision-making was limited to a select group of people (males with **status** [3.53] qualifications). Leadership in religious institutions was "ascribed," based upon heredity and family relationship.

Because of the overarching political nature of ancient religious institutions, regular ritual participation was restricted to the functionaries; most other people had infrequent and occasional direct association with the institution, but continual indirect contact through taxation. The focus of ancient religious institutions revolved around the group; worship consisted of elaborate ritual actions. "Theology" was the province of a small literate elite only, and consisted in second-temple times primarily of apologetic histories (such as 1 Maccabees), textual divination techniques as in the *pesharim* ("prophetic" commentaries) of Qumran, detailed elaborations of cultic-civic rules and requirements in the rabbinic traditions, or elaborate cosmic speculations (apocalyptic scribal traditions like *1 Enoch*). Very often this theology was also a justification or rationalization of existing religious groups or institutions, that is, why they should continue in their positions of **power** [3.44] and privilege or be restored to power and privilege. And often the argument involved the need for the institution to sustain the deity's **patronage** [3.40] and favor. Occasionally in agrarian societies, though, theology became a critical tool for exposing the oppression of the primary political-religious institutions. We think especially of

the cases of the Israelite prophets or of Jesus of Nazareth.

Both **elite** [3.14] and non-elite public religious concerns were, therefore, suffused with **politics** [3.42], since the words "politics, political" refer to the public interactions of families (the primary institutional context in Jesus' day). Every other institution that we moderns distinguish would then have been embedded within or controlled by family organizations. Elite "political religion" refers to elite control over religious symbols and operations that benefit that elite directly. In Jesus' day, this would mean control over theology (defining how God is conceived), over **purity** [3.45] standards (clean/unclean and in-group/out-group), and over ritual (defining how people behave or how things are conducted within the temple). This control sustained the **honor** [3.25] of elite groups (their public recognition and prestige). Control of wealth was necessary for that sustenance as well. Elite political religion, therefore, governed **economy** [3.13] as well. A modern U.S. reader will note that such religion contained few institutionalized checks and balances.

Non-elite religion shifted these emphases somewhat. Non-elite public religion was concerned with recovering the lost honor of families. Non-elite religion encouraged politics by emboldening groups to redefine the meaning of received traditions or even to challenge elite control of religion. This had implications for the economy as well, since elite politics governed the ancient economy.

The Jerusalem Temple and Its Expansion under Herod the Great

The Judean temple in Jerusalem was a political institution in numerous senses, by virtue of its founding by an Israelite **king** [1.13] (Solomon) and refounding later under Persian auspices (Cyrus); by virtue of its privileging a certain **class** [3.7] of people by divine right; and by virtue of its co-optation in Jesus' day by **Herodian** [1.37] and Roman interests.

The course of affairs in first-century Judean religion was continually influenced by memories of the glory days of Israel recounted in the temple psalms and histories of Judean kings. The Law of Moses in Leviticus, of course, gave central place to temple sacrifice (a legal emphasis reached only in the sixth through fifth centuries B.C.E.). The temple of Jesus' day, however, was not the first Israelite temple of King Solomon. Built in the tenth century B.C.E. on Phoenician models (1 Kings 5), Solomon's first temple was destroyed in 587 B.C.E. by Nebuchadnezzar and the Neo-Babylonian army (2 Kgs 25:9). The second temple was founded and finished early in the Persian period (Ezra 6:15; 520 B.C.E.); refurbished by the **Hasmoneans** [1.34] (1 Macc 4:47-48; 164 B.C.E.); and dramatically expanded and remodeled by Herod the Great beginning in 20 B.C.E. (Josephus, *Ant.* 15.380). Herod's temple was the temple of Jesus' time. This temple was destroyed by the Romans in 70 C.E., during the final course of the **First Judean Revolt** [1.28] (66–70 C.E.).

The first temple was political in the sense that it was considered a chapel of the kings of Judah; northern Israelite temples were similarly viewed (Amos 7:13). Prophets arose as occasional critics of palace-sponsored religion. Jeremiah 7 provides a graphic portrayal of such criticism, and Jeremiah 26 the punitive consequences for the prophet.

Early postexilic prophets supported rebuilding the temple (Ezra 5:1-2; Haggai; Zech 4:9). Under the Persians, however, Yehud (no longer Judah) was not reconstituted as before. The royal house of David disappeared; Zerubbabel was not to be Yahweh's Anointed like David. Zechariah 6:11-13 shows that political authority passed to the **high priest** [1.38]. The second temple, as the infrastructure of Judean priestly religion, was to become the new center of Judean power until its destruction.

Memories of prophetic criticism of the temple not surprisingly continued to play a role in Judean affairs around the time of Jesus of Nazareth. The Qumran community's scrolls preserve a comment to Habakkuk 2:5-6 regarding the early Hasmoneans and the temple:

Its interpretation concerns the Wicked Priest who was named after the name of truth when he entered his office. But when he attained rule over Israel, his heart became proud, and he deserted God and acted faithlessly against the law for the sake of riches. He robbed and collected the wealth of the men of violence who rebelled against God. And the wealth of the peoples he seized [out of the temple?],

Prophecy against the Jerusalem Temple

Four years before the war [the First Judean Revolt], when the city was enjoying profound peace and prosperity, there came to the feast at which it is the custom of all Judeans to erect tabernacles to God, Jesus the son of Ananias, an unskilled peasant, who, standing in the temple, suddenly began to cry out, "A voice from the east, a voice from the west, a voice from the four winds; a voice against Jerusalem and the sanctuary, a voice against the bridegroom and the bride, a voice against all the people." Day and night he went about all the alleys with this cry on his lips. . . . So for seven years and five months he continued his wail, his voice never flagging nor his strength exhausted. (Josephus, War 6.300–301, 308; LCL)

so that he heaped sinful iniquity upon himself. (1QpHab 8:8–12; see 4 Macc 4:3, 15-17)

Shortly before the Jerusalem temple's destruction by the Romans in 70 C.E., Jesus son of Ananias cried woe and dishonor against Herod's temple (Josephus, *War* 6.300)—like an Amos of old.

Herod began to expand the temple complex (20 B.C.E.) because of his insatiable ambition (Josephus, *Ant.* 16.153). He also wanted to soften Judean resentment against his harsh regime and building programs (*Ant.* 16.154). He constructed a building to match his enormous ego. It was recognized as one of the wonders of the ancient world.

Archaeology has revealed much of interest and importance about Herod's temple from its remains. While the temple buildings and royal colonnades on top are long gone, still today can be seen the enormous enclosure wall and artificial hill that Herod built as the substructure for the temple. The rabbis called this platform "the mountain of the house"; today it is known as "the Noble Sanctuary" (*Haram esh Sherif*), site of the Muslim Dome of the Rock and Al-Aqsa Mosque. A portion of the enclosure wall on the southwest side is known to modern Jews as the Western Wall. In the nineteenth century, explorers like Edward Robinson, Charles Wilson, and Charles Warren surveyed the ruins and gave names to important features. Warren even sank shafts at the southwest corner of the enclosure wall to explore underground. Nineteenth-century discoveries, though meager, gave impetus to later archaeological work. One important temple inscription, discovered in 1871, will be discussed below. It was not until the late 1960s that Israelis systematically excavated the southwest and south areas adjoining the enclosure wall. The results have been quite revealing.

On the southwest side, archaeologists were able to show that Robinson's Arch had originally belonged not to a bridge crossing to the Upper City of ancient Jerusalem but to a monumental stairway rising from the Tyropoeon Valley below. Adjacent to the archway, archaeologists exposed a Herodian-period street running north-south along the Western Wall. Lying upon the street where they had fallen in 70 C.E. were large blocks of finely carved Herodian masonry from the upper portion of the temple enclosure wall. These had formed the outer wall for the porticoes that rimmed the Court of the Gentiles; the masons had originally shaped the stone into the form of buttressing artificial columns known as pilasters. This was a standard technique in Herodian masonry, as shown from similar elements in Herod's buildings at **Masada** [1.50], Jericho, and Hebron.

The southern wall was adorned by a magnificent staircase leading up to a main temple entrance, the Double Gate. The main staircase extended apparently 105 feet on each side. Farther east, a Triple Gate was accessed by a smaller stairway. In this area, numerous baths associated with ritual purity concerns were unearthed. People entering the temple needed to bathe in order to be in an appropriate state of purity. Several buildings in this area provided housing for visiting pilgrims, and one may have provided meeting space for the **Sanhedrin** [1.71]. During the Crusader period (c. 1099–1291 C.E.), Christian knights stabled horses in vaults under the southeast corner of the temple platform; they called this area "Solomon's Stables," but the stonework of the vaults reveals their original connection to Herod's temple. Perhaps they provided space to warehouse temple goods accessed through the Triple Gate (see further below).

The eastern wall of the temple enclosure has not been cleared away because of tombs near the wall, but it is known that the so-called Golden Gate (from medieval times) stands above an earlier Herodian gate. Archaeologists have also ascertained that seams in the enclosure wall near the south end are due to Herod's extension southward of an earlier Hasmonean enclosure wall (perhaps standing above Solomon's retaining wall). Herod also lengthened the platform northward. Directly north of the temple enclosure stood massive water cisterns: The pool of Israel adjacent to the enclosure wall (now a parking lot) provided much of the water required by the sacrificial rites. The older pools of Bethzatha or Bethesda (John 5), across the Via Dolorosa of the Old City in the courtyard of St. Anne's Church, derive from the second century B.C.E. On the northeast corner of the temple enclosure stood the Antonia Fortress, where Roman troops were stationed during the time of Jesus.

The Western Wall of the temple enclosure had two bridges running to the Upper City of ancient Jerusalem. These bridges show the close connection between the holy place and the dwelling places of powerful Judean families (Herods, Sadducean **priests** [1.62]). The northernmost bridge was named after the first Roman **prefect** [1.61] of Judea, Coponius. The southernmost bridge ran over what is now known as Wilson's Arch (underground today, accessed from a door near the Western Wall).

While the colonnades and temple buildings atop Herod's artificial mountain are no longer intact, some things can be inferred from literary sources about their appearance. The enclosure wall was surrounded on top by colonnades (covered walkways supported by columns). At the south end was a magnificent Royal Portico, a huge entryway with a roof supported by columns. Josephus says of it:

Now the columns (of the portico) stood in four rows, one opposite the other all along—the fourth row was attached to a wall built of stone—and the thickness of each column was such that it would take three men with outstretched arms touching one another to envelop it; its height was twenty-seven feet, and there was a double moulding running round its base. The number of all the columns was a hundred and sixty-two, and their capitals were ornamented in the Corinthian style of carving, which caused amazement by the magnificence of its whole effect. (*Ant.* 15.413–15; LCL)

The Court of the Gentiles, an extensive plaza of about thirty-five acres (Finegan 1992:194), so-called because Gentiles were permitted there, surrounded the temple buildings. This court was separated from the temple by a balustrade, because only Judeans could enter the temple. Gentiles were subject to capital punishment if they tried to cross this line (see Acts 21:28 and the next section below). The temple area inside was divided into three basic areas—one open to men and women, one open only to Judean men, and one open only to priests. The priestly area was divided again into three areas—the place of sacrifices outside the temple building; the holy place just within the temple building (where stood a golden table for the Bread of the Presence, a golden lampstand with seven branches, and a golden incense stand); and the inner room, the Holy of Holies, a dark, completely empty room thirty feet square. The strict separation of all of these areas indi-

cates the overwhelming concern for purity at the core of Judean religion at the time (Malina 2001a:164–65; Sanders 1992).

Archaeology and ancient literature tell us something about the temple of Jesus' day, but its character as a social institution requires further exploration of its social constitution and operation.

The Personnel and Sacrifices of the Jerusalem Temple

As with all ancient institutions, the temple was defined first and foremost by familial ties. The high priest's family was obviously the most important. Generally after the exile, Judean families with great honor and status stood among the priests. Genealogies were therefore extremely important legacies, as evident in the written material from this period, since knowing one's origins was crucial for social standing. Competing with priests for power and privilege were nonpriestly families such as the Herods, or the older Hasmonean and Davidic families. Roman control added another dimension to the politics of Palestine. Even then, only priests had the right by Judean law to enter the temple or to participate in its sacrificial rites.

Four major priestly families had returned to Judea from the Babylonian exile (Ezra 2:36-39). The first high priest after the exile, Joshua, descended from the most prominent family, Jedaiah (Ezra 2:36). With them were other priests, the **Levites** [1.47], who had lost honor, power, and privilege because of the exile (Ezra 2:40-42; see Ezek 44:10-14). By the time of Jesus, high priests were appointed by Rome or its agents from select families only. The ordinary priestly families had by then been organized into twenty-four "courses," that is, divisions (1 Chr 24:7-19; Luke 1:5; Josephus, *Ant.* 7.366; *Life* 2). Levites were also accepted as crucial to the organization and operation of the temple. "Priest" and "Levite" could be used, in Jesus' day, as shorthand for the Judean elite (Luke 10:31-32), though Levites had much less power and standing than the upper-echelon priests.

The high priest and the high priestly families, under the oversight and power of the Roman prefect, played a major role in controlling the temple and its operation. The temple institution can be examined in terms of personnel and operations, with three basic dimensions—administrative, ritual, and economic. We look at ritual personnel and sacrifice here. The administrative and economic dimensions of the temple will be considered more thoroughly in the next section, where the social impact and implications of the temple are taken up. Josephus gives a basic view of temple personnel in *Ant.* 11.128: priests, Levites, musicians, porters, servants, and **scribes** [1.72]. Attention to social structure and institutional need reveals a greater complexity. Figure 5.1, the "Organization Chart for the Temple System," can help to orient the reader in the following discussion.

Besides priests, the high priest had under his authority important administrative and economic functionaries. The priests were charged with maintaining order within the temple complex and even throughout Jerusalem. The chief of everyday temple operations was known as the *stratēgos* (Josephus, *War* 2.409; a military term in Greek: "captain") or *sāgān* (Talmudic Hebrew). It may be that the captain also exercised oversight over the Jerusalem markets, since a comparable functionary did so in earlier times (Hamilton 1964:367).

Under the temple prefect were "police," supplied from the levitical families. These had responsibilities not only for keeping order, but also for maintaining temple purity according to the Law of Moses. Furthermore, since certain areas were off-limits to all but Israelites or priests, the police force had authority to execute transgressors. A temple inscription, originally affixed to a wall separating the Court of Gentiles from the inner courts and temple itself, was discovered in 1871 and published by C. Clermont-Ganneau:

> No outsider is to enter the protective enclosure around the temple; whoever does will have only himself to blame for the death that follows. (Greek text in Schürer 1979:285; Finegan 1992:197)

Levites were also assigned as gatekeepers and garbage collectors for the temple area.

Mosaic Law dealt not only with sacrifice, but also with civil life. Not surprisingly, the temple was closely linked with judicial institutions and authority. The high priest convened the Sanhedrin, the "supreme court" in the time of Jesus. The court was comprised of representatives of priestly families, perhaps with some legal expertise, and various legal experts and advisors from the scribal sectors. It seems that historically the Pharisaic

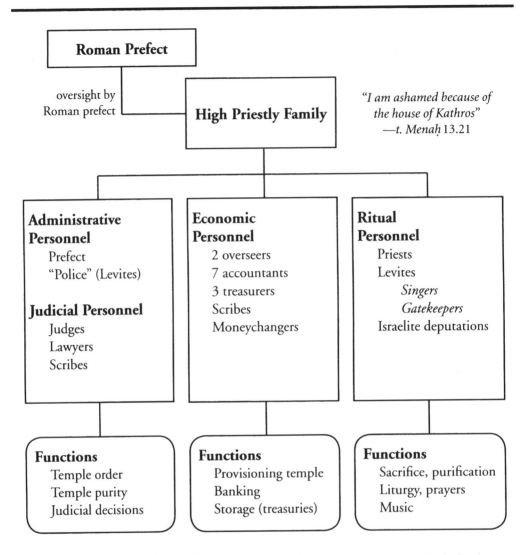

The Roman prefect exercised oversight of the temple and its operations. The high priestly families controlled or occupied the positions of significant power, privilege, or prestige. While personnel and functions can be analytically separated in the system, all participate in the organizational power structures, benefit (more or less) from economic redistribution, and express religious significance. This is what is meant by religion's "embeddedness" in politics or the temple as a political-religious institution.

Figure 5.1 Organization Chart for the Temple System

movement (see below) drew leadership from these scribal lawyers (Mark 2:16). Other judicial and community institutions throughout areas controlled by Judeans would be shaped by temple interests (local courts and **synagogues** [1.81]). The synagogue originated in Judean villages and towns as a communal assembly point (Horsley 1995:223), possibly with regular services paralleling the temple's (Hoenig 1979).

Economic functionaries dealt with the animals and gifts that were essential for the temple's operation. The high priest had at his disposal two general inspectors, seven accountants and other scribes who were responsible for keeping track of offerings and gifts, three major treasurers and people in charge of specific treasuries (bird offerings, libations, clothing for priests), and money changers.

The priests and levitical singers constituted the heart of the Judean temple as a religious operation. Elaborate rituals were centered on the sacrifices mandated in the Law of Moses. Twenty priests were chosen by lot for the daily regular sacrifices, but others were needed to deal with the frequent occasional sacrifices. The twenty-four courses (family groups) each served in succession a week at a time throughout the year (Luke 1:8-9). Altogether, there may have been as many as fifteen hundred priests available for the weekly services (Josephus, *Ant.* 7.363–67; Schürer 1979:246). Courses were controlled by heads of divisions, "fathers' houses," and elders. The Levite families and lay Israelite "deputations" (who witnessed the daily sacrificial activity)

were similarly composed, except that the Levites did not have fathers' houses.

An account of sacrifice in the Hasmonean temple, provided by the second-century B.C.E. *Letter of Aristeas,* is suggestive of the awesome nature of sacrifice in the subsequent Herodian temple:

> The ministering of the priests was absolutely unsurpassable in its vigor and the arrangement of its well-ordered silence: All work hard of their own accord, with much exertion, and each one looks after his appointed task. Their service is unremitting, sharing the sacrifices, some undertaking the carrying of wood, others oil, others wheaten flour, others the sweet spices, others offering burnt offerings of the parts of the flesh—all of them exerting their strength in different ways. . . . A general silence reigns, so that one might think that there was not a single man in the place although the number of ministers in attendance is more than seven hundred, in addition to a large number of the assistants bringing forward the animals for sacrifice. (*Aristeas* 92-95, trans. R. J. H. Shutt, in Charlesworth 1985:19)

Daily in Jesus' time, the priests sacrificed one lamb in the morning and one in the evening, accompanied by meal and drink offerings. This was the *tamîd*, the continuous offering, and represented the basic sacrificial set each day. From Josephus's numbers (*Ant.* 3.224–27), we can calculate that these continuous sacrifices alone required per year nearly twelve hundred animals (bulls, oxen, rams, and lambs).

While the ordinary ritual centered around the whole offerings, there were other categories of sacrifice as well. Chief among these were (1) obligatory sin and purification offerings and (2) so-called freewill offerings. People were constantly bringing their obligatory offerings; their offerings of grain, wine, and oil in satisfaction of vows (the votive offerings); or thank offerings. Numerous priests from the weekly course were needed to assist with these rites. The altar of sacrifice before the temple itself was continuously in use, and the annual requirement for animals probably in the tens or hundreds of thousands.

The regulations for sacrifice in Leviticus and Deuteronomy are elaborate and confusing. It is clear that various sacrificial systems have been combined over the long development and use of these traditions, so that categories are not always entirely distinct. Malina (1996a) argues that the whole system was dedicated to restoring exclusiveness to Judeans before God (thus maintaining the "chosen-ness" of the chosen people). The high concern in sacrificial religion with purity and blood relations (kinship) makes this argument plausible. Figure 5.2 summarizes the daily and occasional sacrificial rituals and important biblical references.

How, specifically, should we understand the sacrificial categories? Anticipating that the question of meaning is not distinct from familial and political relations, we can say at this point that the most holy sacrifices involved whole offerings and also purity and reparation sacrifices. The least holy sacrifices were the communion sacrifices.

Synagogues in First–Century Palestine

The Greek term synagōgos *literally means "gathering place." Modern archaeologists have identified building remains interpreted as first-century synagogues at Capernaum, Chorazin, Masada, Magdala, and Gamla (see also the sidebar on the Theodotus inscription on p. 73). And Josephus mentions synagogue buildings in Caesarea and Galilee (for example,* War *2.285-91;* Life *276–303). Synagogues usually have square or rectangular floor plans, with what look to be staggered seats going entirely around the outside walls. No evidence in these remains suggests sacred space, as is later the case in the Byzantine-period synagogues (with* bema *or "Seat of Moses"). Most likely, these were public gathering spaces, in which weekly prayer services also may have been held. Lee Levine is of the opinion that "[the Judean synagogue] functioned as a community center, housing the activities of school, court, hostel, charity fund, and meeting place for the local Jewish community. . . . Only after the destruction of the Second Temple did the synagogue in Palestine develop and expand as a place of worship" (Levine 1992:1421). In addition to Levine, see Horsley (1995), Hoenig (1979), and Kloppenborg (2005).*

Sacrifices	References
Burnt offering (ʿolāh)	Lev 1:1-17; Pss 20:3b; 66:13, 15
Cereal offering (minḥāh)	Lev 2:1-16; Pss 20:3a; 96:8; Dan 9:21
Peace offerings (zēbaḥ šelāmîm)	Lev 3:1-17; 1 Kgs 3:15; Amos 5:22; Sir 35:1
Purification offering (ḥaṭṭāt)	Lev 4:1-5:13; 2 Kgs 12:16; Ezek 42:13
Reparation offering (ʾāšām)	Lev 5:14—6:7; 19:20-22; Ezek 46:20
Thank offering (tôdāh)	Lev 7:11-14; Neh 12:27; Job 33:19-33; Pss 107:22; 116:17; Jer 30:19; Amos 4:5; Jonah 2:9

Figure 5.2 Temple Sacrifices

The daily whole or burnt offerings belonged entirely to God. These expressed God's exclusive claim upon all goods of life in the form of a divine **tribute** [1.86] or tax. Most of the victim went up, literally, in smoke; but the hide belonged to the officiating priest. In other ways, people indebted themselves to God through vows and oaths. Since these were usually public, thus involving honor or reputation, the Law mandated they be fulfilled as specified by dedicating what was vowed to God before God's elected representatives (priests in Jerusalem). Fulfilling vows was also a matter of expressing loyalty to the divine patron.

The purity and reparation sacrifices were related to the holiness or purity of the temple itself (Milgrom 1976). Milgrom has taken the role of blood seriously in the question of meaning. The purification sacrifice (ḥaṭṭāt; the traditional English translation "sin offering" is not entirely illuminating) might be seen as similar to the modern medical procedure of dialysis. The ancient temple was like a "kidney" that attracted and cleansed impurities in the social body; the ḥaṭṭāt sacrificial blood enabled this "dialysis machine" to work by absorbing and removing the impurities. Other purification offerings (doves after childbirth, Lev 12:8) purged not only the sanctuary, but also restored the postpartum woman to normal life while acknowledging God's sole authority to establish pure blood relations (see Hanson 1993; 1997a).

The reparation sacrifice (ʾāšām; the traditional English translation "guilt offering" is misleading for an **honor–shame culture** [3.25, 3.50]) repaired sanctuary desecrations of various kinds that were felt to dishonor God by imposing fines upon the perpetrators. ʾĀšām sacrifices worked to restore the health of the sanctuary—so necessary (in the priestly view) to maintaining the balance in the divine-human relationship when violations of God's will had transpired. The rites in the temple on the Day of Atonements (Lev 16:1-34; 23:27-32; Num 29:7-11) were magnified versions of the *'āšām*. The priests alone could eat of these two major types of sacrifice (see Hanson 1997a). The meat from the sacrifices was not all consumed by the priests, although some of it was. Talmudic tradition tells us that priests ate so much meat that they suffered from chronic sicknesses (*m. Šeqal.* 5.1; Jeremias 1969:26). Thank offerings and communal sacrifices were consumed by both priests and participants. The remainder of the sacrificial meat was prepared within the temple and distributed within Jerusalem itself (Jeremias 1969:48–49). Huge quantities of salt were needed to preserve the meat in an era without refrigeration (salt was also thought to drive off demons).

The communion sacrifices (either thank offerings or peace offerings), the least holy, were so-called because they were partaken of substantially by lay offerers in familial solidarity or communion with God and one another. This type of sacrifice was characteristic of those at the major festivals of Passover (Exodus 12; Lev 23:5-8; Deut 16:1-8), Pentecost

or Weeks (Exod 23:16; Lev 23:15-21; Deut 16:9-12), and Tabernacles (Lev 23:34-36; Deut 16:13-15). At those times, people gave thanks to God for blessings and celebrated in community. Such celebrations brought great joy and offered times for the whole people of Israel to ask about the meaning of Israel's calling and destiny. Josephus shows that the great festival times were also opportunities for protest against the political subjection to Rome (*War* 2.10//*Ant.* 17.213). This picture is corroborated in the Gospels (Mark 11:15-18).

Our modern conceptions of the temple are rather bloodless and undoubtedly too spiritual. An appropriate analogy is a slaughterhouse. Enormous amounts of animal blood spilled around the altar every day and splashed upon the priests as they worked. The temple architects had to design very special drainage systems to convey the blood down into the depths of the Temple Mount and thence away. Enormous quantities of water were required for this purpose. Aristeas again helps us here:

There were many mouths at the base [of the altar], which were completely invisible

---

The Mishnah on the Temple Personnel

These are the officers who served in the temple: Johanan b. Phineas was over the seals, Ahijah was over the drink offerings, Mattithiah b. Samuel was over the lots, Petahiah was over the bird offerings . . . Ben Ahijah was over the bowel sickness, Nehunyah was the trench digger, Gabini was the herald, Ben Geber was over the cymbal, Hygros b. Levi was over the singing, the House of Garmu was over the preparation of the bread of presence, the House of Abtinas was over the preparation of the incense, Eleazar was over the hangings, and Phineas was over the vestments. (*m. Šeqal.* 5.1; Danby) except for those responsible for the ministry, so that the large amounts of blood which collected from the sacrifices were all cleansed by the downward pressure and momentum. (*Aristeas* 90, trans. by R. J. H. Shutt in Charlesworth 1985:19)

Aristeas afterwards describes the huge conduits and water supply that supported this cleansing mechanism. Archaeology of the Temple Mount area confirms that extensive water facilities were installed. Some of the cisterns still can hold thousands of gallons (see Bahat 1986:26; Rousseau and Arav 1995:298).

The Social Impact and Implications of Herod's Temple

Archaeology and dispassionate description of personnel and sacrifices by themselves are inadequate for a full understanding of Herod's temple. Adequacy at least requires two further considerations: (1) how control of the temple affected the production and distribution of goods in Roman Palestine and (2) under what terms or how willingly most people participated in the temple system. Figure 5.3, "Political Religion in Agrarian Roman Palestine" (see p. 139) extends our appreciation of other social dimensions of the temple system and, together with the preceding organizational chart, helps us to think through major societal impacts and implications for Palestine. The vertical dimension of "Political Religion in Agrarian Roman Palestine" represents the relative power and privilege of the major actors.

Temple and Elite

We have stressed that the temple institution was embedded within kinship and political relationships (Malina 1988:23; 1996:163). The powerful, especially the high priests and important priestly families, controlled the temple and were the primary beneficiaries of it. Other groups (Herods, Romans) struggled for control of the operations and resources within the temple system. Meshorer (1982) has argued that Tyre lost its right (as determined by Rome) to coin "Tyrian" money and that this money began to be minted in Jerusalem in 19 B.C.E. This change correlates with Herod's expansion of the temple complex in 20 B.C.E., showing the power of Herod and the Romans at work to control the temple in new ways. Throughout the time of Jesus, Herod and the Roman prefects appointed the Jerusalem high priests. Herod the Great married successively two women from high priestly families, Mariamme the Hasmonean and Mariamme daughter of Boethus. These priestly **marriages** [3.34] were designed to further consolidate his power and increase his status. The prefects also had control over the high priestly garments (Josephus, *Ant.* 18.93–95; Safrai 1976b:906). The Roman administrative apparatus served as a guarantor of major Roman interests in the Palestinian social system and a check against indigenous attempts to pry free of Roman control.

The indigenous Judean oligarchy was comprised essentially of three groups: the high priests, drawn from only a few elite families and traditionally associated with **Sadducees** [1.70] because of the great prestige of the ancient priestly family of Zaddok

(1 Kgs 1:34); the copyists, recorders, administrators, or legal experts of the system (scribes); and village and town lay nobility tracing their lineage back to important families in Israel's past (elders). Rabbinic tradition could recall the general flavor of this social situation in these words:

> Abba Saul ben Bithnith and Abba Joseph ben Johanan of Jerusalem say, "I am ashamed because of the house of Kathros. Ashamed because of their pen. Ashamed because of the house of Hanin. Ashamed because of their whispering. Ashamed because of the house of Ishmael ben Phabi. For they are high priests, and their sons [are] treasurers, and their sons-in-law [are] supervisors, and their servants come and beat us with staves." (*t. Menaḥ.* 13.21; quoted in Evans 1989b:532–33)

As Saul's and Joseph's laments indicate, the scribes were affiliated in nepotistic fashion with the high priestly families (Evans 1989a:259). There are various lists of these families constructed from Josephus and rabbinic traditions. Josephus highlights Phiabi (Phabi), Boethus, Annas (Hanin), and Kamith, in comparison with the Tosephta's Kathros, Hanin, and Phabi. The Gospels thus give important information when they assert that the "chief priests and the scribes" spearhead the movement to kill Jesus of Nazareth (Mark 14:1) and that Jesus was arrested by "a gang representing the high priests, scribes, and elders bearing swords and clubs" (Mark 14:43). The elders, who were drawn from the towns and villages, had greater ambivalence about Judean politics (compare Jer 26:1-24) and probably had torn loyalties in relation to a figure like Jesus of Nazareth. Joseph of Arimathea was just such a councilor (Mark 15:43). That they were forced into choosing sides is not surprising.

Not all scribes were associated with the Sadducean families. Some took leading roles in the movement of the **Pharisees** [1.57]. This movement encompassed non-priests who attempted to live out the holiness code of the temple in everyday life. The scribes of the Pharisees (see Mark 2:16) were learned in the priestly laws and even came into conflict with priests over how to conduct ritual activities in the temple itself. Rabbinic traditions indicate that two major branches of Pharisees existed in Jesus' day: the Shammaites (followers of Shammai) and the Hillelites (followers of Hillel). Shammai seems to have represented conservative interests of large landowners, while Hillel spoke for non-elite urban dwellers. The Pharisees, as the Gospels show, generally engaged in conflict over matters of ritual purity. The **Essenes** [1.24], another small group whose interests and **values** [3.56] presumably are expressed in the **Dead Sea Scrolls** [2.3] from Qumran, were Judeans similarly concerned with the temple and matters of ritual purity. These, however, are not mentioned in the New Testament, and their relationship to the Jesus movement is unclear. The reader should keep in mind that Sadducees and Pharisees were relatively small but powerful factions that largely neglected the interests of the very large, agrarian, non-elite sector.

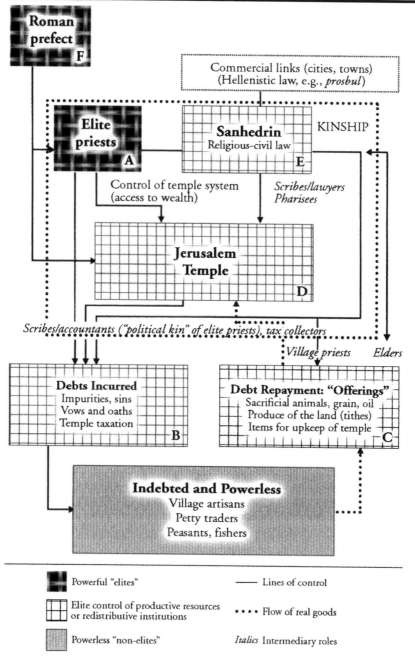

Roman prefect F

Commercial links (cities, towns)
(Hellenistic law, e.g., *prosbul*)

Elite priests A

Sanhedrin
Religious-civil law E

KINSHIP

Control of temple system
(access to wealth)

Scribes/lawyers
Pharisees

Jerusalem Temple D

Scribes/accountants ("political kin" of elite priests), tax collectors

Village priests   *Elders*

Debts Incurred
Impurities, sins
Vows and oaths
Temple taxation B

Debt Repayment: "Offerings"
Sacrificial animals, grain, oil
Produce of the land (tithes)
Items for upkeep of temple C

Indebted and Powerless
Village artisans
Petty traders
Peasants, fishers

Powerful "elites"

Elite control of productive resources
or redistributive institutions

Powerless "non-elites"

—— Lines of control

•••• Flow of real goods

Italics Intermediary roles

Figure 5.3 Political Religion in Agrarian Roman Palestine

First-century Judean religion focused on the Jerusalem temple. Elite priests (A) authorized and delegated power to scribes, who kept track of debts incurred to God by non-priests and collected some through special tax collectors; non-elite Judeans were constantly indebted through impurities, sins, vows, and regular temple taxation (B). Offerings of real goods, specified in religious-civil law (C), repaid the debt; these goods were collected in the temple (D). Law (E) was tied in with the larger legal system of the empire, while high priests involved themselves in interurban commercial affairs. Finally, the Roman prefect (F) was not afraid to intervene in the affairs of the temple or to confiscate temple funds. Power is especially seen here in control of the "means of divine communication" and in the compelling of goods collection and redistribution within the temple institution.

We may identify several important functional groups in Jerusalem, in addition to the priests, who provided economic support to, and received economic benefits from, the temple:

A "logistical group" supplied the temple. Select families made the ritual breads; provided ritually pure oil, flour, wine; made the incense used in the holy place of the temple itself; provided wood for the sacrifices; gathered straw for temple animals; and acquired and kept herds of animals that were ritually acceptable for temple sacrifices (Eppstein 1964).

A "technician group" included architects, engineers, and specialized **artisans** [3.3]. Artisans, for instance, worked on the temple from the time of Herod the Great to just before the First Judean Revolt. When the temple was finished c. 62 C.E., eighteen thousand men were put out of work (Josephus, *Ant.* 20.219). These would have included workers in wood (both carpenters and cabinet makers), stonemasons, metalsmiths, and people concerned with the water supply, roofing, lifting of heavy stones, and so forth. The work of the suppliers and builders required other groups, such as simple laborers and transport personnel who physically moved the temple's provisions.

An "infrastructure group" supported visitors to the holy city: There were innkeepers and food shopkeepers catering to the pilgrims, who especially swelled the indigenous population of Jerusalem during the three great festivals. As today, much of ancient Jerusalem's economic life was devoted to supplying the needs of pilgrims and visitors—room and board, food, the copying of sacred writings (scribal activity) for wealthy pilgrims, and other services.

Many of the sacrifices and material supports for the Jerusalem temple were contributed involuntarily and need thus to be

Item	Primary Geographic Source
Rams	Nabatea
Calves	Sharon
Sheep	Hebron
Doves	Mount of Olives
Incense	Arabia, Mesopotamia
Flour, wine	Judea
Oil	Galilee
Salt	Sodom (Zoar)
Water	Jerusalem (cisterns, aqueducts)

Figure 5.4 Basic Materials Needed for Temple Operations

considered as a form of taxation (Herodian taxation has been treated in chapter 4). Josephus again gives a basic list (*Ant.* 12.140): animals, wine, oil, frankincense, fine flour, wheat, and salt. Materials were obtained from various places in Roman Palestine and eastward. See figure 5.4.

In each of these areas outside of Jerusalem, the Judean oligarchy had an interest in gaining secure control of resources. This was likely done by traditional estate lands in those areas (Galilee) or by longstanding commercial links with powerful families (Nabatea). Judean interests in Nabatea and Galilee involved the need to cooperate with Gentiles.

The temple had perennial "needs" and placed perennial liens. In addition to the various cattle and birds for the sacrifices, wood for the sacrificial fires, and incense for services, these included straw; building materials such as lumber, stone, and precious metals (gold, silver, bronze); cloth for vestments and paraments (linen, wool); and the varieties of grain and fruit crops (tithes and first fruits). In addition, Judean women wove curtains for the temple. Certain Jerusalem families monopolized the provision of wood, incense (family of Abtinas), and the ritual temple "shewbread" (family of Garmu, *m. Šeqal.* 5.1).

Every Judean male throughout the Diaspora in the pre-70 period was expected to support the continuous sacrifices at the temple by paying 2 drachmas or 2 denarii (1/2 shekel) per year. The temple treasuries stored these payments and many other valuables. The temple was in part a **bank** [1.6]

(4 Macc 4:3; Jeremias 1969:56). Lumber, stone, and other building materials dedicated to the temple had to be stored there (*m. 'Arak.* 6.2–5). The temple thus was also a warehouse. Jesus taught in one of the main temple treasuries, the *gazophylakion* (John 8:20; Theissen 1991:120).

The behavior of Roman officials demonstrates this ancillary storage function of the temple. Several Roman prefects, including Pilate (Josephus, *Ant.* 18.60) and Florus (*War* 2.293), usurped funds from the temple. The imperial prefects were auditors and overseers for the system. When the temple was going up in flames through the destruction wrought by Titus's armies in 70 C.E., Titus himself was moved to say:

> We permitted you to exact tribute for God and to collect offerings, without either admonishing or hindering those who brought them—only that you might grow richer at our expense and make preparations with our money to attack us! (*War* 6.335; LCL)

After the temple's destruction, the Romans simply redirected the two-drachma tax to Rome (the *Fiscus Judaicus*), where the money rebuilt the temple to Jupiter on the Capitoline Hill (*War* 7.218; Dio Cassius 66.7.2).

Fernando Belo (1981:44–59) has persuasively argued that the temple **ideology** [3.27] correlated sin and debt such that a constant flow of goods to the temple center remained under the control of the high priestly families. Goodman (1982) outlines how debt operated in Herodian-period Judea, with the **elites** [3.14] acquiring money through debt and mercantile involvements, gaining power over **peasants** [3.41] through loans, controlling more land through debt defaults, and directing enormous agricultural products to their own advantage. The Roman taxation system in Judean Palestine (as seen in chapter 4) and the temple taxation system of the priests were undoubtedly not clearly distinguished in the minds of priests or populace. Heavy and competing taxation systems ensured that debts would increase.

The court system played an important role in enforcing collection on debt. The *prosbul* measure attributed to Hillel (actually originating in **Hellenistic** [1.36] Egyptian law) evaded the prescription of Deuteronomy 15:1-2 and permanently turned the debtor over to the creditor through the agency of the courts (Neusner 1973:16–17; Llewelyn and Kearsley 1992:91–92). Whether understood as collection guaranteed by the judge or as court-forced confiscation of security land, the debtor could be evicted from patrimonial land (becoming "landless") or legally redefined as a tenant. Court situations typically involved debt disputes, as *m. Sanh.* 3.6 indicates. The temple oligarchy controlled not only the Great Sanhedrin, which interpreted the Law, but also the local courts through the elders. ("Sanhedrin" can refer to lower courts as well as the supreme court in Jerusalem.)

The firm enforcement of debt contracts through the courts led to the expansion of large estates under the control of the Judean oligarchy. After default on debt obligations, traditional village lands were added to these estates (as discussed in chapter 4), while tenancy and landlessness increased to significant levels in the period before the First Judean Revolt. The elites, as increasingly big merchants with interests in local commerce and interurban trade (Engle 1977), came to develop cash cropping on their estates. Rabbinic tradition could recall that three merchants (Nakdimon ben Gorion, Kalba Sabbua, and Ben Zizit Hakeset) could supply Jerusalem for ten years (*Lam. Rab.* 1; Applebaum 1976:659, 687).

In relation to the temple system, as with other Palestinian social institutions, we see a powerful minority of elites and the relatively powerless majority of peasants. The powerful, controlling as they did taxation, the courts, debt instruments, and the sacred institution legitimating these arrangements, were established as large landowners and often big merchants as well. The social standing of Judean non-elites became ever more insecure through the one hundred years leading up to the First Judean Revolt.

Temple and Non-elite

How did ordinary villagers feel about this situation? They depended upon the temple and priests for regulating their lives with God and for ensuring the fertility of the land. On the one hand, the temple held power for them. Only if the priests satisfied God's demands would things be well with weather, soil, and crops. Peasant religion has always been *ex opere operato* (based upon performance of sacred ritual) in orientation (Weber 1963:82). When the priestly *opera* (rituals) are done, God supplies the goods of life.

Occasionally, a holy man with a direct line to God comes along (John the Baptizer, Honi the Circle Drawer), but this was rare. On the other hand, the temple held power over them as peasants chafed under God's (and God's representatives') demands.

For many villagers, adequate food consumption was precarious. Not only did the Sadducean oligarchy and their scribes expect enormous supplies to sustain the temple establishment, but lay Judean movements like the Pharisees also increased the expectations at certain points (demanding a second tithe). Judean peasants for their part could not just opt out of supplying these needs or meeting these liens. Freyne and Horsley have noted how Galilean and Judean peasants generally balked at meeting some or all of these obligations (Freyne 1980:282; Horsley 1987:287–88). For this reason, the elites had every incentive to establish rigid control of Judean land. The escalation of debt effected this for them, but contributed to widespread peasant misery and resentment (Oakman 1986:72–80).

Peasants were indebted not only through the need to rectify sins and remove impurities, but also through the heavy expectation of pilgrimage (see the discussion in Malina and Rohrbaugh 1998). According to Deuteronomy 16:16, Judean males were obligated to visit the temple three times a year at the major festivals (Passover, Pentecost, Tabernacles). Philo indicates the force of this expectation in the early first century:

He [Moses] does not permit those who desire to perform sacrifices in their own houses to do so, but he orders all men to rise up, even from the furthest boundaries of the earth, and to come to this temple, by which command he is at the same time testing their dispositions most severely; . . . innumerable companies of men from a countless variety of cities, some by land and some by sea, from east and from west, from the north and from the south, came to the temple at every festival. (*Laws* 1.68–69, trans. by Yonge 1993:540)

The political religion of the temple was expressed comprehensively through personal and communal debts and obligations. Ironically, the same temple that was a source of economic burden and political irritation for the non-elite could also encourage hopes beyond the control of the priests. Pilgrimages were a **strong-group** [3.54] experience, expressions of social solidarity, and not simply reflections of a conscious choice. As "solidarity celebrations," they found their ritual fulfillment in the communion sacrifices previously discussed. The communal sacrifices of the temple brought hope to ordinary people that the God worshiped by Judeans was a God of justice who offered alternative visions for a new household economy. The great pilgrimage festivals, with their *šelāmîm* sacrifices as the prominent feature, were times of communal joy when God provided food for the hungry and when a different kind of redistributive economy was associated with the divine will. At these times of great joy, the ordinary Judean envisioned a new domestic economy of God.

Political Religion, God's Reign, and the Jesus Movement

The temple system as it had developed in the Herodian period within agrarian social structures was oppressive and perceived by many (especially peasants, upon whom rested the primary burden of the tribute) as "banditry." Jesus of Nazareth voiced this perspective when he called the temple a "cave of bandits" (Mark 11:17; Theissen 1976; Horsley 1987).

Jesus' reported action in the temple reflects the ambivalence of his movement toward it. Did Jesus want merely to cleanse the temple or to get rid of it altogether (Malina 1988:10; 1996b:148; see Evans 1989b)? Reference to the temple as a "house of prayer" could imply the abolition of sacrifice (although this is not the case in Isaiah 56); moreover, if no trade can support the institution (John 2:16), then sacrifice on such a scale cannot continue. There are the words of Jesus in Mark 13:2 about the temple's destruction and in John 4:23-24 about spiritual worship. Yet Jesus as a loyal Israelite apparently respected some priestly institutions of the covenant law (Mark 1:44; Luke 17:14), and the Jesus tradition at times assumes temple involvement (Matt 5:23). The harsh words against the temple need only apply to the Herodian buildings and related institutional structure. Certainly, such reforming critique was characteristic of the Israelite prophets (Amos and Jeremiah). The ambiguity suggests the need for seeking more refined alternatives.

It is clear that when Jesus rejected the temple as a cave of bandits, he rejected it as a redistributive institution benefiting only the few. He condemns "qorban" vows that deprive parents of culturally mandated care (Mark 7:11; such vows removed real goods from everyday use). He excoriates scribes (probably temple scribes) who devour widows' houses (Mark 12:40). He remarks regarding the temple tax that "the sons are free" (Matt 17:26). Conversely, Jesus and his disciples were free to glean on the Sabbath, just as David entered the house of God to eat the Bread of the Presence (Mark 2:26). They were also freed from material anxiety by reference to God's rule (Q sayings about anxiety: Matt 6:25-33//Luke 12:22-34). The prayer of Jesus (Lord's Prayer) requests Israel's patron to forgive debts (temple debts might originally have been in mind) (Luke 11:4//Matt 6:12). What kind of institution did Jesus think might benefit the many?

Our previous considerations about religious politics in agrarian societies urge an understanding in which the Jesus faction itself seeks to become the controlling group and beneficiary of the temple institution. In light of Jesus' general message and the values of the Jesus movement, the temple institution must incarnate God's gracious patronage (the reign of God)—on the model of Passover and the *šelāmîm*, where all sacrifice and all share in the sacrifice. "House of prayer" for Jesus, as an alternative to redistributive banditry, implies a place where the patron is accessible and reliable and where needs are met. **Redistribution** [3.47] must serve the needs of the many. In this light, Jesus is remembered to have associated the cup of Passover (perhaps the third cup, the cup of blessing) with the fulfillment of God's reign (Mark 14:24-25).

This vision of Jesus stands in line with old Israelite law that still held up in his day the model of decentralized, simple sacrificial communion with God (Exod 20:24). It also expresses old Israelite hopes for communion of all peoples with God (Isa 56:6-8; Luke 13:29//Matt 8:11). But the vision was not actualized. Jesus himself suffered the fate of all who rebelled against Roman order, the penalty reserved for murderers, rebels, and slaves—crucifixion. In the Herodian temple, Israel's religion was exploited more effectively to enrich the few. The system's increasingly violent nature became ever more apparent as it followed its political course. Jesus' death and the appearance of rebellious brigands in the ensuing period were the warning signs of crisis before the final disaster of 66–70 C.E.

Summary

What consequently stands out about Palestinian society is the centrality of the Herodian temple, especially in maintaining the political-economic system, and the preeminence of the priestly oligarchy in the system's management and benefits. The role of the temple in the life of early Roman Palestine was so pervasive that it should be thought of as an institution intruding into and organizing the social life of every Judean region and settlement. Its effects upon the distribution of social goods within Palestinian society cannot be overemphasized.

The temple was the hub of a redistributive economy: Goods and services, raw materials, crops, animals—all flowed to this central point. There, these goods were redistributed in ways not necessarily benefiting their original producers. Religious ideology legitimated this arrangement. In fact, religious obligation sustained the arrangement.

The temple institution played a crucial role in organizing and governing the life of the Judean peasantry. The peasantry held an ambivalent attitude, to be sure, toward this institution and its representatives (especially if those representatives lived far from the village). Non-elite religion centered by contrast around the great pilgrim festivals when communion sacrifices prevailed. These led to visions of a different distributive institution centered on the temple. The Jesus movement began with a central concern for such institutional reform, but its rapid expansion into the Gentile world, and the destruction of the temple in 70 C.E., relegated such reform impulses to the dustbin of history.

Applying the Perspectives

1. How are kinship concerns evident in both temple religion and the Jesus movement? Reflect on this question in the light of Luke 18:10-13. After reflection, consider the discussion by John H. Elliott (1991).

2. Attitudes about the Hellenistic-Roman temple system are reflected in Judean works prior to and contemporaneous with Jesus:

The interpretation of "your multitude": they are the troops of his garrison [in Jerusale]m, and his "young lions": these are his mighty men . . . and "his prey": the wealth which [the priest]s of Jerusalem have [gathered]. (4QpNah 1:10–11)

Then [after Herod the Great] will rule destructive and godless men, who represent themselves as being righteous, but who will (in fact) arouse their inner wrath, for they will be deceitful men, pleasing only themselves, false in every way imaginable. . . . But really they consume the goods of the (poor), saying their acts are according to justice, (while in fact they are simply) exterminators, deceitfully seeking to conceal themselves so that they will not be known as completely godless because of the criminal deeds (committed) all the day long, saying, "We shall have feasts, even luxurious winings and dinings. Indeed, we shall behave ourselves as princes." (*T. Mos.* 7:3-9, trans. J. Priest in Charlesworth 1983:930)

Can you see similar concerns in the Gospels? How are they reflective of political religion? Do they express elite or non-elite perspectives on the political order? Further, see Evans (1989).

3. Making oaths in public involved reputation and honor. Matthew's special tradition (Matt 5:33-37) recalls that Jesus forbade oaths. Why might Jesus have spoken out on this issue? Consider Jesus' words in Mark about qorban vows (Mark 7:11), or a later rabbinic tradition associated with Rabbi

Judah the Prince (c. 200 C.E.), which indicates that Galileans had a reputation for rash vows:

R. Judah says: The people of Galilee need not assign [transfer control of property through a sacred oath] their share, since their fathers have done so for them already. (*m. Ned.* 5.5)

4. We have explored a number of ways in which the temple affected the economy at the time of Jesus. Can you think of other ways "economy" is reflected in the Gospels in relation to the temple and religion?

5. In what ways does "the separation of church and state" in the United States challenge our readings about "religion" in the New Testament?

6. How does Jesus' critique of the Jerusalem temple fit into the larger picture of prophetic critique of elite power? In what ways is that culture specific? In what ways do you see broader contemporary application?

Suggested Reading

There are a number of scholarly studies available on the temple in the time of Jesus. Among these, we will mention only the following: Safrai (1976b) provides a readable, though detailed, narrative description of the temple priests and rituals. He tends, however, to accept the rabbinic traditions without critical scrutiny. Still quite valuable is Jeremias (1969). An updated edition of Edersheim (1994), while handling source materials uncritically by today's standards, is readily accessible and provides a narrative picture of temple operations. The best available historical discussion of the matters in this chapter is Schürer (1979), but the work is far beyond the introductory level; see also Sanders (1992). Malina (1996a) provides a cross-cultural analysis of sacrifice in the ancient world. For issues of deviance and group process, see Hanson (1997a); for blood symbolism, see Hanson (1993).

The Ritmeyers (1990), Rousseau and Arav (1995:279–313), and Mazar and Cornfeld (1975) summarize archaeological findings since the late 1960s from the temple area. Bahat (2006) discusses the Temple Mount and the New Testament. Older, but still valuable for its detailed commentary on the rabbinic material, is Hollis (1934). Goodman (1987), Salderini (1988), and Stemberger (1995) give useful historical information on the elites of Judea. Rhoads (1976), Horsley (1987), and Price (1992) explore the historical events leading up to the First Judean Revolt.

Masada floor mosaic

"[Herod] placed garrisons throughout the entire people so as to minimize the chance of their taking things into their own hands" (Josephus, *Ant.* 15.295). Masada, located on a high plateau approximately thirty-three miles south-east of Jerusalem, was one of Herod's garrisons. (Photo by Douglas E. Oakman.)

CHAPTER 6

In the Rearview Mirror

Conclusion

The central goal of historical analysis is to explain change, whether that comes in the shape of a war, architectural developments, or a new king's rise to power. What the social sciences help us do, in addition, is to understand the shape and contour of social systems: how they function, what roles individuals and groups play, what values energize them, where the conflicts emerge, and who benefits from the maintenance of the system. Our goal in this volume has been to provide the reader with a clearer picture of these social systems when reading the New Testament and studying the Jesus movement and the earliest churches.

But after learning new vocabulary, engaging models of ancient institutions, and analyzing first-century Palestine with a systems approach, what has been gained? First, *we learn to take seriously the distance between ourselves and the ancients.* The actions of Jesus, Joseph Caiaphas, or Pontius Pilate need to be placed in contexts that make sense for the first century—not only historical contexts, but social contexts. Whatever we have in common with them as humans, they did not grow up in families like ours; they were not motivated by the same values as ours; and they did not participate in the same political, economic, or religious institutions as ours. If those distances are not fully appreciated, then we are simplistically imagining them as variations of modern American individuals.

Second, *we learn to work and think cross-culturally.* This is important for a better understanding of ourselves as well as of the people of first-century Palestine. In the comparisons we can learn something about our own social systems and their limitations. They help us keep in view that ours is not the only way to be human, but only one way. They remind us that our society is not the pinnacle of human development. Everyone does not benefit equally from living in a postindustrial economy. The structures of the "nuclear family" have been less than a total success. And the divisiveness of our religious denominationalism is not a particularly pretty picture. A representative democracy has many weaknesses, but those weaknesses are put in perspective when compared to ancient monarchies.

Third, *by using models we learn to make our assumptions and our approaches explicit.* We do not intend the models employed here to be the last word on these topics. But we hope that we have shown that the use of models is fundamental to working honestly and openly.

Research Tip 6

For fully developed portraits of Jesus that take the social sciences into account, see especially the following:

- William R. Herzog II, *Prophet and Teacher: An Introduction to the Historical Jesus* (2005)
- Pieter F. Craffert, *The Life of a Galilean Shaman: Jesus of Nazareth in Anthropological-Historical Perspective* (2008)

The object of using models is not to force the ancient material into pigeonholes, but to make plain how we understand the objects of our research. Once we make the model explicit, we can modify it as we get new information or we see the relationships differently.

Fourth, *we learn to read the New Testament and other ancient documents in terms of the complex social systems of which they are products.* That is, when we read

- "these are my mother, brothers, and sisters";
- "the man whom you call the King of the Judeans";
- "repay Caesar's things to Caesar and God's to God"; and

- "my house shall be called a house of prayer for all peoples,"

we recognize that the family, the political structures, the political economy, and the political religion assumed in these sayings are whole webs of relations with which we are not immediately familiar. We begin asking questions about how they were configured in first-century Palestine. Even when one passage only provides partial information or assumes the reader knows how the system works, we have to search out what we can discover about the whole system. We want to know what it means to be socialized into and live within these systems.

Fifth, *it becomes clearer that the interests of the elite were often in conflict with the interests of the peasants.* Rather than a harmonious society in which everyone benefits, the social stratification of first-century Palestine calls for an analysis of conflict. Since so many of the ancient documents were the products of elite authors and scribal groups, we must not lose sight of the question "Who benefits?" We want to explore where the tensions were, how the peasants acted subversively or gave in to elite pressures, and what the implications of social stratification were.

Sixth, *we have the tools to look more realistically at how Jesus fit into and reacted to the social systems of first-century Palestine.* A great deal of energy has been expended in the past two hundred years to illuminate "the historical Jesus." Some of these attempts have added considerably to our understanding, while others have been either laughable or simply quaint. It is fair to say that we cannot be clear about what Jesus was affirming, questioning, or criticizing if we do not understand how the systems worked and where the tensions were. While our focus here has not been on drawing a portrait of the historical Jesus, we hope to have shown that a systems approach can contribute considerably to such a task of reading the Gospels with new eyes.

Seventh, *we see more clearly the complexity of the hermeneutical task for contemporary communities of faith that read the New Testament.* We are not in a position to "apply" ancient documents to modern situations if we have not engaged the social systems to which those ancient documents spoke. Roles, values, and institutions do not operate in vacuums but are rooted in social systems. When we practice theology or ideological criticism, we must make our assumptions as clear as when we practice exegesis of ancient documents. In a famous article several decades ago (1962), Krister Stendahl urged that "biblical theology" needed to concern itself with two questions: (1) What did the ancient text mean? and (2) What does it mean? The biblical documents meant something to their communities of origin, and we have shown that those meanings look rather strange to our sensibilities. How then are we to build a bridge from those meanings to the concerns that we bring to reading the biblical documents?

The details cannot be spelled out here, but we suggest expanding Stendahl's questions to four: (1) What in the biblical record is culture-bound and outmoded (for example, women's roles)? (2) What values might we want to attempt to translate (for example,

fictive kinship)? (3) What should we retain without question (for example, commitment to the God whom Jesus proclaimed)? and (4) What is "coming to expression" in the biblical traditions (for example, hopes, visions, dreams)?

We hope we have stimulated your interest to pursue further models in the study of the New Testament. You might think of institutions, occupations, or parts of ancient society that need illumination. Here are some suggestions for continuing:

- ➤ Identify the biblical passages relevant to the topic, using a concordance:
  - words and phrases
  - metaphors
  - conceptualities

- ➤ Read the passages carefully for the following:
  - the identity of the people involved
  - elements of action and interaction
  - values
  - conflicts in the system
  - biases toward other groups
  - unanswered questions

- ➤ Research what biblical scholars have already discovered about the topic:
  - Check Rohrbaugh (1996).
  - See Pilch and Malina (1998).
  - Check the *Biblical Theology Bulletin* for recent "Reader's Guides."
  - Check commentaries on key passages.
  - Check Bible dictionaries and encyclopedias.

- Search the ATLA Religion Index CD-ROM or other indexes.
- Search the World Wide Web and other Internet resources, beginning with our Web site, which is designed to accompany this volume: http://www.fortresspress.com/hansonoakman
- Check Hanson's Greco-Roman bibliography: http://www.kchanson.com/CLASSIFIEDBIB/grstud.html

➤ Research the definitions and models used by anthropologists and macro-sociologists:
- Check dictionaries and encyclopedias of anthropology and sociology.
- Search *Anthropology Abstracts*.
- Modify the models as required by your biblical evidence.

➤ Research the relevant archaeological evidence:
- Check the archaeology dictionaries and encyclopedias (especially Meyers 1997).
- Search the ATLA Religion Index CD-ROM or other indexes.
- Check the indexes of the current issues of *Near Eastern Archaeology* (formerly *Biblical Archaeologist*), *Bulletin of the American Schools of Oriental Research,* and *Biblical Archaeology Review.*

GLOSSARIES

In each of the glossaries, the definitions are provided for the reader to get a sense of how the authors are using the relevant terms. The Hebrew, Greek, and Latin terms (always listed in that order, regardless of the words' origins) are suggestive rather than complete lists of relevant words; some of the word-fields are vast. For the advanced reader, the precise terms will hopefully facilitate searches in concordances, lexicons, and computer databases. The cross-references indicate the glossary number and item number, for example: **scribe** [1.72] means that listing is entry 72 in the first glossary. The biblical references and references to Josephus are representative examples. Bibliographic references for all three glossaries are listed after glossary 3.

The Jerusalem temple steps

"And as he came out of the temple, one of his disciples said to him, 'Look, Teacher, what wonderful stones and what wonderful structures!' And Jesus said to him, 'Do you see these huge structures? No stone will be left on another and not thrown down'" (Mark 13:1-2). The Jerusalem temple was first built by Solomon in approximately 950 B.C.E. It was rebuilt in 520 B.C.E. after the Babylonian Exile. Herod began his massive remodeling and expansion program in 20 B.C.E. (Photo by Douglas E. Oakman)

Ancient Groups, Institutions, Objects, and Events

1.1 Aedile (Greek *agoranomos;* Latin *aedilis*). A city official in the Roman imperial system in charge of controlling and maintaining municipal institutions, such as streets and traffic, markets, weights and measures, archives, public buildings, and public games. In the *cursus honorum,* it was not necessary for a man from a senatorial family to hold this position, but it could be politically expedient. It was an elected position, and it was the lowest rank to confer full senatorial status, although not all *aediles* were senators. Julius Caesar retracted the responsibility for the grain supply from them. Augustus transferred responsibility for public games from *aediles* to *praetors* (**Cursus honorum** [1.16], **Praetor** [1.59], **Senate/senator** [1.73], *Vigintivirus* [1.89]). (See Rom 16:23.)

1.2 Aquila, eagle (Greek *aeotos, akylos;* Latin *aquila*). The silver eagle mounted on a pole carried as a military standard by the *aquiliferi* (eagle-bearer) of the legion. Each Roman legion had one *aquila*, which represented the might of Rome and the legion's membership in the Roman army (**Legion** [1.46], **Standard** [1.80]). (See Luke 17:37; Acts 18:2.)

1.3 Artisan (see 3.3).

1.4 Auxiliary troops (Greek *symmachikon, epikourikos;* Latin *auxiliarius milites*). The Roman troops recruited from noncitizens and therefore outside the organization of legions. Under Augustus there were approximately 130,000 auxiliary troops in the empire, organized in units of either 500 or 1,000. These troops wore different uniforms, and they were paid less than Roman legionaries: approximately one-third for foot soldiers and two-thirds for cavalrymen. After serving for twenty-five years, an auxiliary soldier was eligible for Roman citizenship for himself, his family, and his descendants (**Cavalry** [1.9], **Citizen/ship** [1.11], **Cohort** [1.14], **Diploma** [1.19], **Legion** [1.46], **Soldier** [1.79], *Turma* [1.87]). (See Acts 23:23; Josephus, *War* 4.598; *Ant.* 14.128.)

1.5 Bandits (see **Social Bandits** [3.51]).

1.6 Bank/er, Treasury (Greek *trapēza/trapēzitēs, tamieion, gazophylakion, thēsaurus;* Latin *argentaria/argentarius*). Depositories for money and bullion (unminted copper, silver, or gold), for both elite investors and the state or temple. These banks were located in the urban centers, such as Jerusalem, Sepphoris, Tiberias, and Caesarea (**Economy/Economics** [3.13]). (See Sir 29:12; 1 Macc 3:29; 2 Macc 3:28; Matt 25:27; Luke 19:23; John 8:20; Josephus, *Life* 68, 295.)

1.7 Bar Kokhba Revolt. The war of independence fought by the Judeans against Rome (132–135 C.E.), also known as the Second Judean Revolt. The military-political leader was Shimeon bar Kosiba (but also called Bar Kokhba, "son of a star," or negatively Bar Koziba, "son of a liar"). Bar Kokhba captured Jerusalem, was declared "Prince of Israel," and minted new coins. By the end of the war, the army of the Roman emperor Hadrian had recaptured Jerusalem and built a new city over the ruined capital, renaming it Aelia Capitolina. Native Judeans were thereafter banned from living in the city (**First Judean Revolt** [1.28], **Messiah** [1.51]).

1.8 Broker (see 3.6).

1.9 Cavalry (Greek *hippeus, hippikos, hippos, hippeōn ilēs;* Latin *equistris, ala*). The mounted units of Roman legions. The cavalry in each legion was divided into four units (*turmas*); each turma was composed of thirty soldiers and led by a *decurion*. An aux-iliary cavalry unit (an *ala*) was composed of either 500 or 1,000 troops, divided into 16 or 24 *turmas* respectively, and commanded by a prefect (**Auxiliary troops** [1.4], **Decurion** [1.17], **Legion** [1.46], **Prefect** [1.61], **Turma** [1.87]). (See 1 Macc 1:17; 2 Macc 10:24; Acts 23:23; Rev 9:16; Josephus, *Ant.* 18.87; *Life* 214, 420.)

1.10 Centurion (Greek *kentyrion, hekatontarchēs;* Latin *centurio*). The commander of a Roman infantry unit (a "century") consisting of approximately eighty fighting troops and twenty support troops. Each legion had ten cohorts; the first cohort had five senior centurions, and the other nine had six junior centurions each. Since a legion, therefore, had fifty-five to sixty centurions, they were of varying statuses. The commanding centurion (*primus pilus*) commanded his own century as well as the other centurions. Centurions were normally free-born Roman citizens but not of the equestrian class (**Cohort** [1.14], **Legion** [1.46]). (See Matt 8:5-13; Mark 15:39; Luke 7:2; Acts 10:1; Josephus, *War* 2.63.)

1.11 Citizen/ship (Greek *politēs/politeia;* Latin *civis/civitas*). The legal status of a fully enfranchised member of Roman society. During the Principate, citizenship was granted to ever-widening circles outside of Italy. But in 48 C.E., only about 5.9 million were citizens in an empire of 60 to 80 million inhabitants. One could become a Roman citizen either by being born into a family with citizenship or by having it conferred by the state. The emperor or Senate might confer it in a number of situations: for individuals, cities, or territories that had acted in the interests of Rome; to create clients of local monarchs or other elites; for payment; for completion of military service in an auxiliary unit; or for someone freed from slavery by an owner who was a citizen (**Auxiliary troops** [1.4], **Class** [3.7], **Order** [1.53], **Principate** [1.63], **Veteran** [1.88]). (See 2 Macc 4:9; Acts 22:25-29; Josephus, *Life* 423.)

1.12 Client (see 3.8).

1.13 Client–king (Greek *basileus*; Latin *regulus*). A ruler of a monarchy who owes allegiance and tribute to an emperor. Such vassals had limited *imperium* (legal, financial, and military authority). They were, however, often in hereditary positions, subject to Roman approval. After the death of his father (Herod the Great), Archelaus, for example, was reduced from client-king to *ethnarch* of Judea (**Client** [3.8], **Emperor** [1.21], **Ethnarch** [1.25], **Imperium** [1.41], **Queen** [1.67], **Tribute** [1.86]). (See Matt 2:3, 22; Luke 3:1-2; Josephus, *War* 2.93.)

1.14 Cohort (Greek *speira*; Latin *cohors*). The tenth part of a Roman legion. The first (senior) cohort of a legion was ideally led by five centurions, commanding 160 infantrymen each. The second through tenth cohorts were ideally composed of six "centuries" (each led by a centurion) of approximately 80 infantrymen. By the first century B.C.E., the term had also broadened to include the entourage of a provincial governor. Auxiliary troops under the command of a prefect

(Pontius Pilate, for example) were also called cohorts. They could be composed of either 500 troops (*cohortes quingenariae*) or 1,000 troops (*cohortes milliariae*). Auxiliary cohorts were occasionally *cohortes equitatae*: a mixed cohort of infantry and cavalry. Josephus also used these terms for the Palestinian troops during the First Judean Revolt (**Auxiliary troops** [1.4], **Cavalry** [1.9], **Centurion** [1.10], **Legion** [1.46], **Militiae** [1.52], **Prefect** [1.61], **Soldier** [1.79]). (See Acts 10:1; 21:31; 27:1; Josephus, *Life* 214.)

1.15 Consul (Greek *stratēgos, hypatos*; Latin *consul ordinarius, consul suffectus*). The chief magistrate and top office of the *cursus honorum* in Roman public life for those of senatorial rank. Two consuls held office at one time as a balance of power and were appointed for two- to four-month terms by the emperor (during the Republic they were elected by the Senate for one-year terms). In 81 B.C.E. the dictator Sulla decreed that the minimum age for consuls would be forty-two and that they must have previously held the positions of *quaestor* and *praetor* in order to ensure that they had sufficient governmental experience; during the Principate, however, this was not always followed. The emperors occasionally appointed themselves, or even their children, to the post. After serving as consul, a senator was often appointed proconsul over a province. Tradition has it that the office of consul was instituted at the beginning of the Roman Republic in 509 B.C.E.; it survived in the Western Roman Empire until 534 C.E. An *ordinarius* was a regularly appointed consul, while a *suffectus* was a replacement in the case of resignation, illness, or death (**Cursus honorum** [1.16], **Praetor** [1.59], **Proconsul** [1.64], **Quaestor** [1.66], **Senate/senator** [1.73], **Vigintivirus** [1.89]). (See 1 Macc 8:16; 15:16; Josephus, *War* 2.205; 7.82; *Ant.* 14.144.)

1.16 Cursus honorum. Latin for "course/path of honors." It is the technical designation for the sequence by which Roman men of the senatorial class moved up the social ladder by holding public offices. After service in the army, generally as a tribune, the beginning step was *aedile, vigintivirus,* or *quaestor,* and the top position was consul of Rome. This hierarchical system was instituted by the dictator Sulla in 81 B.C.E. (**Aedile** [1.1], **Consul** [1.15], **Quaestor** [1.66], **Militiae** [1.52], **Praetor** [1.59], **Proconsul** [1.64], **Senate/senator** [1.73], **Social stratification** [3.52], **Tribune** [1.85], **Vigintivirus** [1.89]).

1.17 Decurion (Greek *dekanos, dekatarchēs, dekadarchos;* Latin *decurio*). The commander of a Roman cavalry squadron (*turma*). A legion ideally had four *decurions,* each commanding a squadron of thirty horse-soldiers. During the Principate, this term also came to refer to the members of municipal senates in the provinces, with thirty to several hundred members who had paid for the honor (**Cavalry** [1.9], **Elites** [3.14], **Equestrian** [1.23], **Legion** [1.46], **Turma** [1.87]).

1.18 Denarius (pl. *denarii;* Greek *dēnarion;* Latin *denarius*). The basic unit of

coinage used throughout the Roman Empire (**Economy/Economics** [3.13], **Sestertius** [1.75], **Shekel** [1.76]). (See Matt 20:2-15; John 6:7; 12:5.)

1.19 Diploma (Latin *diplomata*). The pair of small bronze plates given soldiers (especially auxiliaries) at the completion of their service. These inscriptions designated their privileges and status: citizenship (if they were not already citizens), legal status for their marriages, and civic rights for their descendants (**Auxiliary troops** [1.4], **Soldier** [1.79], **Veteran** [1.88]).

1.20 Elites (see 3.14).

1.21 Emperor (Hebrew *melek gādôl;* Greek *sebastos, basileus megas, autokratōr, kaisar;* Latin *caesar, imperator*). A monarch who rules over an empire (such as the Roman Empire) composed of provinces and other dependent monarchies. Caesar Augustus (Octavian) became the first Roman emperor in 27 B.C.E. (**Client-king** [1.13], **Imperial province** [1.40]). (See Luke 2:1; 1 Pet 2:13, 17; Josephus, *War* 1.402-3.)

1.22 Eparch (Greek *eparchos*). The governor of a province or a regional district (**Governor** [1.33]). (See 1 Esd 6:3; Josephus, *Life* 33, 46.)

1.23 Equestrian (Greek *tagma tōn hippeōn;* Latin *equester*). This is the second order of Roman citizens (after senators), originally making up the cavalry. They were normally freeborn and could demonstrate wealth equal to at least 400,000 sesterces; and they were free to intermarry with senatorial families. By the first century C.E., as Roman citizenship was granted to elites throughout the empire, wealthy landholders in municipalities and Greek cities were granted equestrian status, including Israelites. As the empire grew, the most influential equestrians were invited into the senatorial class (**Decurion** [1.17], **Elites** [3.14], ***Militiae*** [1.52], **Order** [1.53], **Senate/senator** [1.73]). (See Josephus, *Ant.* 18.2.)

1.24 Essenes (Greek *Essēnoi.*) A priestly sect of Israelites, presumably associated with the collection and writing of the Dead Sea Scrolls (**Dead Sea Scrolls** [2.3], **Faction** [3.19], **Pharisees** [1.57], **Sadducees** [1.70]). (See Josephus, *War* 2.119–61; *Ant.* 18.18–22; Philo, *Every Good Man Is Free* 75–80; *Apology for the Judeans* 11.1–18.)

1.25 Ethnarch (Greek *ethnarchēs.*) Literally, "a ruler over a people." It was a status lower than client-king since it embodied less independence and authority. Hyrcanus II (the Hasmonean) and Archelaus (Herod the Great's son) were each accorded this rank (**Client–king** [1.13], **Governor** [1.33], **Hasmoneans** [1.34]). (See 1 Macc 14:47; 15:1-2; Josephus, *War* 2.93.)

1.26 Fall of Jerusalem. At the end of the First Judean Revolt, the Romans laid siege to and captured Jerusalem and destroyed the Jerusalem temple in 70 C.E. This was carried out by the general Titus, later to be the Roman emperor (**First Judean Revolt**

[1.28], **Josephus** [2.7], **Masada** [1.50], **Sicarii** [1.77], **Zealots** [1.90]). (See Mark 13:1-19; Josephus, *War* 6.1–442.)

1.27 Fasces. The Latin term referring to the symbol of authority carried by a *lictor* in procession before a Roman official. These were made of bundles of elm or birch rods tied with red thongs, sometimes around an ax. The number of *fasces* carried symbolized the relative status of the official: twelve for emperors and consuls, six for *praetors*, and fewer for those with delegated *imperium* (**Imperium** [1.41], **Lictor** [1.48]).

1.28 First Judean Revolt. The war fought by the Judeans and Galileans against Rome from 66 to 73 C.E. While the final rebels were not defeated until 73 or 74 at Masada, the main fighting was completed with the capture of Jerusalem and the destruction of the temple in 70. Vespasian was the Roman general at the beginning of the war; but when he was called to Rome to become emperor, his son Titus took command (**Bar Kokhba Revolt** [1.7], **Fall of Jerusalem** [1.26], **Josephus** [2.7], **Masada** [1.50], **Sicarii** [1.77], **Zealots** [1.90]). (See Josephus, *War* 3–7.)

1.29 Freedman/woman (Greek *apeleutheros/apeleuthera, libertinos/libertina;* Latin *libertus/liberta*). The official status of one freed from slavery, and the lowest of the four traditional Roman orders. Individuals were released (manumitted) from slavery after either lengthy service or the raising of their purchase-price to pay their owners. One of this status owed lifetime allegiance as a client to his or her former owner. Freedmen played a significant role in the administration of the Roman Empire: from the emperor's staff to governors like Festus, the Judean procurator (**Client** [3.8], **Order** [1.53], **Patron** [3.40]). (See Acts 6:9; 1 Cor 7:22.)

1.30 Friendship (see 3.20).

1.31 Garrison (Greek *phroura*; Latin *praesidium*). An unspecified number of military troops stationed in a village, town, or city for its defensive and policing powers (**Praetorium** [1.60]). (See 1 Macc 4:61; 10:75; Josephus, *War* 1.210; *Life* 347, 411.)

1.32 General (or commander) (Greek *stratēgos, archistratēgos*). The leader of an army or large military unit. Josephus was the commander of the Palestine forces in Galilee at the beginning of the First Judean Revolt (**Legate** [1.45]). (See Jdt 4:1; 1 Macc 8:10; Josephus, *Life* 341.)

1.33 Governor. The ruler over a district, region, or province, usually as delegated by a king, emperor, or the Roman Senate. English translators use this term for a variety of Hebrew, Aramaic, Greek, and Latin terms (**Decurion** [1.17], **Eparch** [1.22], **Ethnarch** [1.25], **General** [1.32], **Legate** [1.45], **Prefect** [1.61], **Proconsul** [1.64], **Procurator** [1.65], **Tetrarch** [1.83], **Toparch** [1.84]). Note also the Greek terms *archōn, despotēs, dynastēs, epimeletēs, epitropos, hēgemōn, prostatēs, prōtos, satrapēs, stratēgos,* and *turranos*, which may designate magis-trates, chieftains, leaders, and rulers of small regions or independent cities during the Hellenistic, Hasmonean, and Roman periods.

1.34 Hasmoneans. The priestly family who led the Judean war of independence (Maccabean Revolt) against Syrian (Seleucid) rule of Palestine (165–162 B.C.E.). After the revolt they controlled the high priesthood and then became kings, queens, and ethnarchs. The Herodian family began as military leaders and governors in the service of the Hasmoneans; but when Herod the Great took power as Judean king, he consolidated his royal honor by marrying Mariamme from the Hasmonean family (**Ethnarch** [1.25], **Hellenism** [1.36], **Herodians** [1.37], **High priest** [1.38], **Maccabean Revolt** [1.49], **Queen** [1.67]). (See *m. Mid.* 1.6.)

1.35 Head of the synagogue (Hebrew *r'ōš ha-keneseth*; Greek *archisynagōgos*). The leader of a synagogue responsible for the service arrangements and organization (**Synagogue** [1.81]). (See Mark 5:21-43; Luke 13:14; Acts 13:15.)

1.36 Hellenism (Greek *hellēnismos*). The adoption of Greek cultural forms by non-Greeks: language, values, education, institutions, customs, and so forth. Beginning with the conquests of Alexander the Great in 323 B.C.E., Hellenism supplied important elements to construct ideology and imperial policy of rulers throughout the eastern Mediterranean and Middle East. The process of changing customs from native to Greek is called "hellenization." Reaction

against hellenization played a major role in the Maccabean Revolt and the rise to power of the Hasmoneans in Judea (**Hasmoneans** [1.34], **Maccabean Revolt** [1.49]). (See 2 Macc 4:13.)

1.37 Herodians (Greek *Hērōdianoi*). The family of Herod the Great who governed Palestine (or its parts) for almost two centuries (c. 80 B.C.E.–100 C.E.). But the designation "Herodians" also refers more broadly to the clients (political "kin") who supported these rulers' interests. From the time of Herod's grandfather, Antipater, they were a family of power and prestige, moving from military leaders to governors to kings and tetrarchs of Palestine and its parts. They originally belonged to the ethnic group of Idumeans (the southern section of Palestine, originally called "Edom"). Along with other Idumeans, the Herodians had converted to the Israelite state religion (**Hasmoneans** [1.34]). (See Matt 22:16; Mark 3:6; 12:13.)

1.38 High priest (Hebrew *kōhēn gadôl*; Greek *archiereus*). The chief official of Judah's state temple in Jerusalem. During the Roman era (and several centuries preceding it), this person was chosen from among several leading priestly families. Because of the hereditary character of priesthood and the control of these families, they are often lumped together as "chief priests." Since Judea was a subject state and the high priesthood was a political position, the officeholders were chosen by (and thus, in some sense, clients of) the Roman emperors, the Herodians, or governors. The high priest's major roles were

to head the organization of the temple personnel, officiate at major festivals (especially the Day of Atonements), and preside over the Sanhedrin. He would also be associated with the Sadducee faction (Acts 5:17) (**Levite** [1.47], **Priest** [1.62], **Religion** [3.48], **Sadducees** [1.70], **Sanhedrin** [1.71]). (See Lev 9:1-24; Sir 50:1-15; John 11:47-53; Acts 4:5-22; Josephus, *Ant.* 20.197-98, 222-23; *m. Yoma 7.5*.)

1.39 Hospitality (see 3.26).

1.40 Imperial province (Latin *provincia*). A Roman province (such as Judea) that was under the direct jurisdiction of the Roman emperor rather than the Senate. These provinces were the ones most distant from Rome itself and were governed by prefects, procurators, or legates, depending on the era and whether legions were stationed in them (**Emperor** [1.21], **Prefect** [1.61], **Procurator** [1.64], **Legate** [1.45], **Senatorial province** [1.74]). (See Acts 23:34; 25:1.)

1.41 Imperium. The Latin term for the authority of Roman office in terms of the administration of law, financial management, or military power. Having *imperium* meant that full authority was vested in the holder by the emperor or Senate. *Imperium* was typically held by emperors, consuls, proconsuls, legates, *praetors*, prefects, and procurators. The physical symbol of having *imperium* was the presence of attendants (*lictors*) holding the *fasces*. Other than that held by the emperor, Roman *imperium* was usually granted for a limited period of time (one to three years) and had to be renewed if necessary (**Client-king** [1.13], **Fasces** [1.27], **Lictor** [1.48], **Power** [3.44]). (See Luke 20:20; 3 Macc 7:12; 4 Macc 4:6; Josephus, *Ant.* 18.2.)

1.42 Inheritance (see 3.29).

1.43 Judeans (Hebrew *Yehûdîm;* Greek *Ioudaioi;* Latin *Iudaei*). Those connected to the ethnic group from the land of Judah/Judea. This term has multiple meanings, referring in different contexts to (1) the inhabitants of Judah (as opposed to the other territories of Palestine); (2) all the inhabitants of Palestine (Judea, Samaria, Galilee, Perea, Idumea, and the northern territories); (3) all those in the Mediterranean and Middle East with ethnic connections to Judah; (4) all those professing allegiance to the state religion of Judah (even if converts); or (5) the elites of Judah (as opposed to the peasants). Which of these senses is meant in any given context depends upon who is speaking of whom, and in what context. This term is preferable to "Jews" when speaking of the first-century situation, since "Jews" has specifically "religious" connotations for modern readers, with different social indices. With the formation of the Mishnah (c. 200 C.E.) and the Babylonian Talmud (c. 550 C.E.), "rabbinic Judaism" took shape as a religious phenomenon, no longer connected to the geographical and political region of Judea (**Talmud** [2.18]).

1.44 King (see **Client-king** [1.13]).

1.45 Legate (Greek *dikaiodotēs, hēgemōn, tagma;* Latin *legatus*). The governor of a major Roman imperial province. The regions of Palestine (Judea, Galilee, Samaria, and others) were indirectly under the supervision of the legate of Syria, since he controlled the closest Roman legions. This position parallels the proconsul in senatorial provinces and prefect in Egypt (**Imperial province** [1.40], **Governor** [1.33], **Legion** [1.46], **Prefect** [1.61], **Proconsul** [1.64]). (See Luke 2:2; Josephus, *Life* 347, 373.)

1.46 Legion (Greek *legiōn, tagma;* Latin *legiones*). A division of the Roman army. In the first century, Rome had twenty-five legions (according to Tacitus). Each legion was ideally composed of 5,000 infantrymen and 120 cavalrymen. A legion was usually headed by a legate, but in Egypt by a prefect. Each legion carried both the Roman eagle (*aquila*) and an individualized legionary standard (**Aquila** [1.2], **Auxiliary troops** [1.4], **Cavalry** [1.9], **Centurion** [1.10], **Legate** [1.45], **Prefect** [1.61], **Soldier** [1.79], **Standard** [1.80]). (See Matt 26:53; Mark 5:9; Josephus, *War* 2.66–67.)

1.47 Levite (Hebrew *lēvî;* Greek *leuitēs;* Latin *levites*). One identified with the "tribe" of Levi. During the second temple period, males from this group could serve in the Jerusalem temple, but they did not have the full status of priests; they served as musicians, singers, custodians, and attendants (**High priest** [1.38], **Priest** [1.62]). (See Luke

10:32; John 1:19; Acts 4:36; Josephus, *Ant.* 20.215–18; *m. Pe'ah* 1.6.)

1.48 Lictor (Latin *lictores*). The attendants of Roman officials, especially consuls, proconsuls, legates, prefects, magistrates, and priests. In public these attendants carried the *fasces* as a symbol of their official's *imperium*. The number of *lictors* assigned to an official depended upon the rank and size of his administrative duties; a proconsul might have as many as twelve (**Fasces** [1.27], **Imperium** [1.41]).

1.49 Maccabean Revolt. The Judean war of independence fought against the Seleucid (Syrian) Empire (165–162 B.C.E.), taking its name from the "general," Judah the Maccabee (Hammer). The Seleucids, led by King Antiochus IV Epiphanes, had rededicated the Jerusalem temple to Zeus Olympus. After recapturing Jerusalem, the Maccabeans cleansed the temple, built a new altar, and reinstituted worship of the Israelite God, Yahweh. They also refortified the city. The eight-day Israelite festival of Hanukkah (Dedication) celebrates this rededication (**Hasmoneans** [1.34]). (See 1 Macc 4:52-61; 2 Macc 2:19-22; John 10:22.)

1.50 Masada. The palace and fortress built by Herod the Great on a plateau near the Dead Sea. This fortress became the last holdout of revolutionaries at the end of the First Judean Revolt. After a siege by the Roman general Silva, it finally fell c. 73–74 C.E. As Josephus tells the story, the Judeans committed mass suicide rather than surrender to the Romans, with only one woman and two children surviving (**Fall of Jerusalem** [1.26], **First Judean Revolt** [1.28], **Zealots** [1.90]). (See Josephus, *War* 7.252–406.)

1.51 Messiah (Hebrew *māšîaḥ*; Greek *christos*). The term for a Judean king, meaning "anointed one." Part of the Judean royal ideology was that the king was the (adopted) son of Yahweh. Many Judeans looked forward to a coming messiah (a king in the tradition of David) as a function of having been a subject people without independent leadership. The image of the messiah in some texts is confusing, for example, the dual epithet "messiah of Aaron and Israel" in the Community Rule from the Dead Sea Scrolls (1QS 9.10). The anticipated leadership in the Judean community (not always identified as "messiah") was often attributed to the resurgence of archetypal models: royal (David), prophetic (Moses or Elijah), and priestly (Aaron). (See 1 Sam 9:16; 2 Sam 7:14-15; 1 Kgs 1:39; Pss 2:7; 89:26-27; John 1:41; 2 Esd 7:28; *1 Enoch* 48:1-10; *Pss Sol* 17:21-43; 18:5; *2 Bar* 39:1, 40:4; Josephus, *Ant.* 18.63–64; *m. Ber.* 1.5; *m. Soṭ.* 9.15.)

1.52 Militiae. Latin for "military service." It is the technical term for the equestrian ladder of promotion parallel to the senatorial *cursus honorum*. By the mid-first century C.E., the three common steps were prefect of a cohort, legionary tribune, and cavalry tribune. Equestrians could also rise to be prefects of provinces—Pontius Pilate in

Judea, for example (**Cavalry** [1.9], ***Cursus honorum*** [1.16], ***Diploma*** [1.19], **Equestrian** [1.23], **Prefect** [1.61], **Soldier** [1.79], **Tribune** [1.85]).

1.53 Order (Greek *tagma;* Latin *ordo*). Rank, class, group, or status. Ancient Rome recognized four closely defined orders: senatorial, equestrian, free citizens, and freedmen/women. During Augustus's reign the identity of the equestrian class was weakened in terms of offices held, as well as membership, which was opened up to many provincials (**Citizen** [1.11], **Class** [3.7], **Equestrian** [1.23], **Freedman/woman** [1.29], **Senate/senator** [1.73], **Status** [3.53]). (See Josephus, *Ant.* 18.2.)

1.54 Ossuary (Latin *ossuarium*). Bone boxes used for secondary burials in Palestine.

1.55 Patron (see 3.40).

1.56 Peasant (see 3.41).

1.57 Pharisees (Hebrew *perûšîm;* Greek *pharisaioi*). The Judean faction that taught that the laity should live by priestly standards of purity. They evidently began developing out of pietistic groups during the Maccabean Revolt. Their focus on Law interpretation, purity, and piety became the basis for the development of rabbinic Judaism in later eras (**Essenes** [1.24], **Faction** [3.19], **Maccabean Revolt** [1.49], **Sadducees** [1.70], **Scribe** [1.72]). (See Matt 23:13-36;

Acts 23:6-10; Josephus, *War* 2.162–66; *Ant.* 18.12–15; *m. Ḥag.* 2.7; *m. Soṭ.* 3.4.)

1.58 Poor (Hebrew *anawîm;* Greek *ptōchoi, aporoi;* Latin *inops, mendicus*). Those who could not maintain their inherited status in society and thus became destitute due to drought and famine, war, widowhood, or taxation. (See Mark 12:41-44; Josephus, *Ant.* 18.37; *Life* 66; *m. Pe'ah* 8.7.)

1.59 Praetor. A Roman judicial post of senatorial rank. The *praetor urbanus* was the chief judicial officer within Rome. The *praetor peregrinus* (literally "praetor of foreigners") dealt with legal cases in which one or both parties were foreigners (***Cursus honorum*** [1.16], **Senate/senator** [1.73]).

1.60 Praetorium (Greek *praitorion;* Latin *praetorium*). The official residence of a Roman regional governor, whatever his rank. In biblical texts, it may sometimes refer to the Roman barracks or garrison (**Garrison** [1.31], **Governor** [1.33], **Legate** [1.45], **Prefect** [1.61], **Procurator** [1.64]). (See Mark 15:16; John 18:28; Acts 23:35.)

1.61 Prefect (Greek *epitropos, epimelētēs, hēgemōn, hipparchēs;* Latin *praefectus*). A provincial governor of the equestrian class. This was a military rank that also had responsibility for collecting tribute for Rome. Pontius Pilate was the prefect over Judea, as demonstrated from an inscription bearing his name and rank found in Caesarea. After 44 C.E., governors of Judea held the title of procurator.

Herod the Great was made *epimelētēs* of Coele-Syria by Cassius. It could also be used for a commander of a large cavalry unit (*praefectus equitum* = *hipparchēs*) (**Equestrian** [1.23], **Governor** [1.33], *Miltiae* [1.52], **Procurator** [1.64], **Tribute** [1.86]). (See Matt 27:2; Josephus, *War* 2.291; *Ant.* 18.55.)

1.62 Priest (Hebrew *kohēn;* Greek *hiereus;* Latin *sacerdos*). A hereditary office of ritual functionaries in Judean tradition, traditionally from the "tribe" of Levi, and in the tradition of Aaron. Prior to the first century, there were so many eligible males that they were organized into twenty-four groups or "courses" that rotated responsibility for the performance of the daily temple sacrifices and rituals (**High priest** [1.38], **Levite** [1.47]). (See Exod 29:1-46; 1 Chr 24:1-19; Luke 1:5; John 1:19; Josephus, *Ant.* 3.151–87; 7.363–67; *m. Sukk.* 5.7–8; *m. Ned.* 11.3.)

1.63 Principate. The period of the Roman Empire, beginning with Caesar Augustus (27 B.C.E.), distinguished from the earlier period of the Republic. Augustus chose the single word *Princeps* ("Principal" or "Preeminent One") to describe his status; it was not an official title but harked back to an ancient designation of honor for the senator at the top of the Senate roll, *Princeps Senatus* ("First Senator"), a title he was given in 28 B.C.E. Subsequent emperors assumed the designation *Princeps* themselves at their accession; it was not granted by the Senate (**Emperor** [1.21], **Republic** [1.69], **Senate/senator** [1.73]).

1.64 Proconsul (Greek *anthypatos;* Latin *proconsul*). A governor of a Roman senatorial province who acts "for the consul." These were normally senior senators, appointed after finishing a term as consul. This position parallels that of a legate in the imperial provinces (**Consul** [1.15], *Cursus honorum* [1.16], **Governor** [1.33], **Legate** [1.45], **Senate/senator** [1.73], **Senatorial province** [1.74]). (See Acts 13:7-12; 18:12; 19:38.)

1.65 Procurator (Greek *hēgemōn, epitropos, dioikētēs;* Latin *procurator.*) A Roman provincial governor, particularly charged with collecting Roman tribute and taxes. They could be either of equestrian rank or freedmen. Tacitus and the Gospels use this designation for Pontius Pilate, but it is anachronistic for governors of Judea before 44 C.E. when Fadus was appointed to this office. During the First Judean Revolt, Josephus refers to Modius as the *dioikētēs* over the northern territories for Agrippa I (*Equestrian* [1.23], **Freedman/woman** [1.29], **Governor** [1.33], **Legate** [1.45], *Militiae* [1.52], **Prefect** [1.61], **Tribute** [1.86]). (See Matt 27:11; Acts 23:24; 24:27; Josephus, *Life* 74, 126.)

1.66 Quaestor. A midlevel Roman bureaucratic position held by someone serving as a criminal magistrate or prosecutor, state treasurer, or paymaster. *Quaestor* was often the position in the *cursus honorem* that some-one from the senatorial class would hold after *vigintivirus* (**Cursus honorum** [1.16], **Senate/senator** [1.73], **Vigintivirus** [1.89]).

1.67 Queen (Hebrew *malkāh;* Greek *basilissa, basilidos*). The wife or consort of a client-king, independent king, or emperor (Berenice, wife of Herod of Chalcis, for example). But this may also designate an independent female ruler (the Hasmonean Alexandra Salome, or the Candace of Ethiopia) (**Client-king** [1.13], **Hasmoneans** [1.34]). (See Neh 2:6; Acts 8:27; Josephus, *War* 1.107–19.)

1.68 Rabbi. The Hebrew term for teacher; the Aramaic form is "Rabboni." While this came to have a technical meaning in later eras, identifying one who was a master interpreter of Israelite law, during the first century C.E. it seems to have been a general designation for any respected teacher. After c. 200 C.E., sayings and Law discussions of the rabbis were collected and organized into the Mishnah and Talmuds. Later Jewish tradition organized the rabbis into eras: the "Tannaim" are the rabbis from c. 10 to 220 C.E.; the "Amoraim" are those from c. 200 to 550 C.E. (**Talmud** [2.18]). (See Matt 23:7-8; Mark 10:51; John 1:38; 9:2.)

1.69 Republic (Latin *respublica*). The representative form of government of Rome beginning c. 509 B.C.E. with the expulsion of the Etruscan monarchy. Two magistrates (in a later period called consuls) were elected annually from the patrician class to rule for one year. The poorer class was called the plebians. The Twelve Tables were drawn up c. 450 B.C.E., forming the basis of future Roman law. The Republic came to an end with the Senate's appointment of Augustus as emperor (**Consul** [1.15], **Emperor** [1.21], **Principate** [1.63], **Senate/senator** [1.73]).

1.70 Sadducees (Hebrew *seddûqîm;* Greek *saddukaioi*). The Judean faction centering around the interests of the Jerusalem priestly elite (**Essenes** [1.24], **Faction** [3.19], **High priest** [1.38], **Pharisees** [1.57]). (See Mark 12:18; Acts 5:17; 23:6-10; Josephus, *Ant.* 18.16–17; 20.199; *m. Erub.* 6.2; *m. Mak.* 1.6.)

1.71 Sanhedrin (Hebrew *sanhedrîn;* Greek *synedrion, gerousia, boulē*). A Judean council. In Jerusalem there was a "supreme council," which had administrative, judicial, and legislative functions over public affairs throughout Palestine; it had seventy-one members and normally met in the Hall of Hewn Stone in the temple area. The high priest was the convener. Local councils also bore this name and traditionally had twenty-three members each. Jerusalem had two of these local sanhedrins (**High priest** [1.38], **Pharisees** [1.57], **Sadducees** [1.70], **Scribe** [1.72]). (See Matt 5:22; Mark 15:1; John 11:47; Acts 5:21-41; Josephus, *Ant.* 14.167; *Life* 368, 381; *m. Sanh.* 1.5–6.)

1.72 Scribe (Hebrew *sophēr;* Greek *grammateus;* Latin *scriba*). Scribes played a central role in the social world of Jesus. Scribes emerged during the second temple period as important leaders. Scribes served many functions, including copying sacred texts, drawing up legal documents, and serving as accountants, administrators, and even legal advisors. Scribal education was formal and repetitious. Most ancient scribes were not well educated by modern standards, though a few could master the intricate detail of Israelite law or compose complex works such as those found in the Judean Pseudepigrapha. These latter were among the elite scribal sector, while village non-elite scribes played only very simple roles, like drawing up debt contracts or marriage contracts by rote (**High priest** [1.38], **Pharisees** [1.57], **Sadducees** [1.70]). (See Sir 38:24; 39:1-11; Matt 13:52; 23:13-36; Josephus, *Ant.* 11.128.)

1.73 Senate/senator (Greek *gerousia/ gerōn, bouleuō/bouleutēs;* Latin *senatus/senator*). The administrative and judicial body of the Roman Empire and its members. It was traditionally composed of Roman men born to families of senatorial rank who had come of age and had a minimum personal wealth of one million sesterces. Major governmental posts were normally open only to members of this rank. The Senate had direct rule over several of the provinces not on the frontiers of the empire until the emperors eventually took over even these. During the Principate the Senate was opened to elites from the provinces, and the emperors had the power to appoint members. During the early Republic the Senate consisted of 300 members; Sulla

expanded it to 600 (81 B.C.E.), Julius Caesar increased it to 900, and Augustus reduced it to 600 (**Cursus honorum** [1.16], **Elites** [3.14], **Order** [1.53], **Principate** [1.63], **Republic** [1.69], **Sestertius** [1.75]). (See 1 Macc 8:15; 12:3; Josephus, *War* 1.174; 2.205-14; 4.596, 600.)

1.74 Senatorial province. One of approximately ten Roman provinces under the jurisdiction of the Senate and governed by proconsuls—Achaea, for example (**Imperial province** [1.40], **Proconsul** [1.64], **Senate/senator** [1.73]).

1.75 Sestertius. The basic unit of Roman money; it was copper, and it equaled one-fourth of a (silver) denarius. A Roman senator needed to demonstrate at census personal wealth equal to one million sesterces (250,000 denarii), and an equestrian 400,000 sesterces (100,000 denarii) (**Denarius** [1.18], **Economy/ Economics** [3.13], **Shekel** [1.76]).

1.76 Shekel (Hebrew *šekel;* Greek *siklos, statēr*). A unit of weight and later coinage. The Tyrian shekel was the silver standard in Roman Palestine (**Denarius** [1.18], **Economy/ Economics** [3.13], **Sestertius** [1.75]). (See Josephus, *Ant.* 3.194; *m. Bek.* 8.7.)

1.77 Sicarii (Greek *sicarioi;* Latin *sicarii*). A group of assassins who operated in the period just prior to the First Judean Revolt. Their name derives from the Latin word for the type of short dagger they were known to use: a *sica*. Their political agenda was to assassinate or kidnap for ransom urban elites and their families (beginning with the high priest Jonathan in 37 C.E.) in retaliation for their cooperation with Roman control of Judea (**First Judean Revolt** [1.28], **Zealots** [1.90]). (See Acts 21:38; Josephus, *War* 2.254–56; 4.400–405; 7.253–62; *Ant.* 20.208.)

1.78 Social bandits (see 3.51).

1.79 Soldier (Hebrew *gibbûr*; Greek *stratiōtēs, pezos, hoplitēs*; Latin *miles, legionarius*). A member of a Roman legion or auxiliary troop. In the first century C.E., service was extended from sixteen to twenty years, in addition to five years as a veteran (who could be recalled in an emergency). Soldiers were paid 225 denarii per year. Veterans who retired were given grants of land and other perquisites (**Auxiliary troops** [1.4], **Cavalry** [1.9], **Cohort** [1.14], **Denarius** [1.18], **Legion** [1.46], **Veteran** [1.88]). (See Ps 33:16; Jer 51:57; Matt 8:9; John 19:2; Acts 12:4; 23:23; Josephus, *Ant.* 18.87.)

1.80 Standard (Hebrew *degel, nēs;* Greek *sēma;* Latin *vexillum*). A staff with insignia symbolizing a military unit. Each Roman legion had both the Roman eagle (*aquila*), symbolizing its imperial status (carried by an *aquiliferi*), and an individualized legionary standard (*vexillum*) with its name, number, and images of the emperor or zodiac (carried by a *vexillarius*). These legionary standards were part of the imperial cult; sol-

diers anointed them and sacrificed before them when they entered the legion as an act of allegiance and solidarity (**Aquila** [1.2], **Legion** [1.46]). (See Josephus, *War* 2.169–74//*Ant.* 18.55–59.)

1.81 Synagogue (Hebrew *'edah, qahal, beth-ha-keneseth, beth-ha-tephillāh;* Greek *synagōgē, proseuchē;* Latin *synagoga*). The local gathering of Judeans for community affairs, prayer, and Scripture reading and exposition. These were eventually formal buildings but seemed to have developed from the functions of the town square (**Head of the synagogue** [1.35]). (See Matt 4:23; 6:2; 10:17; 23:6; John 18:20; Acts 6:9; Philo, *Ag. Flacc.* 41, 53; Josephus, *War* 2.289; *Life* 277; *m. Ber.* 7.3.)

1.82 Tannaim/Tannaitic (see **Rabbi** [1.68]).

1.83 Tetrarch (Greek *tetrarchēs;* Latin *tetrarches*). A ruler over a region. It originally referred to ruling one-fourth of a kingdom but came to be used loosely for any small region or part of a province. Herod the Great and his brother Phasaelus were made tetrarchs over sections of Palestine by Mark Antony, as Herod Antipas (Galilee and Perea) and Herod Philip (northern territories) were later by Augustus (**Client–king** [1.13], **Ethnarch** [1.25], **Governor** [1.33], **Toparch** [1.84]). (See Matt 14:1; Luke 3:1; Acts 13:1; Philo, *Ag. Flacc.* 25; Josephus, *War* 1.244; 2.94–95.)

1.84 Toparch (Greek *toparchēs*). The administrator of a "toparchy" or district. During the first century, Judea was divided into ten or eleven of these districts (**Client-king** [1.13], **Ethnarch** [1.25], **Governor** [1.33], **Tetrarch** [1.83]). (See 1 Macc 10:30, 38; 11:28; Josephus, *Ant.* 13.125.)

1.85 Tribune (Greek *chiliarchos;* Latin *tribunus militum*). A commander of a cohort. Six of these senior army officers were attached to each legion. During the Principate two types of tribunes were distinguished on the basis of birth: the *laticlavii* (those of the broad stripe) from the more prestigious senatorial families, and the *angusticlavii* (those of the narrow stripe) from the equestrian families. These designations refer to the purple stripes on the edges of their robes that indicated their relative status. The six tribunes would rotate the direct command of the legion every two months; therefore the commanding tribune could also be called the *tribunus semestris* (literally, "tribune of one-sixth of the year"). Young men of the senatorial class were expected to hold one of these positions before becoming a *vigintivirus* (**Cohort** [1.14], **Equestrian** [1.23], **Legion** [1.46], **Militiae** [1.52], **Senate/senator** [1.73], **Vigintivirus** [1.89]). (See Mark 6:21; Acts 21:31-37; 22:22-29; 25:23.)

1.86 Tribute (Greek *phoros;* Latin *tributum*). The payments in goods and money paid by subject peoples to a foreign empire (the Judeans to the Romans, for example).

(See Matt 17:25; Luke 20:22; 1 Macc 1:29; Josephus, *Ant.* 12.141–44.)

1.87 Turma. A Roman cavalry squadron of thirty soldiers. A legion included four *turmas*, each commanded by a *decurion*. Auxiliary cavalry could include sixteen to twenty-four *turmas* (**Auxiliary troops** [1.4], **Cavalry** [1.9], **Decurion** [1.17], **Equestrian** [1.23]).

1.88 Veteran (Greek *ouetranos;* Latin *veteranus*). A legionary soldier who had successfully completed twenty years of military service, or an auxiliary soldier with twenty-five years of service. This status was held for five years, during which time the veteran could be called up for service in emergencies. Veterans were normally granted land and a tax exemption, along with citizenship (if they were not already citizens) (**Auxiliary troops** [1.4], **Cavalry** [1.9], **Citizen/ship** [1.11], **Diploma** [1.19], **Soldier** [1.79]).

1.89 Vigintivirus. An entry-level public office for the Roman senatorial class. This general title could provide any number of public functions: civil magistrate, maintenance of streets, administration of a mint, or management of prisons and executions. A young senatorial class male normally held one of these positions before moving on to *quaestor* (**Aedile** [1.1], **Consul** [1.15], **Cursus honorum** [1.16], **Order** [1.53], **Quaestor** [1.66], **Senate/senator** [1.73]).

1.90 Zealots (Greek *zelotai*). A revolutionary faction during the First Judean Revolt. In earlier eras this term seems to have been merely a general designation for those "zealous for the Law," that is, extraordinarily pious (**Faction** [3.19], **Fall of Jerusalem** [1.26], **First Judean Revolt** [1.28], **Sicarii** [1.77]). (See 1 Macc 2:27; 2 Macc 4:2; Luke 6:15; Gal 1:14; Josephus, *War* 4.196–223.)

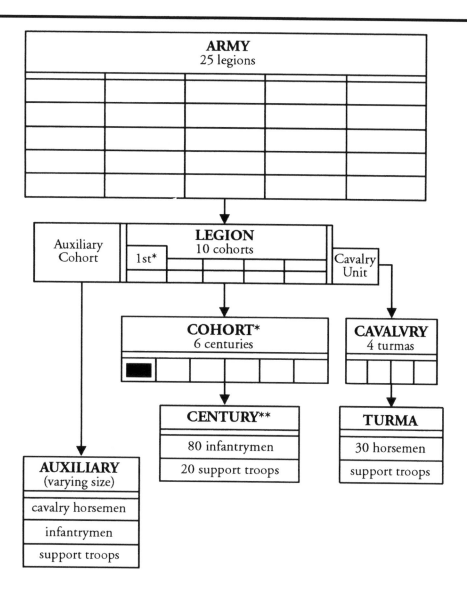

*The first cohort was composed of five (instead of six) centuries and centurions, and those five centuries were double in size: 160 infantrymen and (presumably) 40 support troops each.

**The five senior centurions of each cohort commanded a century of double size: 160 rather than 80 infantrymen.

Figure G.1 Roman Imperial Army: Military Units

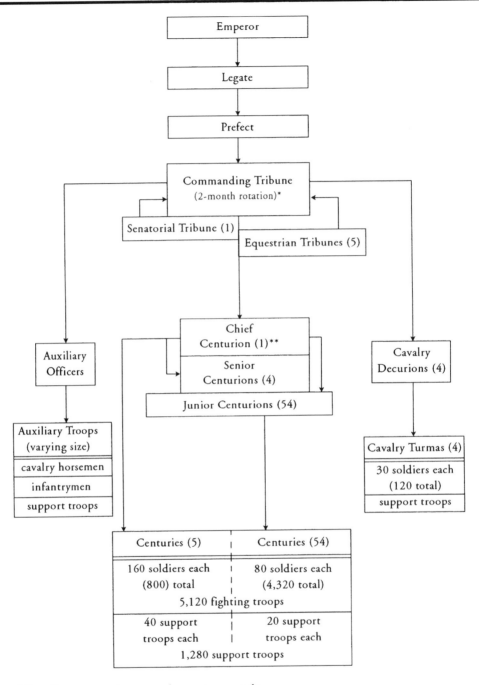

Emperor

Legate

Prefect

Commanding Tribune
(2-month rotation)*

Senatorial Tribune (1)

Equestrian Tribunes (5)

Chief
Centurion (1)**

Senior
Centurions (4)

Junior Centurions (54)

Auxiliary
Officers

Cavalry
Decurions (4)

Auxiliary Troops
(varying size)

cavalry horsemen

infantrymen

support troops

Cavalry Turmas (4)

30 soldiers each
(120 total)

support troops

Centuries (5)	Centuries (54)
160 soldiers each (800 total)	80 soldiers each (4,320 total)
5,120 fighting troops	
40 support troops each	20 support troops each
1,280 support troops	

*The tribunes rotated command every two months.

**The chief centurion commanded the senior and junior centurions.

Figure G.2 Roman Imperial Army: Chain of Command

Ancient Documents, Collections, and Authors

2.1 Apocrypha. Israelite writings used by Diaspora Israelites and therefore in the "Alexandrian Canon" (the books accepted by Israelites in Egypt), as witnessed in the Septuagint. Many of these works were originally composed in Hebrew and translated into Greek, but they were not included in the Hebrew Bible. Also known as "Deuterocanonical Works," they are included in Roman Catholic, Eastern Orthodox, and ecumenical translations, but not in Protestant Bibles. During the Protestant Reformation, Luther (following the lead of Carlstadt's treatise on the canon) accorded them secondary status by gathering them together at the end of his German translation in 1534. But in France and England, Protestants did not want them included at all. Especially important for Judean narrative history are 1 Maccabees and 2 Maccabees; and important in terms of social values of the Judeans during the Hellenistic period are Sirach and Wisdom of Solomon (**Hebrew Bible** [2.6], **Old Testament** [2.10], **Septuagint** [2.15]).

2.2 Babatha Archive. A collection of personal documents dating 92–132 C.E. that provide important insights into Judean social life during the late first century. This collection belonged to a Judean woman named Babatha and was hidden in the "Cave of Letters" in Naḥal Ḥever (just west of the Dead Sea, in Israel) from the period between the First Judean Revolt and the beginning of the Bar Kokhba Revolt. They were first discovered by Palestinian bedouin in 1959 and then excavated by the Israeli archaeologist Yigael Yadin in 1960. Numbered as "*p. Yadin*," they include a variety of forms: letters, dowry and marriage documents, legal disputes, and receipts. The documents appear in the three languages used during this period: Greek, Aramaic, and Hebrew (**Bar Kokhba Revolt** [1.7], **First Judean Revolt** [1.28]). For an English translation, see Lewis et al. (1989).

2.3 Dead Sea Scrolls. A group of documents (most of which are fragmentary) written on leather scrolls from the period c. 150 B.C.E.–70 C.E. discovered near the northwest shores of the Dead Sea in caves near Khirbet Qumran. Their discovery began with a chance find by a Palestinian bedouin goatherd, Muhammed Ahmed el-Hamed (also known as Muhammed ed-Dhib, "the Wolf"), from the Ta'amireh tribe, in 1947. Most of them were excavated in the period 1948–58 from the Qumran caves, but also from caves in nearby Wadi Murabba'at. These documents in Hebrew, Aramaic, and Greek are not a cohesive collection but include some documents typical of Israelite theology during this period (for example, biblical scrolls); some that are "sectarian," representing a priestly sect (for example, scriptural commentaries); and some that are of unclear provenance (for example, the Temple Scroll). The dominant scholarly opinion has associated the settlement at Qumran and the scrolls with the Essene sect described by Josephus, but this has come under increasing scrutiny. Some of the scrolls tell of a dispute over the high priesthood (the Habakkuk commentary), and others speak of the priestly qualifications for community leadership (the Community Rule) (**Essenes** [1.24], **First Judean Revolt** [1.28], **Hebrew Bible** [2.6], **High priest** [1.38], **Targumim** [2.19]). For English translations, see García Martínez (1996), Gaster (1976), and Vermes (1997).

2.4 Elephantine Papyri. Documents written on papyrus discovered on the Egyptian island of Elephantine (Aramaic: Yeb) in the Nile River. They were written in Aramaic by the Judeans associated with the Persian military colony. They include dowry and marriage contracts, as well as other legal, financial, and personal documents. One of the most interesting documents is a letter from the priests in Elephantine to the Jeru-

salem priests requesting funds for rebuilding their temple to Yah. But the "mundane" documents relating the family affairs of Mibtachiah are also of great interest. They date primarily from the fifth century B.C.E. For English translations, see Cowley (2005), Driver (2005), Ginsberg (1969), and Porten (1986 and 1996).

2.5 *Gospel of Thomas*. A "sayings gospel" (that is, it includes no narratives) discovered in Egypt, first in the 1890s at Oxyrhynchus in Greek fragmentary papyri, then in 1945 at Nag Hammadi in a complete Coptic copy. *Thomas* is important for Jesus research because it represents a tradition independent of the New Testament Gospels and seems to include several authentic Jesus sayings that are not in the New Testament. Furthermore, several sayings in *Thomas* seem to be in older forms than in the New Testament Gospels (**Nag Hammadi Library** [2.9], **Oxyrhynchus Papyri** [2.11], **Q (Sayings Source)** [2.14]). For English translations, see Layton (1987), Meyer (1992), Miller (1994), and Robinson (1996).

2.6 Hebrew Bible. The collection of books generated by the ancient Israelite and Judean communities in the Hebrew language (with some Aramaic sections). In modern Jewish tradition these books are referred to either as "the Bible" or "Tanak" (T-N-K is an acronym for the three parts of the canon: *Torah* [Law], *Nevi'îm* [Prophets], and *Kethuvîm* [Writings]). This collection of "authorized" scriptures represents what was eventually sanctioned by the Palestinian rabbis. Israelites in the Diaspora often read these books in either Greek (Septuagint) or Aramaic (Targumim) translations (**Apocrypha** [2.1], **Old Testament** [2.10], **Septuagint** [2.15], **Targumim** [2.19]).

2.7 Josephus (c. 37–100 C.E.). The first-century Judean author of *The Judean War against the Romans* (*Historia Ioudaikou polemou pros Rōmaious*), which covers the Hasmonean and Herodian eras; *Judean Antiquities* (*Ioudaikē archaiologias*), which retells the Old Testament narratives and continues through the Herodian era; Josephus's *Life* (*Iōsēpou bios*), his autobiography; and *Against Apion* (*Contra Apionem*), his defense against an anti-Judean author. According to his autobiography, he was from a priestly family, was distantly related to the Hasmoneans, identified with the faction of Pharisees, and served as the military commander/governor of Galilee during the First Judean Revolt. After being captured by the Romans, Josephus became the client of the Roman generals and emperors Vespasian, Titus, and Domitian, whose family name (Flavius) he adopted (**First Judean Revolt** [1.28], **Hasmoneans** [1.34], **Pharisees** [1.57], **Priest** [1.62]). For English translations, see Feldman (2004), Mason (1992), Thackeray (1926; 1927–28); Thackeray et al. (1927–28 and 1930–65); Whiston (1987).

2.8 Mishnah (see **Talmud** [2.18]). For an English translation, see Danby (1933).

2.9 Nag Hammadi Library. The remnants of a Coptic gnostic library discovered near Nag Hammadi, Egypt. They were first dug up by an Egyptian farmer, Muhammed Ali, in 1945, and excavations were carried out through the 1970s. They include a diversity of books: early Christian Gospels (for example, *Gospel of Thomas*), philosophical treatises (for example, Plato's *Republic*), gnostic Christian writings (for example, *Dialogues of the Savior*), and other writings of unknown origin (**Gospel of Thomas** [2.5], **Oxyrhynchus Papyri** [2.11]). For an English translation, see Robinson (1996).

2.10 Old Testament. The Christian designation for the writings generated by the ancient Israelite and Judean communities, and consciously contrasted to the New Testament. The designations "Old Testament" and "New Testament" were first used by Tertullian (c. 165–230 C.E.) and Origen (c. 185–254 C.E.). "Old Testament" can refer to the same books as the Hebrew Bible, or it can be used in its broader sense to include the longer list of books in the Septuagint, used by Judeans and early Christian communities, which includes books now designated as the Apocrypha (**Apocrypha** [2.1], **Hebrew Bible** [2.6], **Septuagint** [2.15]).

2.11 Oxyrhynchus Papyri. Documents predominantly from the third and fourth centuries C.E. written in Greek on papyrus. Many of them are fragmentary, but more than 4,000 documents were excavated. They were discovered in a trash heap near Oxyrhynchus, Egypt, in the late nineteenth and early twentieth centuries. They are important for New Testament research because they include early fragments of Gospels (including the *Gospel of Thomas*), four epistles, and Revelation. But the letters, legal documents, and receipts provide insight into Roman administration and social phenomena of provincial Egypt during the Principate (**Gospel of Thomas** [2.5], **Nag Hammadi Library** [2.9]). No handy English translation is available; the papyri have appeared over the past one hundred years and in more than sixty volumes.

2.12 Philo (c. 20 B.C.E.–50 C.E.). An Israelite author who lived in Alexandria, Egypt, at the time of Jesus. Philo attempted to synthesize Hellenistic (Greek) and Israelite cultural conceptions. The approximately forty short books of his that survive include theology, scriptural commentary, philosophy, and polemical defenses of Israelites against their detractors. Philo's works also provide historical information about Roman imperial policies toward Judea, as well as important first-century events. His status is demonstrated by his leadership of a delegation to Rome in 39 to 40 C.E. (recounted in his book *The Legation to Gaius*). Furthermore, his family honor and influence are manifested in the marriage of his nephew Marcus Julius Alexander to the Herodian princess Berenice, the daughter of King Agrippa I of Judea (Josephus, *Ant.* 19.277). For English translations, see Colson and Whitaker (1929–62) and Yonge (1993).

2.13 Pseudepigrapha. A collec-

tion of Israelite writings "falsely ascribed" to ancient heroes (for example, *1 Enoch*), but written during the Hellenistic and Roman periods (c. 300 B.C.E.–100 C.E.). In antiquity these never formed a collection, but they have been brought together in the modern era for study of ancient Israelite literature. Many of these writings attest to a competitive pluralism among ancient Israelite groups. Ideologically, several of these groups were oriented to visionary apocalyptic (revelatory) traditions that often promise a reversal of honor and status with the imminent arrival of God's reign (*malkutha*). For English translations, see Charlesworth (1983 and 1985).

2.14 Q (Sayings Source). A large number of Jesus sayings in Matthew and Luke (but not in Mark) attest to the existence of a written tradition of Jesus' words in Greek earlier than the four canonical Gospels. This reconstructed Q source has been studied intensively in the last century and provides important insights into the Galilean social milieu of Jesus. Q was taken up into Matthew's and Luke's gospels independently. Luke is generally thought by scholars to give the order and readings closest to the original form of Q (thus the citation Q 12:33 refers to a Q saying found in Luke 12:33). The designation Q stems from the German word *Quelle* (source) (**Gospel of Thomas** [2.5]). For an isolation and reconstruction of the Q document, see Miller (1994:253–300) and Robinson et al. (2000). For a detailed analysis, see Kloppenborg (1987 and 2000).

2.15 Septuagint. The Hellenistic

Greek translation of the Hebrew Scriptures that was produced by numerous scribes c. 200–63 B.C.E., often represented by the sign LXX (the Roman numeral 70). A legend, preserved in the *Letter of Aristeas* (in the Pseudepigrapha), and urging the authoritative status of this translation, tells how seventy-two Israelite translators in Alexandria, Egypt, produced the translation in seventy-two days with remarkable unanimity. The term *Septuagint* may refer to the translation of just the Law or of the larger Hebrew Bible and additional books in Greek. The Septuagint is often cited in the Greek New Testament and represents the authoritative scriptures of the New Testament writers. Other Greek translations (associated with the names Aquila, Symmachus, and Theodotion) were produced in the second century C.E. to replace the Septuagint (**Apocrypha** [2.1], **Hebrew Bible** [2.6], **Old Testament** [2.10], **Pseudepigrapha** [2.13]). For an English translation, see Brenton (1986).

2.16 Suetonius (Gaius Suetonius Tranquillis, c. 69–130 C.E.). Roman historian born to the equestrian class. He worked as a lawyer, but became an imperial administrator through the intervention of his patron, Pliny the Younger. His administrative posts provided him with access to the imperial archives, and he wrote *Lives of the Caesars* (*De vita Caesarum*) c. 117–120 C.E., covering Julius Caesar to Domitian in eight volumes. These "Lives" provide important details about the events and imperial policies of the first-century emperors. In *Claudius* 25.4 he writes: "He [Claudius] expelled from

Rome the Judeans who had been riled up by Chrestus."

2.17 Tacitus, Cornelius (born c. 56 C.E.). Roman historian and a major source for the history of the early Roman Empire. Tacitus is best known for his two great works, *The Annals* and *The Histories*. Neither has been preserved in its entirety. *The Annals* covers the period from the death of Augustus to the beginning of the First Judean Revolt. *The Histories* begins with the Roman Civil War of 69 C.E. and ends with Domitian at the end of the first century (**First Judean Revolt** [1.28]).

2.18 Talmud. The great codifications of Israelite legal discussion, which went through several "editions." The core of the Talmud is the Mishnah, which was written down under the sponsorship of Rabbi Judah the Prince of Sepphoris around 200 C.E. The Mishnah gets its name from the fact that the rabbis of the second century committed voluminous discussions and controversies over Israelite law to memory and taught students to repeat (Hebrew *mishneh*) them. A second codification, called Tosefta, appeared in the early fourth century C.E. The Talmud represents additional discussions or commentary (Aramaic *gemara*) upon the Mishnah. Two versions exist, the Jerusalem Talmud (also known as "Yerushalmi" or "Talmud of the Land of Israel") from the fifth century C.E., and the much more extensive Babylonian Talmud (also known as "Bavli") from the sixth century C.E. (**Mishnah** [2.8]). For an English translation of Bavli, see the

unfinished multivolume edition by Stein-saltz (1989–).

2.19 Targumim (sing. *targum*). The translations of and commentaries on the Hebrew Bible in the Aramaic language. The primary targum on the Torah is called Onkelos, attributed by the Talmud to a rabbi of the late first and early second centuries C.E.; it tends to stay very close to the Hebrew readings. The Talmud attributes Targum Jonathan on the Prophets to the first century C.E.; it tends to paraphrase and comment on each passage rather than simply translating the Hebrew. The Jerusalem Targum and the Fragmentary Targum come from somewhat later eras but are difficult to date. Ancient Aramaic fragments of Leviticus and Job were found in Qumran Caves 4 and 11 (**Dead Sea Scrolls** [2.3], **Talmud** [2.18]).

2.20 Zenon Papyri. The Zenon Papyri were discovered in 1915 by peasants digging in the ruins of ancient Philadelphus in Lower (northern) Egypt. These papyri contained the archives of a certain Zenon who worked for Apollonios, the chief financial officer of Ptolemy II Philadelphus (ruled 283–246 B.C.E.). The correspondence between Zenon and Apollonios is especially valuable for shedding light on the political and economic conditions of Palestine during the Hellenistic period. Ptolemaic policy, for instance, encouraged the development of large estates producing cash crops for export to Egypt. Ptolemaic institutional patterns heavily influenced the subsequent royal arrangements of the Hasmoneans and Herodians. For translations, see White (1986:27–52).

Social–Scientific and Cross–Cultural Terms

3.1 Agrarian society. A society in which primary production and subsistence center around agriculture (such as all of those in the ancient Mediterranean), as opposed to hunter-gatherer, fishing, or industrial societies. "Advanced agrarian" societies are identified by their use of iron tools, the dominance of the plow over the hoe, and the use of large animals (oxen, donkeys, horses) for plowing and carting. (See 1 Sam 13:19-21; Jer 52:16; Luke 9:62; 1 Cor 9:10.)

3.2 Anachronism. To misunderstand events, persons, or other social phenomena by placing them in a historical context in which they do not belong. An example would be to interpret the status, role, and authority of ancient Roman emperors (like Augustus) as if they were analogous to elected presidents in the United States (**Ethnocentrism** [3.16]).

3.3 Artisan (Hebrew *ḥakam, ḥaras*; Greek *tektōn, teknitēs*; Latin *artifex, opifex*). A craftsperson who does hand fabrication, usually of a complete product, such as a pot or table (**Class** [3.7], **Elites** [3.14], **Patron** [3.40]). (See Exod 35:35; Sir 9:17; 38:27-34; Mark 6:3; Acts 19:24.)

3.4 Benefactor (see **Broker** [3.6], **Client** [3.8], **Friend/ship** [3.20], **Network** [3.37], **Patron** [3.40]).

3.5 Bridewealth (Hebrew *mohar, kethubâh*; Greek *hedna*). The transfer of goods from the groom's family to the bride's family following marriage negotiations. This practice is evidenced throughout the ancient eastern Mediterranean but not the West (**Dowry** [3.12], **Indirect dowry** [3.28], **Kinship** [3.31], **Usufruct** [3.55]). (See Exod 22:17; 1 Sam 18:25.)

3.6 Broker (Hebrew *mêlîs*; Greek *mesitēs, diallaktēr*; Latin *interpres*). An intermediary between a patron and a client, that is, one who provides access to other people who can provide concrete benefits. This role was often necessary to bridge the distance between people of different social strata, a god and humans, or just those from different groups or factions. Note other closely related Greek terms: "peacemaker" (*eirēnopoios*), "delegate" or "ambassador" (*presbeia*), "apostle" (*apostolos*), "angel" (*angelos*), "reconciliation" (*kattalagē*), "intervention" (*energeia*), and "intervene" (*metaxu histemi*) (**Client** [3.8], **Friend/ship** [3.20], **Network** [3.37], **Patron** [3.40]). (See Isa 43:27; Job 33:23; Luke 7:3; John 12:20-22; 1 Tim 2:5; Heb 9:15.)

3.7 Class (Greek *genos;* Latin *classis, ordo*). The stratum of society to which one belongs (for example, ruling elites, priests, peasants, merchants, artisans, the destitute). People of the same class have the same general social status. Class can be formalized, as with the Roman orders, or remain informal, as in Palestinian society. While modern discussions of class focus on economic considerations, this was not the primary variable in antiquity (**Artisan** [3.3], *Cursus honorum* [1.16], **Elites** [3.14], *Equestrian* [1.23], **Freedman/woman** [1.29], *Militiae* [1.52], **Order** [1.53], **Patron** [3.40], **Priest** [1.62], **Senate/senator** [1.73]). (See Jer 26:11, 17; Mark 6:21; Josephus, *Life* 196–97.)

3.8 Client (Greek *pelatēs, proxenia;* Latin *cliens, socius*). A free individual obligated and loyal to a patron. In Roman society patronage/clientage was a clearly defined relationship between individuals of different status for their mutual benefit. While this could be an informal arrangement, Roman law mandated and regulated the duty (*obsequium*) and services (*officia*) between freedmen/women and their former owners. A client could appeal to a patron for help (*beneficium, charis*) with bureaucratic, legal, financial, or other social

arrangements (**Broker** [3.6], **Friend/ship** [3.20], **Freedman/woman** [1.29], **Network** [3.37], **Patron** [3.40]). (See Luke 7:2-10; Philemon.)

3.9 Cultural System. The configuration of language, values, ideas, and historical information conditioned by environmental adaptation and technological developments. The cultural system "envelops" the social system, and the social system makes values, norms, statuses, and roles of the cultural system operational (**Ideology** [3.27]).

3.10 Descent. The series of links that connects the members of a kin-group to a common ancestor. The three types of descent principles identified by anthropologists are (a) patrilineal, tracking links through male ancestors; (b) matrilineal, through female ancestors; and (c) cognatic, a combination of male and female ancestors (**Genealogy** [3.22]).

3.11 Domain. An institutional system or constellation of social institutions. Every society manifests the domains of politics, kinship, economics, and religion, but in different configurations and relationships. In ancient Mediterranean societies, economics and religion were embedded in either politics or kinship, which are the only two explicit domains (**Economy/Economics** [3.13], **Institution** [3.30], **Kinship** [3.31], **Politics** [3.42], **Religion** [3.48]).

3.12 Dowry (Hebrew *šilluḥim, melog, ṣôn barzel;* Greek *meilia, proix, phernarion,* *domata;* Latin *dos*). The property a bride's family provides the bride or couple (usually under the control of her husband) at the time of marriage as her share of the family's inheritance. It might be movable property, immovable property, cash, or a combination of these (**Bridewealth** [3.5], **Indirect dowry** [3.28], **Inheritance** [3.29], **Kinship** [3.31], **Marriage** [3.34], **Usufruct** [3.55]). (See 1 Kgs 9:16; 2 Macc 1:14.)

3.13 Economy/Economics (Greek *oikonomia*). Literally, "household management." The social domain of all types of exchange: buying and selling; bartering and trading; borrowing and lending; tax, tribute, and tolls; mints and money; rents and leases; debts and redemption. Ancient economic institutions were embedded in kinship or political institutions, so that the word relates primarily to the provisioning of the household rather than (as today) to individual decisions about allocating scarce resources to a variety of ends (**Denarius** [1.18], **Domain** [3.11], **Extractive economy** [3.18], **Institution** [3.30], **Limited good** [3.32], **Market economy** [3.33], **Reciprocity** [3.46], **Redistribution** [3.47], **Sestertius** [1.75], **Shekel** [1.76]). (See 1 Macc 15:5-6; Josephus, *War* 7.285–303).

3.14 Elites (Greek *prōtoi, megistanoi, kratistoi, dynatoi, lamproi, prostatoi, dokimoi, gnōrimoi, epiphanestatoi*). A general word denoting those in a superior social position, especially over peasants and artisans. They have prestige, social standing, leadership roles, political office, power, or wealth.

Depending upon the historical or literary context, these terms may refer to everyone from large estate-holders, to members of the town council, to the Roman emperor (**Artisan** [3.3], **Class** [3.7], *Cursus honorum* [1.16], **Extractive economy** [3.18], **Honor** [3.25], *Militiae* [1.52], **Order** [1.53], **Patron** [3.40], **Social stratification** [3.52]). (See Mark 6:21; Acts 13:50; 25:5; Josephus, *Life* 32–36, 64–67.)

3.15 Endogamy. Marriage within one's own kin-group, a form of homogamy. In the ancient (and modern) Mediterranean, this was usually between cousins but could also be between an uncle and niece (**Exogamy** [3.17], **Homogamy** [3.24], **Marriage** [3.34]).

3.16 Ethnocentrism. Misconstruing social phenomena from another group by interpreting them in terms of one's own ethnic group and social experience. An example would be to interpret Judean state "religion" as if it were analogous to a modern Protestant denomination (**Anachronism** [3.2]).

3.17 Exogamy. Marriage between people who are not kin. Exogamous marriages could be arranged to advance a family's honor or strengthen its network by associating with a powerful family, or to recruit clients by associating with a weaker family (**Endogamy** [3.15], **Homogamy** [3.24], **Marriage** [3.34]).

3.18 Extractive economy. Taking "surplus" product from peasants and artisans so that production and consumption benefit elites rather than the peasants and artisans; also known as a "tributary economy." The extraction of goods and services was managed from the top down at the level of the Roman Empire, the Herodians, the priests, and the large estate-holders. The elites viewed the territories under their control as their "household" to use at their discretion (**Economy/Economics** [3.13], **Elites** [3.14], **Market economy** [3.33], **Reciprocity** [3.46], **Redistribution** [3.47], **Tribute** [1.86]).

3.19 Faction (Greek *stasis, hairesis;* Latin *factio*). A coalition of persons recruited by a leader to compete against opposing factions for honor, power, or control of resources. In the first century, the Jesus group can be classified as a faction, as can the various Pharisee groups (**Group** [3.23], **Movement** [3.36], **Network** [3.37]). (See Luke 5:29-34; 1 Cor 11:19; Josephus, *War* 2.119-21; *Life* 33.)

3.20 Friend/ship (Hebrew *ḥābēr, rêaʾ, sôd;* Greek *philos/philia, syntrophos, synekdēmos, hetairos, synēthēs;* Latin *amicus/amicitia, socius/societas*). A social relation of commitment and solidarity for mutual benefit, often referring to a patron/client relationship. The Romans distinguished between friends of greater, equal, and lower status. These terms could apply to the relationship of either individuals or groups (**Broker** [3.6], **Client** [3.8], **Network** [3.37], **Patron** [3.40]). (See Matt 26:50; Mark 5:19; Luke 7:34; Acts 19:29; Sir 6:5-17; 37:1-6; 1 Macc

8:20; 9:28; 14:40; Josephus, *Life* 79, 204, 274.)

3.21 Gender division. The social separation of males and females in terms of roles, behaviors, expectations, and physical space (**Patriarchy** [3.39], **Role** [3.49], **Social stratification** [3.52], **Status** [3.53]). (See Luke 10:38-42; John 4:1-30; Philo, *Laws* 3.169-71.)

3.22 Genealogy (Hebrew *tôlēdāh;* Greek *genealogia, genesis;* Latin *stirps*). A listing of relatives over two or more generations. This can be presented as a "lineal genealogy" (one ancestor per generation) or "segmented genealogy" (multiple family members in a given generation) (**Descent** [3.10], **Kinship** [3.31]). (See Matt 1:1-18; Luke 3:23-38; Josephus, *War* 1.181, 562-63; 2.220-22; *Ant.* 18.130-42.)

3.23 Group. Any collection of people that shares a sense of membership and common goals (**Faction** [3.19], **Movement** [3.36], **Network** [3.37], **Strong-group orientation** [3.34], **Weak-group orientation** [3.57]).

3.24 Homogamy. Marriage within the group of one's own social status, class, or ethnic group. Endogamy is one form of homogamy (**Endogamy** [3.15], **Exogamy** [3.17], **Marriage** [3.34]). (See Luke 1:5.)

3.25 Honor (Hebrew *kabod, ašrê;* Greek *timē, makarios;* Latin *dignitas, honorus, honos*). The conjunction of one's status claim (in terms of power, sexual status, and the sacred) with one's social group's acknowledgment of that claim. Honor takes two basic forms: "ascribed honor," which one possesses because of who one is, and "acquired honor," based upon what one has done. Being a Roman male born in the senatorial class would provide one with a grant of ascribed honor. Appointment as a prefect of Judea on the basis of influence, one's previous offices, or demonstrated expertise would be acquired honor (**Cursus honorum** [1.16], **Militiae** [1.52], **Order** [1.53], **Shame** [3.50]). (See Mark 6:7; John 4:44; Rom 2:7; Phil 2:29-30.)

3.26 Hospitality (Greek *philoxenia;* Latin *hospitium*). The conversion of strangers into guests. In the ancient Mediterranean, this term did not refer to something one extended to friends and family, but to outsiders due to need, networking, and so on. (**Broker** [3.6], **Client** [3.8], **Network** [3.37], **Patron** [3.40]). (See Wis 19:14; Luke 10:4; 22:35; Rom 12:13; 1 Tim 5:10; Heb 13:2; 3 John.)

3.27 Ideology. A system of beliefs and perspectives that a culture or subgroup shares. It is the integration of the group's stories, wisdom, customs, and values that are used to interpret experience and social life (**Cultural system** [3.9], **Group** [3.23], **Norms** [3.38], **Values** [3.56]).

3.28 Indirect dowry. The property or money given by a groom's kin, either directly to the bride or indirectly through her kin. It may constitute all or part of the bridewealth (**Bridewealth** [3.5], **Dowry** [3.12], **Kinship** [3.31], **Marriage** [3.34], **Usufruct** [3.55]). (See Gen 24:53.)

3.29 Inheritance (Hebrew *naḥalāh;* Greek *klēros, klēronomia;* Latin *hereditas*). The distribution of goods, property, and money to relatives, patrons, slaves, or friends, usually at death. Every society has different laws and customs with regard to which relatives are included in this distribution and in what order (**Dowry** [3.12], **Kinship** [3.31]). (See Deut 21:17; Luke 12:13; Gal 3:18.)

3.30 Institution. A system of interrelated behaviors, relationships, roles, and exchanges created in response to persistent social needs. Examples: marriage (which integrates sexuality, childrearing, dowry, residential patterns), law courts (which integrate law, arbitration, punishment, property transfer, and community authority), and kingship (which integrates social stratification, taxation, military control, and administration of bureaucracy) (**Cultural system** [3.9], **Domain** [3.11]).

3.31 Kinship (Greek *syngeneia;* Latin *consanguinitas*). The social domain that includes all the relationships and transactions regarding families: genealogy and descent, marriage and divorce, childbearing and -rearing, adoption, dowry and inheritance, and social roles (for example, mother, daughter, sister, wife, daughter-in-law) (**Descent** [3.10], **Domain** [3.11], **Genealogy** [3.22], **Inheritance** [3.29], **Marriage** [3.34]).

3.32 Limited good. The view in agrarian societies that all goods, tangible and intangible, are in limited supply (land, water, honor, for example). (See Luke 19:12-27.)

3.33 Market economy. An economic system in which production and distribution of goods and services are controlled by supply and demand in price-setting markets (like those in modern democracies) rather than by the elite or the mechanisms of a centralized bureaucracy (**Economy/Economics** [3.13], **Extractive economy** [3.18]).

3.34 Marriage. The binding relationship between a man and woman contracted, in peasant societies, by their families. While it creates a new social unit, it may have political, economic, and religious implications as well (**Bridewealth** [3.5], **Dowry** [3.12], **Endogamy** [3.15], **Exogamy** [3.17], **Homogamy** [3.24], **Indirect dowry** [3.28], **Kinship** [3.31]).

3.35 Model. A conceptual representation of reality. Models may be isomorphic (representing every detail) or homomorphic (representing only important or strategic details). The models in this book are usually homomorphic social models, informed by comparative social sciences, that show key patterns, functions, or interrelationships. Use of comparative social sciences is necessary for modeling ancient societies because social models developed out of monocultural or monosocial experiences tend to be anachronistic and ethnocentric.

3.36 Movement. The ideology of a group with enduring purposes that sustain the group's identity over time. Movements may draw in people of different social strata. Central to the New Testament is the Jesus movement group, which began as a Galilean faction centered around Jesus. Jesus of Nazareth first articulated the group's purposes (symbolized in the phrase "reign of God") around 29 C.E.; these sustained the group and allowed it to survive his death and to develop into the form of early Christian churches. We emphasize in this book that the Jesus movement group was far more concerned with addressing familial, political, and economic issues than might be envisioned by modern people interested in purely religious meanings (**Faction** [3.19], **Group** [3.23], **Network** [3.37], **Strong-group orientation** [3.54]).

3.37 Network. A web of relationships between any combination of friends, clients, brokers, and patrons that acts over time with numerous exchanges of gifts, favors, and commitments. Networks may vary in size, mutuality, and duration (**Broker** [3.6], **Client** [3.8], **Friend/ship** [3.20], **Patron** [3.40]). (See Luke 14:12.)

3.38 Norms. Binding behavioral rules, very often contingent upon or related to status. In Mediterranean societies like Roman Palestine, strong groups prevailed so that norms and roles were widely shared and rigidly enforced (**Strong-group orientation** [3.54], **Values** [3.56]).

3.39 Patriarchy. Literally "father's rule." More generally, it relates to male control or domination over women in public life, and older males over younger males (**Gender division** [3.21], **Social stratification** [3.52]).

3.40 Patron (Greek *euergetēs, dōrētēs;* Latin *patronus, pater*). A person (male or female) in a position to provide "first order" benefits to others (for example, land, a job, judicial clemency, citizenship) usually due to superior honor, power, role, wealth, and influence. In return for these benefits, a patron could expect public displays of honor, information, and political support from clients. Modeling family relationships, a common term for a patron was *father.* Brokers provide access to patrons ("second order" benefits) for clients (**Broker** [3.6], **Client** [3.8], **Friend/ship** [3.20], **Network** [3.37]). (See Matt 6:9; Acts 4:34-37; 10:38; Rom 16:2; Wis 19:14; 2 Macc 4:2; Josephus, *Life* 244, 368.)

3.41 Peasant (Hebrew *'am ha-'areṣ, perazôn, 'ikkar,* Greek *geōrgos, agroikos;* Latin *agricola, rusticus, colonus*). A farmer or animal herder in an agrarian society; one whose livelihood derives directly from the land. At a higher level of abstraction, "peasants" can describe all non-elites in an agrarian society, both in villages and cities, including fishers and artisans, potters, weavers, woodworkers, ironsmiths, and so on. Terms of derision were often used of peasants by the elite, for example: "insignificant ones" (*asēmatatoi; Josephus, Life* 35) and "the masses" (*hoi polloi;*

Josephus, *Ant.* 20.255) (**Agrarian society** [3.1], **Artisan** [3.3], **Class** [3.7], **Elites** [3.14]). (See Judg 5:7, 11; Jer 31:24; 2 Esd 9:17; Sir 38:25-26; 2 Tim 2:6.)

3.42 Politics. The domain of collective action. It may relate to the matters of the state or, more broadly, to group goal-setting and the exercise of power. This includes the holding of official positions, but also informal means of control, coercion, influence, and patronage (**Domain** [3.11], **Elites** [3.14], *Imperium* [1.41], **Institution** [3.30], **Network** [3.37], **Patron** [3.40], **Power** [3.44]).

3.43 Poor (see 1.58).

3.44 Power (Hebrew *koaḥ, 'oz;* Greek *dynamis, exousia;* Latin *auctoritas, potestas, imperium*). The exercise of control over others in order to achieve personal, group, or societal ends (**Elites** [3.14], *Imperium* [1.41], **Politics** [3.42]). (See Mark 9:1; Luke 4:36; Phil 3:21; 1 Macc 10:71.)

3.45 Purity/Pollution. An ideology and system of regulating the proper place for everything: clean/unclean, sacred/profane, normal/deviant, in-group/out-group. This applies to objects, people, times, places, animals, and food, and these categories are often arranged in hierarchies. It provides a society with meaning, orientation, and maps of behavior and belonging (**Cultural system** [3.9], **Ideology** [3.27]). (See Mark 7:1-5; Acts 10:9-35.)

3.46 Reciprocity. The give-and-take of both tangible and intangible items between individuals or groups. "Generalized reciprocity" refers to the sharing that families and other tightly knit groups do without strict accounting. "Balanced reciprocity" means that what one gives is based upon what one receives (*quid pro quo,* a "fair price"). "Negative reciprocity" refers to taking advantage of the other: getting a bargain, manipulating, tricking, or stealing (**Economy/Economics** [3.13], **Extractive economy** [3.18], **Redistribution** [3.47]).

3.47 Redistribution. The redistributive exchange mechanisms that collect agricultural products or manufactured goods at a central point and distribute them for social ends governed by elite decisions. Taxation and temple offerings reflect redistribution in Roman Palestine, since taxes were controlled by Rome and offerings by the priests of Jerusalem (**Economy/Economics** [3.13], **Extractive economy** [3.18], **Reciprocity** [3.46]).

3.48 Religion (Greek *eusebēia, theosebēia, thrēskeia, latreia;* Latin *religio*). In Latin, literally "binding back"; so, in Roman culture, a bond or constraint to observe sacred rites. Generally, this is the social domain in which cultural arrangements are legitimated and provided with ultimate meaning and reference to the divine. Anthropologists have defined religion as symbolic forms and actions that relate human beings to the ultimate conditions of existence (Bellah), or symbol systems providing notions of general order and supporting long-lasting moods and motivations (Geertz). Ancient religious institutions were embedded in kinship or political institutions, so that the overlap of meaning is limited when compared to modern arrangements of voluntary associations of individuals unconcerned with the larger shaping of society (**Domain** [3.11], **Institution** [3.30], **Power** [3.44]).

3.49 Role. The social expectations and behavior patterns specifying obligations or privileges dependent upon one's social status. Social roles in Roman Palestine were defined in relationship to gender (male, female), place in the family (mother, oldest son, cousin), power (elite, non-elite), and vocation (peasant, priest, scribe) (**Gender division** [3.21], **Norms** [3.38], **Order** [1.53], **Social stratification** [3.52], **Status** [3.53]).

3.50 Shame (Hebrew *bôšeth, kelimmah;* Greek *aischynē;* Latin *ignominia, pudor*). As it relates to society in general, shame is the negative correlate of honor: to lose honor, be humiliated, be ashamed, act shamefully, be disgraced, be ridiculed. In terms of gender, shame is that which the female protects through her virginity, chastity, or continence, so that for her to "lack shame" or "be shameless" is to fail at protecting the family honor through her sexuality (**Gender division** [3.21], **Honor** [3.25]). (See Prov 9:13; Sir 4:21; Luke 14:9; 1 Cor 1:27.)

3.51 Social bandits (Hebrew *gedûd*; Greek *lēstai*; Latin *latrunculi*). Members of a renegade band who prey especially upon elites and their estates or upon military outposts. Groups of these bandits are most often composed of those displaced or disenfranchised by elites, precipitated by a combination of persecution, debt, heavy taxation, confiscation of lands, and forced shifts in the economy. (Robin Hood in medieval England is an example.) Rather than common thieves, they are groups that form for survival and protest against the elites. Bandits of this type helped force the First Judean Revolt (**Extractive economy** [3.18], **First Judean Revolt** [1.28], *Sicarii* [1.77], **Zealots** [1.90]). (See Judg 11:1-3; 1 Sam 22:1-2; Mark 15:27; John 18:40; Josephus, *War* 1.204, 304–14; 2.232–40; *Ant.* 20.5.)

3.52 Social stratification. The "layering" of social statuses and roles in terms of power, privilege, office, influence, wealth, or some other social value. Family origin and power were key variables in the social stratification of ancient societies (**Gender division** [3.21], **Order** [1.53], **Patriarchy** [3.39], **Power** [3.44], **Role** [3.49], **Status** [3.53]).

3.53 Status. The position of a person relative to his or her group and the society at large, based upon such things as family, gender, ethnicity, religious affiliation, trade, group solidarity, and honorable behavior. One's status may also involve fulfilling defined roles, belonging to a trade associa-

tion, or living in an urban center (**Gender division** [3.21], **Honor** [3.25], **Order** [1.53], **Patriarchy** [3.39], **Role** [3.49], **Social stratification** [3.52]).

3.54 Strong–group orientation. A characteristic of societies (like those in the ancient Mediterranean) that socialize their members to a high degree of group identification, solidarity, conformity, and commitment. Correspondingly, individualism, autonomy, and the pursuit of goals not oriented to the group are discouraged, shamed, or punished (**Gender division** [3.21], **Honor** [3.25], **Patriarchy** [3.39], **Shame** [3.50], **Weak-group orientation** [3.57]).

3.55 Usufruct. The technical term for a husband's management of dowry property that belongs to his wife and her heirs (**Bride-wealth** [3.5], **Dowry** [3.12], **Indirect dowry** [3.28], **Marriage** [3.34]).

3.56 Values. The general social directions and the most basic expectations of specific cultures. Every culture has core values (operative in every interaction) and peripheral values (limited to specific interactive contexts). Values are realized through normative behaviors and institutional structures (**Cultural system** [3.9], **Ideology** [3.27], **Norms** [3.38]).

3.57 Weak–group orientation. A characteristic of (primarily modern Western) societies that manifest a high degree of social and geographical mobility and thus socialize their members to pursue personal goals (for example, career and spousal choices). These societies expect less group conformity and (proportionately) less intensive group commitments than "strong groups"; and they manifest a large percentage of individuals moving from one set of relationships to another (for example, divorce, denominational changes, moving neighborhoods) and belonging to a number of groups simultaneously with varying degrees of commitment (church, PTA, service organization, Neighborhood Watch, softball team, political party, professional association). The high percentage of marriages ending in divorce in the United States is one index of this (**Strong-group orientation** [3.34]).

BIBLIOGRAPHY 1

Ancient Documents

Brenton, Lancelot C. L., translator. 1986. *The Septuagint with Apocrypha: Greek and English.* Peabody, Mass.: Hendrickson.

Charlesworth, James H., editor. 1983 and 1985. *The Old Testament Pseudepigrapha.* 2 vols. Garden City, N.Y.: Doubleday.

Colson, F. H., and G. H. Whitaker, translators. 1929–62. *Philo.* LCL. New York: Putnam.

Danby, Herbert, translator. 1933. *The Mishnah.* Oxford: Oxford University Press.

Driver, G. R., translator. 1965. *Aramaic Papyri of the Fifth Century B.C.* 3rd ed. Reprint, Eugene, Ore.: Wipf & Stock, 2005.

Elliott, J. K., translator. 1993. *The Apocryphal New Testament: A Collection of Apocryphal Christian Literature in an English Translation.* Oxford: Clarendon.

Feldman, Louis H., translator and commentator. 2000. *Flavius Josephus: Judean Antiquities 1–4.* Flavius Josephus 3. Leiden: Brill.

Frey, Jean-Baptiste, editor. 1936–52. *Corpus inscriptionum iudaicarum.* Reprint, Library of Biblical Studies. New York: Ktav, 1975.

García Martínez, Florentine, translator. 1996. *The Dead Sea Scrolls Translated: The Qumran Texts in English.* Translated by W. G. E. Watson. 2nd ed. Leiden: Brill.

Gaster, Theodor H., translator. 1976. *The Dead Sea Scriptures.* 3rd ed. Garden City, N.Y.: Doubleday.

Layton, Bentley, translator. 1987. *The Gnostic Scriptures.* Garden City, N.Y.: Doubleday.

Lewis, Naphtali, editor. 1989. *The Documents from the Bar Kokhba Period in the Cave of Letters: Greek Papyri.* JDS. Jerusalem: Israel Exploration Society.

Mason, Steve, translator and commentator. 2003. *Life of Josephus.* Flavius Josephus 9. Leiden: Brill.

Meyer, Marvin, translator. 1992. *The Gospel of Thomas: The Hidden Sayings of Jesus.* Commentary by Harold Bloom. San Francisco: HarperSanFrancisco.

Miller, Robert J., editor. 1994. *The Complete Gospels: Annotated Scholar's Version.* Rev. ed. Sonoma, Calif.: Polebridge.

Moore, Clifford F., and John Jackson, translators. 1962. *Tacitus: The Histories; The Annals.* 4 vols. LCL. Cambridge: Harvard University Press.

Porten, Bezalel, et al., editors. 1996. *The Elephantine Papyri in English: Three Millennia of Cross-Cultural Continuity and Change.* Leiden: Brill.

Pritchard, James B., editor. 1969. *Ancient Near Eastern Texts Relating to the Old Testament.* 3rd ed. Princeton: Princeton University Press.

Robinson, James M., editor. 1996. *The Nag Hammadi Library in English.* 4th ed. Leiden: Brill.

Robinson, James M., Paul Hoffmann, and John S. Kloppenborg. 2000. *The Critical Edition of Q.* Hermeneia Supplements. Minneapolis: Fortress Press.

Rolfe, John Carew, translator. 1959–60. *Suetonius.* 2 vols. LCL. Cambridge: Harvard University Press.

Steinsaltz, Adin, translator and commentator. 1989–. *The Talmud: The Steinsaltz Edition.* New York: Random House.

Thackeray, H. S. J., translator. 1926. *Josephus: The Life; Against Apion.* LCL 186. Cambridge: Harvard University Press.

———. 1927–28. *Josephus: The Jewish War.* 2 vols. LCL 203, 210. Cambridge: Harvard University Press.

Thackeray, H. S. J., Ralph Marcus, and Louis H. Feldman, translators. 1930–65. *Josephus: Antiquities of the Jews.* 6 vols. LCL 242, 281, 326, 365, 433, 456. Cambridge: Harvard University Press.

Vermes, Geza. 1997. *The Complete Dead Sea Scrolls in English.* New York: Allen Lane.

Whiston, William, translator. 1987. *The Complete Works of Josephus.* Rev. ed. Peabody, Mass.: Hendrickson.

White, John L. *Light from Ancient Letters.* Foundations & Facets: New Testament. Philadelphia: Fortress Press, 1986.

Yonge, C. D., translator. 1993. *The Works of Philo.* Rev. ed. Peabody, Mass.: Hendrickson.

BIBLIOGRAPHY 2

Social–Science Theory and Terminology

Barnard, Alan, and Jonathan Spencer. 1996. *Encyclopedia of Social and Cultural Anthropology.* London: Routledge & Kegan Paul.

Barrett, Stanley R. 1996. *A Student's Guide to Theory and Method.* Toronto: University of Toronto Press.

Bellah, Robert N. 1970. *Beyond Belief: Essays on Religion in a Post-traditional World.* New York: Harper & Row.

Elliott, John H. 1993. *What Is Social Scientific Criticism?* GBS. Minneapolis: Fortress Press.

Geertz, Clifford. 1973. *Interpretation of Cultures.* New York: Basic.

Honigmann, John J., editor. 1973. *Handbook of Social and Cultural Anthropology.* Chicago: Rand McNally.

Ingold, Tim, editor. 1994. *Companion Encyclopedia of Anthropology.* London: Routledge.

Kuper, Adam, and Jessica Kuper, editors. 1995. *The Social Science Encyclopedia.* London: Routledge & Kegan Paul.

Levinson, David, and Melvin Ember, editors. 1996. *Encyclopedia of Cultural Anthropology.* 4 vols. New York: Holt.

Malina, Bruce J. 1986. *Cultural Anthropology and Christian Origins: Models for Biblical Interpretation.* Atlanta: John Knox.

———. 1993. *The New Testament World: Insights from Cultural Anthropology.* Rev. ed. Louisville, Ky.: Westminster John Knox.

Nolan, Patrick, and Gerhard Lenski. 2006. *Human Societies: A Macrosociological Approach.* 10th ed. New York: McGraw-Hill.

Parsons, Talcott. 1966. *Societies: Evolutionary and Comparative Perspectives.* Foundations of Modern Sociology Series. Englewood Cliffs, N.J.: Prentice-Hall.

———. 1971. *The System of Modern Societies.* Englewood Cliffs, N.J.: Prentice-Hall.

Pilch, John J., and Bruce J. Malina, editors. 1993. *Biblical Social Values and Their Meaning: A Handbook.* Peabody, Mass.: Hendrickson.

Sills, David L., editor. 1968. *International Encyclopedia of the Social Sciences.* New York: Free Press.

Theodorson, George A., and Achilles G. Theodorson. 1969. *A Modern Dictionary of Sociology.* New York: Harper & Row.

BIBLIOGRAPHY 3

References Consulted or Cited

[Abbreviations are those of the *Journal of Biblical Literature*.]

Aharoni, Y., M. Avi-Yonah, Anson F. Rainey, and Ze'ev Safrai. 1993. *The Macmillan Bible Atlas*. 3rd ed. New York: Macmillan.

Applebaum, Shimon. 1976. "Economic Life in Palestine." In *The Jewish People in the First Century: Historical Geography, Political History, Social, Cultural and Religious Life and Institutions*, edited by S. Safrai and M. Stern, 631–700. CRINT 2. Philadelphia: Fortress Press.

———. 1977. "Judaea as a Roman Province; Countryside as a Political and Economic Factor." In *ANRW* II.8:355–96. Berlin: de Gruyter.

Austin, M. M., and P. Vidal-Naquet. 1977. *Economic and Social History of Ancient Greece: An Introduction*. Translated by M. M. Austin. Berkeley: University of California Press.

Aviam, Mordechai. 2004. "First-Century Jewish Galilee: An Archaeological Perspective." In *Religion and Society in Roman Palestine: Old Question, New Approaches*, edited by Douglas R. Edwards, 7–27. London: Routledge.

Avi-Yonah, Michael. 1977. *The Holy Land: From the Persian to the Arab Conquest (536 B.C.– A.D. 640)*. Rev. ed. Grand Rapids, Mich.: Baker.

Bahat, Dan. 1986. *Carta's Historical Atlas of Jerusalem*. Jerusalem: Carta.

———. 2006. "Jesus and the Herodian Temple Mount." In *Jesus and Archaeology*, edited by James H. Charlesworth, 300–308. Grand Rapids, Mich.: Eerdmans.

Balch, David, and Carolyn Osiek, editors. 2003. *Early Christian Families in Context: An Interdisciplinary Dialogue*. Grand Rapids. Mich.: Eerdmans.

Barnard, Alan. 1994. "Rules and Prohibitions: The Form and Content of Human Kinship." In *Companion Encyclopedia to Anthropology*, edited by Tim Ingold, 783–12. London: Routledge.

Belo, Fernando. 1981. *A Materialist Reading of the Gospel of Mark.* Translated by Matthew J. O'Connell. Maryknoll, N.Y.: Orbis.

Bernett, Monika. 2007. "Roman Imperial Cult in the Galilee: Structures, Functions, and Dynamics." In *Religion, Ethnicity, and Identity in Ancient Galilee: A Region in Transition*, edited by Jürgen Zangenberg et al., 337–56. WUNT 1/210. Tübingen: Mohr/Siebeck.

Boissevain, Jeremy. 1974. *Friends of Friends: Networks, Manipulators and Coalitions.* New York: St. Martin's.

Boissevain, Jeremy, and J. Clyde Mitchell, editors. 1973. *Network Analysis: Studies in Human Interaction.* The Hague: Mouton.

Brisay, K. W. de, and K. A. Evans, editors. 1975. *Salt: The Study of an Ancient Industry.* Colchester: Colchester Archaeological Group.

Broshi, Magen. 1987. "The Role of the Temple in the Herodian Economy." *JJS* 38:31–37.

Brown, Raymond E. 1993. *The Birth of the Messiah: A Commentary on the Infancy Narratives in the Gospels of Matthew and Luke.* New updated ed. New York: Doubleday.

Carney, Thomas F. 1975. *The Shape of the Past: Models and Antiquity.* Lawrence, Kans.: Coronado.

Chancey, Mark A. 2002. *The Myth of a Gentile Galilee.* SNTSMS 118. Cambridge: Cambridge University Press.

———. 2005. *Graeco-Roman Culture and the Galilee of Jesus.* SNTSMS 134. Cambridge: Cambridge University Press.

———. 2007. "The Epigraphic Habit of Hellenistic and Roman Galilee." In *Religion, Ethnicity, and Identity in Ancient Galilee: A Region in Transition*, edited by Jürgen Zangenberg et al., 83–98. WUNT 1/210. Tübingen: Mohr/Siebeck.

Charlesworth, James H., editor. 1983. *The Old Testament Pseudepigrapha.* Vol. 1: *Apocalyptic Literature and Testaments.* Garden City, N.Y.: Doubleday.

———, editor. 1985. *The Old Testament Pseudepigrapha.* Vol. 2: *Expansions of the "Old Testament" and Legends, Wisdom and Philosophical Literature, Prayers, Psalms and Odes, Fragments of Lost Judeo-Hellenistic Works.* Garden City, N.Y.: Doubleday.

———. 2006a. "The Historical Jesus and Biblical Archaeology: Reflections on New Methodologies and Perspectives." In *Jesus and Archaeology*, edited by James H. Charlesworth, 692–95. Grand Rapids, Mich.: Eerdmans.

———, editor. 2006b. *Jesus and Archaeology.* Grand Rapids, Mich.: Eerdmans.

———. 2006c. "Jesus Research and Archaeology: A New Perspective." In *Jesus and Archaeology*, edited by James H. Charlesworth, 11–63. Grand Rapids, Mich.: Eerdmans.

Chilton, Bruce D. 1992. *The Temple of Jesus: His Sacrificial Program within a Cultural History of Sacrifice.* University Park: Pennsylvania State University Press.

Chilton, Bruce D., and Craig A. Evans, editors. 1999a. *Authenticating the Activities of Jesus.* NTTS 28/2. Leiden: Brill.

————, editors. 1999b. *Authenticating the Words of Jesus.* NTTS 28/1. Leiden: Brill.

Cohen, Shaye J. D. 1993. *The Jewish Family in Antiquity.* BJS 289. Atlanta: Scholars.

————. 1999. *The Beginnings of Jewishness: Boundaries, Varieties, Uncertainties.* Berkeley: University of California Press.

Collins, Randall. 1988. *Theoretical Sociology.* San Diego: Harcourt Brace Jovanovich.

Coote, Robert B. and Mary P. Coote. 1990. *Power, Politics, and the Making of the Bible: An Introduction.* Minneapolis: Fortress Press.

Corcoran, Thomas H. 1957. "The Roman Fishing Industry of the Late Republic and Early Empire." Ph.D. dissertation. Northwestern University.

————. 1963. "Roman Fish Sauces." *Classical Journal* 58:204–10.

Corley, Kathleen. 1993. *Private Women, Public Meals: Social Conflict in the Synoptic Tradition.* Peabody, Mass.: Hendrickson.

Craffert, Pieter F. 2008. *The Life of a Galilean Shaman: Jesus of Nazareth in Anthropological-Historical Perspective.* Matrix. Eugene, Ore.: Cascade Books.

Crossan, John Dominic. 1973. *In Parables: The Challenge of the Historical Jesus.* San Francisco: Harper & Row.

————. 1991. *The Historical Jesus: The Life of a Mediterranean Jewish Peasant.* San Francisco: HarperSanFrancisco.

————. 1994. *Jesus: A Revolutionary Biography.* San Francisco: HarperSanFrancisco.

Crossan, John Dominic, and Jonathan L. Reed. 2001. *Excavating Jesus: Beneath the Stones, Behind the Texts.* San Francisco: HarperSanFrancisco.

Curtis, Robert L. 1991. *Garum and Salsamenta: Production and Commerce in Materia Medica.* Studies in Ancient Medicine 3. Leiden: Brill.

Cutting, Charles L. 1955. *Fish Saving: A History of Fish Processing from Ancient to Modern Times.* London: Hill.

Dalman, Gustav. 1964. *Arbeit und Sitte in Palästina.* 7 vols. 1928–39. Reprint, Hildesheim: Olms.

Daly, Herman, and John B. Cobb Jr. 1994. *For the Common Good: Redirecting the Economy toward Community, the Environment, and a Sustainable Future.* 2nd ed. Boston: Beacon.

Danker, Frederick W. 1982. *Benefactor: Epigraphic Study of a Graeco-Roman and New Testament Semantic Field.* St. Louis, Mo.: Clayton.

D'Arms, John H. 1984. "Control, Companionship, and Clientela: Some Social Functions of the Roman Common Meal." *Echos du monde classique* 18:327–48.

Delaney, Carol. 1986. "The Meaning of Paternity and the Virgin Birth Debate." *Man* 21:494–513.

————. 1987. "Seeds of Honor, Fields of Shame." In *Honor and Shame and the Unity of the Mediterranean,* edited by David D. Gilmore, 35–48. SPAAA 22. Washington, D.C.: American Anthropological Association.

Destro, Adriana, and Mauro Pesce. 1995. "Kinship, Discipleship and Movement: An Anthropological Study of John's Gospel." *BibInt* 3:266–84.

Downing, F. Gerald. 1988. *Christ and the Cynics: Jesus and Other Radical Preachers in First-Century Tradition.* Sheffield: Sheffield Academic.

———. 2004. "In Quest of First-Century C.E. Galilee." *CBQ* 66:78–97.

Duling, Dennis C. 1995. "Matthew and Marginality." *HTS* 51:358–87.

———. 1999. "The Jesus Movement and Social Network Analysis (Part I: The Spatial Network)." *BTB* 29:156–75.

———. 2000. "The Jesus Movement and Social Network Analysis (Part II: The Social Network)." *BTB* 30:3–14.

———. 2002. "The Jesus Movement and Network Analysis." In *The Social Setting of Jesus and the Gospels,* edited by Wolfgang Stegemann et al., 301–32. Minneapolis: Fortress Press.

———. 2003. *The New Testament: History, Literature, and Social Context.* Belmont, Calif.: Wadsworth/Thomson.

Edelstein, Gershon. 1990. "What's a Roman Villa Doing Outside Jerusalem?" *BAR* 16/6:32–42.

Edersheim, Alfred. 1994. *The Temple: Its Ministry and Services.* Updated ed. Peabody, Mass.: Hendrickson.

Edwards, Douglas R., editor. 2004. *Religion and Society in Roman Palestine: Old Question, New Approaches.* London: Routledge.

———. 2007. "Identity and Social Location in Roman Galilean Villages." In *Religion, Ethnicity, and Identity in Ancient Galilee: A Region in Transition,* edited by Jürgen Zangenberg et al., 357–74. WUNT 1/210. Tübingen: Mohr/Siebeck.

Edwards, Douglas R., and C. Thomas McCullough, editors. 1997. *Archaeology and the Galilee: Texts and Contexts in the Graeco-Roman and Byzantine Periods.* SFSHJ 143. Atlanta: Scholars.

Eisenstadt, S. N. 1963. *The Political Systems of Empires.* New York: Free Press.

Eisenstadt, S. N., and Louis Roniger. 1980. "Patron-Client Relations as a Model of Structuring Social Exchange." *CSSH* 22:42–77.

———, editors. 1984. *Patrons, Clients and Friends: Interpersonal Relations and the Structure of Trust in Society.* New York: Cambridge University Press.

Elliott, J. K. 1993. *The Apocryphal New Testament: A Collection of Apocryphal Christian Literature in an English Translation.* Oxford: Clarendon.

Elliott, John H. 1987. "Patronage and Clientism in Early Christian Society: A Short Reading Guide." *Forum* 3/4:39–48. Reprinted in *The Social Sciences and the New Testament,* edited by Richard L. Rohrbaugh, 144–56. Peabody, Mass.: Hendrickson, 1996.

———. 1991. "Temple versus Household in Luke-Acts: A Contrast in Social Institutions." In *The Social World of Luke-Acts: Models for Interpretation,* edited by Jerome H. Neyrey, 211–40. Peabody, Mass.: Hendrickson.

———. 2005. A *Home for the Homeless: A Social-Scientific Criticism of 1 Peter, Its Situation and Strategy, with a New Introduction.* 1990. Eugene, Ore.: Wipf & Stock.

———. 2007. "Jesus the Israelite Was Neither a 'Jew' nor a 'Christian': On Correcting Misleading Nomenclature." *JSHJ* 5/2:119–54.

Engle, Anita. 1977. "An Amphorisk of the Second Temple Period." *PEQ* 109:117–22.

Eppstein, Victor. 1964. "The Historicity of the Gospel Account of the Cleansing of the Temple." *ZNW* 55:42–58.

Eshel, Esther, and Douglas R. Edwards. 2004. "Language and Writing in Early Roman Galilee: Social Location of a Porter's Abecedary from Khirbet Qana." In *Religion and Society in Roman Palestine: Old Question, New Approaches*, edited by Douglas R. Edwards, 49–55. London: Routledge.

Evans, Craig A. 1989a. "Jesus' Action in the Temple: Cleansing or Portent of Destruction?" *CBQ* 51:237–70.

———. 1989b. "Jesus' Action in the Temple and Evidence of Corruption in the First-Century Temple." In *SBLSP*, 522–39. Atlanta: Scholars.

———. 1992. "Opposition to the Temple: Jesus and the Dead Sea Scrolls." In *Jesus and the Dead Sea Scrolls*, edited by James H. Charlesworth, 235–53. ABRL. New York: Doubleday.

———. 2003. *Jesus and the Ossuaries: What Jewish Burial Practices Reveal about the Beginning of Christianity.* Waco, Tex.: Baylor University Press.

———. 2006. "Excavating Caiaphas, Pilate, and Simon of Cyrene: Assessing the Literary and Archaeological Evidence." In *Jesus and Archaeology*, edited by James H. Charlesworth, 323–40. Grand Rapids, Mich.: Eerdmans.

Evans, Craig A., and Stanley E. Porter, editors. 2000. *Dictionary of New Testament Background.* Downers Grove, Ill.: InterVarsity.

Falk, Zeev Wilhelm. 1974. "Jewish Private Law." In *The Jewish People in the First Century: Historical Geography, Political History, Social, Cultural and Religious Life and Institutions*, edited by S. Safrai and M. Stern, 504–34. CRINT 1. Philadelphia: Fortress Press.

Fiensy, David A. 1991. *The Social History of Palestine in the Herodian Period.* SBEC 20. Lewiston, N.Y.: Mellen.

———. 2007. *Jesus the Galilean: Sounding in a First-Century Life.* Piscataway, N.J.: Gorgias.

Finegan, Jack. 1992. *The Archaeology of the New Testament: The Life of Jesus and the Beginning of the Early Church.* Rev. ed. Princeton: Princeton University Press.

Finley, Moses, I. 1981. "Marriage, Sale and Gift in the Homeric World." In *Economy and Society in Ancient Greece*, 233–45. New York: Penguin.

———. 1985. *The Ancient Economy.* 2nd ed. London: Hogarth.

Foster, George. 1965. "Peasant Society and the Image of Limited Good." *AmAnth* 67:293–315.

———. 1967. "The Image of Limited Good." In *Peasant Society: A Reader,* by J. Potter, M. Diaz, and G. Foster, 300–323. Boston: Little, Brown.

Freyne, Seán. 1980. *Galilee from Alexander the Great to Hadrian 323 B.C.E. to 135 C.E.* Wilmington, Del.: Glazier.

———. 1988a. "Bandits in Galilee: A Contribution to the Study of Social Conditions in First-Century Palestine." In *The Social World of Formative Christianity and Judaism: Essays in Tribute to Howard Clark Kee,* edited by Jacob Neusner et al., 50–68. Philadelphia: Fortress Press.

———. 1988b. *Galilee, Jesus and the Gospels: Literary Approaches and Historical Investigations.* Philadelphia: Fortress Press.

———. 1994. "The Geography, Politics, and Economics of Galilee and the Quest for the Historical Jesus." In *Studying the Historical Jesus: Evaluations of the State of Current Research,* edited by C. Evans and B. Chilton, 75–121. NTTS 19. Leiden: Brill.

———. 1995. "Herodian Economics in Galilee: Searching for a Suitable Model." In *Modelling Early Christianity: Social-Scientific Studies of the New Testament in Its Context,* edited by Philip F. Esler, 23–46. London: Routledge.

———. 1997. "Galilean Questions to Crossan's Mediterranean Jesus." In *Whose Historical Jesus?* edited by William E. Arnal and M. Desjardins, 63–91. SCJ 7. Waterloo, Ont.: Wilfrid Laurier University Press.

———. 2000. *Galilee and Gospels: Collected Essays.* WUNT 125. Tübingen: Mohr/Siebeck.

———. 2002a. "Galilee and Judea in the First Century—the Social World of Jesus and His Ministry." In *Texts, Contexts and Cultures: Essays on Biblical Topics,* 122–52. Dublin: Veritas. Reprinted in *The Face of New Testament Studies: A Survey of Recent Research,* edited by Scot McKnight and Grant R. Osborn, 21–35. Grand Rapids, Mich.: Baker Academic, 2004.

———. 2002b. "The Quest for the Historical Jesus—Some Theological Reflections." In *Texts, Contexts and Cultures: Essays on Biblical Topics,* 106–21. Dublin: Veritas.

———. 2002c. *Texts, Contexts and Cultures: Essays on Biblical Topics.* Dublin: Veritas.

———. 2006. "Archaeology and the Historical Jesus." In *Jesus and Archaeology,* edited by James H. Charlesworth, 64–83. Grand Rapids, Mich.: Eerdmans.

———. 2007a. "Galilean Studies: Old Issues and New Questions." In *Religion, Ethnicity, and Identity in Ancient Galilee: A Region in Transition,* edited by Jürgen Zangenberg et al., 13–29. WUNT 1/210. Tübingen: Mohr/Siebeck.

———. 2007b. "Galilee as Laboratory: Experiments for New Testament Historians and Theologians." *NTS* 53:147–64.

Galbraith, John Kenneth. 1977. *The Age of Uncertainty: A History of Economic Ideas and Their Consequences.* Boston: Houghton Mifflin.

Garnsey, Peter. 1976. "Peasants in Ancient Roman Society." *JPS* 3:221–35.

————, editor. 1980. *Non-slave Labour in the Greco-Roman World.* Cambridge: Cambridge Philological Society.

Garnsey, Peter, Keith Hopkins, and C. R. Whittaker, editors. 1983. *Trade in the Ancient Economy.* Berkeley: University of California Press.

Garnsey, Peter, and Richard Saller. 1987. *The Roman Empire: Economy, Society and Culture.* Berkeley: University of California Press.

Geertz, Hildred. 1979. "The Meaning of Family Ties." In *Meaning and Order in Moroccan Society*, edited by Clifford Geertz et al., 315–91. CSCS. New York: Cambridge University Press.

Gellner, Ernest, and John Waterbury, editors. 1977. *Patrons and Clients in Mediterranean Societies.* London: Duckworth.

Gilmore, David D. 1982. "Anthropology of the Mediterranean Area." *ARA* 11:175–205.

————, editor. 1987. *Honor and Shame and the Unity of the Mediterranean.* SPAAA 22. Washington, D.C.: American Anthropological Association.

Ginsberg, H. L., translator. 1969. "Aramaic Papyri from Elephantine." In *Ancient Near Eastern Texts Relating to the Old Testament*, edited by James B. Pritchard, 222–23. 3rd ed. Princeton: Princeton University Press.

Gnuse, Robert. 1985. *You Shall Not Steal: Community and Property in the Biblical Tradition.* Maryknoll, N.Y.: Orbis.

Goodman, Martin. 1982. "The First Jewish Revolt: Social Conflict and the Problem of Debt." *JSS* 33:417–27.

————. 1987. *The Ruling Class of Judaea: The Origins of the Jewish Revolt against Rome* A.D. *66–70.* Cambridge: Cambridge University Press.

————. 1999. "Galilean Judaism and Judaean Judaism." In *The Cambridge History of Judaism.* Vol. 3: *The Early Roman Period*, edited by William Horbury et al., 596–619. Cambridge: Cambridge University Press.

Goody, Jack. 1973. "Bridewealth and Dowry in Africa and Eurasia." In *Bridewealth and Dowry*, 1–58. CPSA 7. Cambridge: Cambridge University Press.

Gordon, Cyrus H. 1965. *The Ancient Near East.* New York: Norton.

————. 1977. "Paternity at Two Levels." *JBL* 96:101.

————. 1978. "The Double Paternity of Jesus." *BAR* 4/2:26–27.

Gowan, Donald E. 1987. "Wealth and Poverty in the Old Testament: The Case of the Widow, the Orphan, and the Sojourner." *Int* 41:341–53.

Greene, Kevin. 1986. *The Archaeology of the Roman Economy.* Berkeley: University of California Press.

Guijarro, Santiago. 1997. "The Family in First-Century Galilee." In *Constructing Early Christian Families: Family as Social Reality and Metaphor*, edited by Halvor Moxnes, 42–65. London: Routledge & Kegan Paul.

Hachili, Rachel. 1983. "Jewish Funerary Customs during the Second Temple Period in the Light of the Excavations at the Jericho Necropolis." *PEQ* 115:109–32.

———. 1997. "A Jericho Ossuary and a Jerusalem Workshop." *IEJ* 47 (1997): 238–47.

Hamilton, Neill Q. 1964. "Temple Cleansing and Temple Bank." *JBL* 83:365–72.

Hanson, K. C. 1989a. "The Herodians and Mediterranean Kinship, Part I: Genealogy and Descent." *BTB* 19:75–84.

———. 1989b. "The Herodians and Mediterranean Kinship, Part II: Marriage and Divorce." *BTB* 19:142–51.

———. 1990. "The Herodians and Mediterranean Kinship, Part III: Economics." *BTB* 20:10–21.

———. 1993. "Blood and Purity in Leviticus and Revelation." *Listening* 28:215–30.

———. 1994. "BTB Reader's Guide: Kinship." *BTB* 24:183–94.

———. 1997a. "Sin, Purification, and Group Process." In *Problems of Biblical Theology: Essays in Honor of Rolf Knierim*, edited by H. T. C. Sun et al., 167–91. Grand Rapids, Mich.: Eerdmans.

———. 1997b. "The Galilean Fishing Economy and the Jesus Tradition." *BTB* 27:99–111.

———. 2002. "Jesus and the Social Bandits." In *The Social Setting of Jesus and the Gospels*, edited by Wolfgang Stegemann, Bruce J. Malina, and Gerd Theissen, 283–300. Minneapolis: Fortress Press.

Hellerman, Joseph H. 2001. *The Ancient Church as Family*. Minneapolis: Fortress Press.

Harrell, Stevan, and Sara A. Dickey. 1985. "Dowry Systems in Complex Societies." *Ethnology* 24:105–20.

Hengel, Martin. 1977. *Crucifixion in the Ancient World and the Folly of the Message of the Cross*. Translated by John Bowden. Philadelphia: Fortress Press.

Hennecke, Edgar, and Wilhelm Schneemelcher. 1963. *New Testament Apocrypha*. Vol. 1: *Gospels and Related Writings*. Translated by R. McL. Wilson. Philadelphia: Westminster.

———. 1965. *New Testament Apocrypha*. Vol. 2: *Writings Relating to the Apostles*. Translated by R. McL. Wilson. Philadelphia: Westminster.

Herzog, William R., II. 1994. *Parables as Subversive Speech: Jesus as Pedagogue of the Oppressed*. Atlanta: Westminster John Knox.

———. 2005a. *Prophet and Teacher: An Introduction to the Historical Jesus*. Louisville, Ky.: Westminster John Knox.

———. 2005b. "Why Peasants Responded to Jesus." In *Christian Origins*, edited by Richard A. Horsley, 47–70. PHC 1. Minneapolis: Fortress Press.

Hezser, Catherine. 2001. *Jewish Literacy in Roman Palestine*. TSAJ 81. Tübingen: Mohr/Siebeck.

———. 2003. *Rabbinic Law in Its Roman and Near Eastern Context*. TSAJ 97. Tübingen: Mohr/Siebeck.

Hirschfeld, Yizhar. 2006. "Ramt Hanadiv and Ein Gedi: Property in Judea before 70." In *Jesus and Archaeology*, edited by James H. Charlesworth, 384–92. Grand Rapids, Mich.: Eerdmans.

Hirschfeld, Yizhar, and R. Birger-Calderon. 1991. "Early Roman and Byzantine Estates Near Caesarea." *IEJ* 41:81–111.

Hobsbawm, Eric J. 1959. *Primitive Rebels: Studies in Archaic forms of Social Movements in the 19th and 20th Centuries.* New York: Norton.

———. 1974. "Social Banditry." In *Rural Protest: Peasant Movements and Social Change*, edited by H. Landsberger, 142–57. London: Macmillan.

———. 1981. *Bandits.* Rev. ed. New York: Pantheon.

Hoehner, Harold W. 1972. *Herod Antipas.* SNTSMS 17. Cambridge: Cambridge University Press.

Hoenig, Sidney B. 1979. "The Ancient City-Square: The Forerunner of the Synagogue." In *ANRW* II 19.1:448–76. Berlin: de Gruyter.

Hohlfelder, Robert L. 1992. "Caesarea." In *ABD* 1:798–803.

Hollis, A. H. T. 1934. *The Archaeology of Herod's Temple, with a Commentary on the Tractate 'Middoth.'* London: Dent.

Holum, Kenneth G., et al. 1988. *King Herod's Dream—Caesarea on the Sea.* New York: Norton.

Horsley, Richard A. 1979. "Josephus and the Bandits." *JSJ* 10:37–63.

———. 1986. "Popular Prophetic Movements at the Time of Jesus: Their Principal Features and Social Origins." *JSNT* 26:3–27.

———. 1987. *Jesus and the Spiral of Violence: Popular Jewish Resistance in Roman Palestine.* Reprint, Minneapolis: Fortress Press, 1993.

———. 1988. "Bandits, Messiahs, and Longshoremen: Popular Unrest in Galilee around the Time of Jesus." In *SBLSP,* 183–99. Atlanta: Scholars.

———. 1989a. *The Liberation of Christmas: The Infancy Narratives in Social Context.* Reprint, Eugene, Ore.: Wipf & Stock, 2006.

———. 1989b. *Sociology and the Jesus Movement.* New York: Crossroad.

———. 1995a. "Archaeology and the Villages of Upper Galilee: A Dialogue with Archaeologists." *BASOR* 297:5–16, 27–28.

———. 1995b. *Galilee: History, Politics, People.* Valley Forge, Pa.: Trinity.

———. 1996. *Archaeology, History and Society in Galilee: The Social Context of Jesus and the Rabbis.* Valley Forge, Pa.: Trinity.

———. 2003. *Jesus and Empire: The Kingdom of God and the New World Disorder.* Minneapolis: Fortress Press.

———. 2004. "The Pharisees and Jesus in Galilee and Q." In *When Judaism and Christianity Began: Essays in Memory of Anthony J. Saldarini.* Vol. 1: *Christianity in the Beginning*, edited by Alan J. Avery-Peck et al., 117–45. JSJSup 85. Leiden: Brill.

————. 2005. "Jesus Movement and the Renewal of Israel." In *Christian Origins*, edited by Richard A. Horsley, 23–46. PHC 1. Minneapolis: Fortress Press.

————. 2007. *Scribes, Visionaries, and the Politics of Second Temple Judea*. Louisville, Ky.: Westminster John Knox.

Horsley, Richard A., and John S. Hanson. 1985. *Bandits, Prophets, and Messiahs: Popular Movements at the Time of Jesus*. San Francisco: Harper & Row.

Isaac, B. 1984. "Bandits in Judaea and Arabia." *HSCP* 88:171–203.

Jensen, Morten Hoerning. 2006. *Herod Antipas in Galilee: The Literary and Archaeological Sources on the Reign of Herod Antipas and Its Socio-economic Impact on Galilee*. WUNT 2/215. Tübingen: Mohr/Siebeck.

————. 2007. "Message and Minting: The Coins of Herod Antipas in Their Second Temple Context as a Source for Understanding the Religio-political and Socio-economic Dynamics of Early First-Century Galilee." In *Religion, Ethnicity, and Identity in Ancient Galilee: A Region in Transition*, edited by Jürgen Zangenberg et al., 277–313. WUNT 1/210. Tübingen: Mohr/Siebeck.

Jeremias, Joachim. 1969. *Jerusalem in the Time of Jesus*. Translated by F. H. Cave and C. H. Cave. Philadelphia: Fortress Press.

————. 1972. *The Parables of Jesus*. 2nd ed. Translated by S. H. Hooke. New York: Scribner.

Johnson, Marshall D. 2002. *The Purpose of the Biblical Genealogies*. 2nd ed. SNTS Monograph Series 8. 1988. Reprint, Eugene, Ore.: Wipf & Stock.

Kautsky, John H. 1982. *The Politics of Aristocratic Empires*. Chapel Hill: University of North Carolina Press.

Kee, Howard C. 1983. *Understanding the New Testament*. 4th ed. Englewood Cliffs, N.J.: Prentice-Hall.

Keesing, Roger M. 1975. *Kin Groups and Social Structure*. New York: Holt, Rinehart and Winston.

Kloppenborg, John S. 1987. *The Formation of Q: Trajectories in Ancient Wisdom Collections*. Studies in Antiquity and Christianity. Philadelphia: Fortress Press.

————. 2000. *Excavating Q: The History and Setting of the Sayings Gospel*. Minneapolis: Fortress Press.

————. 2006. "The Theodotus Synagogue Inscription and the Problem of First-Century Synagogue Buildings." In *Jesus and Archaeology*, edited by James H. Charlesworth, 236–82. Grand Rapids, Mich.: Eerdmans.

Koester, Helmut. 1995. *Introduction to the New Testament*. Vol. 1: *History, Culture and Religion of the Hellenistic Age*. 2nd ed. New York: Gruyter.

————. 2003. "The Synoptic Sayings Gospel Q in the Early Communities of Jesus' Followers." In *Early Christian Voices in Texts, Traditions and Symbols: Essays in Honor of François Bovon*, edited by David Warren et al., 45–58. BibIntSer 66. Leiden: Brill.

Koliopoulos, J. 1979. *Brigands with a Cause*. Oxford: Oxford University Press.

Kraemer, Ross Shepard, and Mary Rose D'Angelo, editors. 1999. *Women and Christian Origins*. New York: Oxford University Press.

Kreissig, Heinz. 1969. "Die landwirtschaftliche Situation in Palästina vor dem judäischen Krieg." *Acta Antiqua* 17:223–54.

———. 1970. *Die sozialen Zusammenhänge des judä3ischen Krieges: Klassen und Klassenkampf im Palästina des 1. Jahrhunderts v. u. Z.* Berlin: Akademie.

Lendon, J. E. 1997. *Empire of Honour: The Art of Government in the Roman World*. Oxford: Clarendon.

Lenski, Gerhard E. 1984. *Power and Privilege: A Theory of Social Stratification*. 2nd ed. Chapel Hill: University of North Carolina Press.

Lernau, Hanan, and Omri Lernau. 1989. "Fish Bone Remains." In *Excavations in the South of the Temple Mount: The Ophel of Biblical Jerusalem*, 155–59. Qedem 29. Jerusalem: Hebrew University.

Lerner, Gerda. 1986. *The Creation of Patriarchy*. New York: Oxford University Press.

Levine, Amy-Jill. 2007. "Theory, Apologetic, History: Reviewing Jesus' Jewish Context." *AusBR* 55:57–78.

Levine, Lee I. 1975a. *Caesarea under Roman Rule*. SJLA 7. Leiden: Brill.

———. 1975b. *Roman Caesarea: An Archaeological-Topographical Study*. Jerusalem: Institute of Archaeology, Hebrew University of Jerusalem.

———. 1992. "The Sages and the Synagogue in Late Antiquity: The Evidence of the Galilee." In *The Galilee in Late Antiquity*, edited by Lee I. Levine, 201-22. Cambridge: Harvard University Press.

———. 2004. "The First-Century Synagogue: Critical Reassessments and Assessments of the Critical." In *Religion and Society in Roman Palestine: Old Question, New Approaches*, edited by Douglas R. Edwards, 70–102. London: Routledge.

Lewis, Naphtali. 1983. *Life in Egypt under Roman Rule*. Oxford: Clarendon.

Lewis, Naphtali, and Meyer Reinhold, editors. 1990. *Roman Civilization*. Vol. 2: *The Empire*. 3rd ed. New York: Columbia University Press.

Lewis, Naphtali, Yigael Yadin, and Jonas C. Greenfield, editors. 1989. *The Documents from the Bar Kokhba Period in the Cave of Letters*. Jerusalem: Israel Exploration Society.

Llewelyn, S. R., and R. A. Kearsley. 1992. *New Documents Illustrating Early Christianity*. Vol. 6. Marrickville, Australia: Macquarie University Ancient History Documentary Research Centre.

Mack, Burton L. 1993. *The Lost Gospel: The Book of Q and Christian Origins*. San Francisco: HarperSanFrancisco.

Madden, F. W. 1967. *A History of Jewish Coinage*. 1864. Reprint, Library of Biblical Studies. New York: Ktav.

Malina, Bruce J. 1980. "What Is Prayer?" *TBT* 18:14–20.

———. 1986. " 'Religion' in the World of Paul." *BTB* 16:92–101.

———. 1987. "Wealth and Poverty in the New Testament and Its World." *Int* 41:354–67.

———. 1988. "Patron and Client: The Analogy behind Synoptic Theology." *Forum* 4/1:2–32.

———. 1989. "Christ and Time: Swiss or Mediterranean?" *CBQ* 51:1–31.

———. 1990. "Mother and Son." *BTB* 20:54–64.

———. 1991a. "First-Century Personality: Dyadic, Not Individual." In *The Social World of Luke-Acts: Models for Interpretation*, edited by Jerome H. Neyrey, 67–96. Peabody, Mass.: Hendrickson.

———. 1991b. "Interpretation: Reading, Abduction, Metaphor." In *The Bible and the Politics of Exegesis: Essays in Honor of Norman K. Gottwald on His Sixty-fifth Birthday*, edited by David Jobling et al., 253–66. Cleveland, Ohio: Pilgrim.

———. 1995. "Pain, Power, and Personhood: Ascetic Behavior in the Ancient Mediterranean." In *Asceticism,* edited by Vincent L. Wimbush and Richard Valantasis, 162–77. New York: Oxford University Press.

———. 1996a. "Mediterranean Sacrifice: Dimensions of Domestic and Political Religion." *BTB* 26:26–44.

———. 1996b. "Patron and Client: The Analogy behind Synoptic Theology." In *The Social World of Jesus and the Gospels,* 143–75. London: Routledge.

———. 2001a. *The New Testament World: Insights from Cultural Anthropology.* 3rd ed. Louisville, Ky.: Westminster John Knox.

———. 2001b. *The Social Gospel of Jesus: The Kingdom of God in Mediterranean Perspective.* Minneapolis: Fortress Press.

Malina, Bruce J., and Jerome H. Neyrey. 1988. *Calling Jesus Names: The Social Value of Labels in Matthew.* Sonoma, Calif.: Polebridge.

Malina, Bruce J., and Richard L. Rohrbaugh. 1998. *Social-Science Commentary on the Gospel of John.* Minneapolis: Fortress Press.

———. 2003. *Social-Science Commentary on the Synoptic Gospels.* 2nd ed. Minneapolis: Fortress Press.

Marquis, Timothy Luckritz. 2007. "Re-presenting Galilean Identity: Josephus's Use of 1 Maccabees 10:25–45 and the Term *Ioudaios.*" In *Religion, Ethnicity, and Identity in Ancient Galilee: A Region in Transition,* edited by Jürgen Zangenberg et al., 55–67. WUNT 1/210. Tübingen: Mohr/Siebeck.

Mason, Steve. 2007. "Jews, Judaeans, Judaizing, Judaism: Problems of Categorization in Ancient History." *JSJ* 38:452–512.

———. 1992. *Josephus and the New Testament.* Peabody, Mass.: Hendrickson.

Mastermann, E. W. G. 1908. "The Fisheries of Galilee." *PEF* 40:40–51.

Mattern, Susan P. 1999. *Rome and the Enemy: Imperial Strategy in the Principate.* Berkeley: University of California Press.

May, David M. 1997. "'Drawn from Nature or Common Life': Social and Cultural Reading Strategies for the Parables." *RevExp* 94:199–214.

Mazar, Benjamin, Gaalyah Cornfeld, and David N. Freedman, editors. 1975. *The Mountain of the Lord: Excavating in Jerusalem.* Garden City, N.Y.: Doubleday.

Mendels, Doron. 1992. *The Rise and Fall of Jewish Nationalism: Jewish and Christian Ethnicity in Ancient Palestine.* ABRL. New York: Doubleday.

Meshorer, Yaakov. 1967. *Jewish Coins of the Second Temple Period.* Translated by I. H. Levine. Tel Aviv: Am Hassefer.

———. 1982. *Ancient Jewish Coinage.* 2 vols. Dix Hills, N.Y.: Amphora.

Meyers, Eric M., editor. 1997. *Oxford Encyclopedia of Archaeology in the Near East.* 5 vols. New York: Oxford University Press.

———, editor. 1999. *Galilee through the Centuries: Confluence of Cultures.* Duke Judaic Studies Series. Winona Lake, Ind.: Eisenbrauns.

Milgrom, Jacob. 1976. "Sacrifices and Offerings, OT." In *IDBSup,* 763–71.

Miller, Stuart S. 1984. *Studies in the History and Traditions of Sepphoris.* SJLA 37. Leiden: Brill.

———. 2007. "Priest, Purities, and the Jews of Galilee." In *Religion, Ethnicity, and Identity in Ancient Galilee: A Region in Transition,* edited by Jürgen Zangenberg et al., 375–402. WUNT 1/210. Tübingen: Mohr/Siebeck.

Moore, Henrietta L. 1994. "Understanding Sex and Gender." In *Companion Encyclopedia to Anthropology,* edited by Tim Ingold, 813–30. London: Routledge.

Moreland, Milton C. 2001. "Q and the Economics of Early Roman Galilee." In *The Sayings Source Q and the Historical Jesus,* edited by Andreas Lindemann, 561–75. BETL 158. Leuven: Peeters.

———. 2004. "The Galilean Response to Earliest Christianity." In *Religion and Society in Roman Palestine: Old Question, New Approaches,* edited by Douglas R. Edwards, 37–48. London: Routledge.

———. 2006. "The Jesus Movement in the Villages of Roman Galilee: Archeology, Q, and Modern Anthropological Theory." In *Oral Performance, Popular Tradition, and Hidden Transcript in Q,* edited by Richard A. Horsley, 159–80. Semeia Studies 60. Atlanta: Society of Biblical Literature.

———. 2007. "The Inhabitants of Galilee in the Hellenistic and Early Roman Periods: Probes into the Archaeological and Literary Evidence." In *Religion, Ethnicity, and Identity in Ancient Galilee: A Region in Transition,* edited by Jürgen Zangenberg et al., 133–59. WUNT 1/210. Tübingen: Mohr/Siebeck.

Moxnes, Halvor. 2001. "The Construction of Galilee as a Place for the Historical Jesus [2 parts]." *BTB* 31:27–37; 64–77.

———. 2003. *Putting Jesus in His Place: A Radical Vision of Household and Kingdom.* Louisville, Ky.: Westminster John Knox.

Murphy-O'Connor, Jerome. 1992. *The Holy Land: An Archaeological Guide from the Earliest Times to 1700.* 3rd ed. Oxford: Oxford University Press.

Neusner, Jacob. 1973. *From Politics to Piety: The Emergence of Pharisaic Judaism.* Reprint, Eugene, Ore.: Wipf & Stock, 2003.

Neyrey, Jerome H., editor. 1991. *The Social World of Luke-Acts: Models for Interpretation.* Peabody, Mass.: Hendrickson.

———. 1996. "John 18–19: Honor and Shame and the Passion Narrative." *Semeia* 68:113–37.

———. 1998. *Honor and Shame in the Gospel of Matthew.* Louisville, Ky.: Westminster John Knox.

Nun, Mendel. 1989. *The Sea of Galilee and Its Fishermen in the New Testament.* Kibbutz Ein Gev, Israel: Kinnereth Sailing Co.

Oakman, Douglas E. 1985. "Jesus and Agrarian Palestine: The Factor of Debt." In *SBLSP*, 57–73. Atlanta: Scholars.

———. 1986. *Jesus and the Economic Questions of His Day.* SBEC 8. Lewiston, N.Y.: Mellen.

———. 1991a. "The Ancient Economy in the Bible." *BTB* 21:34–39.

———. 1991b. "The Countryside in Luke-Acts." In *The Social World of Luke-Acts: Models for Interpretation*, edited by Jerome H. Neyrey, 151–79. Peabody, Mass.: Hendrickson.

———. 1992. "Was Jesus a Peasant? Implications for Reading the Samaritan Story (Luke 10:30–35)." *BTB* 22:117–25.

———. 1993. "Cursing Fig Trees and Robbers' Dens: Pronouncement Stories within Social-Systemic Perspective (Mark 11:11–25 and Parallels)." *Semeia* 64:253–72.

———. 1994. "The Archaeology of First-Century Galilee and the Social Interpretation of the Historical Jesus." In *SBLSP*, 220–51. Atlanta: Scholars.

———. 1996. "The Ancient Economy." In *The Social Sciences and New Testament Interpretation*, edited by Richard L. Rohrbaugh, 126–43. Peabody, Mass.: Hendrickson.

———. 2008. *Jesus and the Peasants.* Matrix. Eugene, Ore.: Cascade Books.

O'Collins, Gerald G. 1992. "Crucifixion." In *ABD* 1:1207–10.

Olami, Yaakov, and Yehudah Peleg. 1977. "The Water Supply System of Caesarea Maritima." *IEJ* 27:127–37.

Osiek, Carolyn. 1992. *What Are They Saying about the Social Setting of the New Testament?* Rev. ed. Mahwah, N.J.: Paulist.

———. 1996. "The Family in Early Christianity: 'Family Values' Revisited." *CBQ* 58:1–24.

———. 2005. "Family Matters." In *Christian Origins*, edited by Richard A. Horsley, 201–20. PHC 1. Minneapolis: Fortress Press.

Osiek, Carolyn, and David L. Balch. 1997. *Families in the New Testament World: Households and House Churches.* The Family, Religion, and Culture. Louisville, Ky.: Westminster John Knox.

Osiek, Carolyn, and Margaret Y. MacDonald, with Janet Tulloch. 2006. *A Woman's Place: House Churches in Earliest Christianity.* Minneapolis: Fortress Press.

Parassoglou, G. M. 1987. "A Lease of Fishing Rights." *Aegyptus* 67:89–93.

Parente, F., and Joseph Sievers, editors. 1994. *Josephus and the History of the Greco-Roman Period.* Studia Post-Biblica 41. Leiden: Brill.

Parker, Anthony J. 1984. "Shipwrecks and Trade in the Ancient Mediterranean." *Archaeological Review from Cambridge* 3:99–113.

Parsons, Talcott. 1966. *Societies: Evolutionary and Comparative Perspectives.* Foundations of Modern Sociology Series. Englewood Cliffs, N.J.: Prentice-Hall.

———. 1971. *The System of Modern Societies.* Englewood Cliffs, N.J.: Prentice-Hall.

———. 1978. *Action Theory and the Human Condition.* New York: Free Press.

Pastner, Carroll McC. 1981. "The Negotiation of Bilateral Endogamy in the Middle Eastern Context: The Zikri Baluch Example." *JAR* 37:305–18.

Patai, Raphael. 1959. *Sex and Family in the Bible and the Middle East.* New York: Macmillan.

Patterson, Stephen J. 1993. "Wisdom in Q and Thomas." In *In Search of Wisdom: Essays in Memory of John G. Gammie*, edited by Leo G. Perdue, Bernard Brandon Scott, and William Johnston Wiseman, 187–221. Louisville, Ky.: Westminster John Knox, 1993.

———. 1998. *The God of Jesus: The Historical Jesus and the Search for Meaning.* Harrisburg, Pa.: Trinity.

Pearson, Birger A. 2004. "A Q Community in Galilee?" *NTS* 50:476–94.

Peristiany, J. G., editor. 1965. *Honour and Shame: The Values of Mediterranean Society.* London: Weidenfeld & Nicholson.

Peristiany, J. G., and Julian Pitt-Rivers, editors. 1992. *Honour and Grace in Anthropology.* Cambridge: Cambridge University Press.

Perkins, Pheme. 1984. "Taxes in the New Testament." *JRE* 12:182–200.

Pilch, John J. 1980. "Praying with Luke." *TBT* 18:221–25.

———. 2000. *Healing in the New Testament: Insights from Medical and Mediterranean Anthropology.* Minneapolis: Fortress Press.

———, editor. 2001. *Social Scientific Models for Interpreting the Bible: Essays by the Context Group in Honor of Bruce J. Malina.* BibIntSer. Leiden: Brill.

————. 2007. *Hear the Word.* Vol. 2: *Introducing the Cultural Context of the New Testament.* 1991. Reprint, Eugene, Ore.: Wipf & Stock.

Pilch, John J., and Bruce J. Malina, editors. 1998. *Handbook of Biblical Social Values.* 2nd ed. Peabody, Mass.: Hendrickson.

Pitt-Rivers, Julian. 1968. "Pseudo-Kinship." In *The International Encyclopedia of the Social Sciences,* edited by David L. Sills, 408–13. New York: Free Press.

Polanyi, Karl, Conrad M. Arensberg, and Harry W. Pearson. 1957. *Trade and Market in the Early Empires: Economies in History and Theory.* Glencoe, Ill.: Free Press.

Powell, Marvin A. 1992. "Weights and Measures." In *ABD* 6:897–908.

Price, Jonathan J. 1992. *Jerusalem under Siege: The Collapse of the Jewish State, 66–70 C.E.* BSJS 3. Leiden: Brill.

Purcell, Nicholas. 1996. "Livia." In *Oxford Classical Dictionary*, edited by Simon Hornblower and Antony Spawforth, 876. 3rd ed. Oxford: Oxford University Press.

Rapinchuk, Mark. 2004. "The Galilee and Jesus in Recent Research." *CBR* 2/2:197–222.

Reed, Jonathan L. 2000. *Archaeology and the Galilean Jesus: A Re-examination of the Evidence.* Harrisburg, Pa.: Trinity.

————. 2006. "Archaeological Contributions to the Study of Jesus and the Gospels." In *The Historical Jesus in Context*, edited by Amy-Jill Levine, Dale C. Allison Jr., and John Dominic Crossan, 40–54. PRR. Princeton: Princeton University Press.

Rhoads, David. 2008. *Israel in Revolution, 66–74 C.E.: A Political History Based on the Writings of Josephus.* 2nd ed. Eugene, Ore.: Cascade Books.

Richardson, Peter. 1996. *Herod: King of the Jews and Friend of the Romans.* Reprint, Minneapolis: Fortress, 1999.

————. 2006. "Khirbet Qana (and Other Villages) as a Context for Jesus." In *Jesus and Archaeology*, edited by James H. Charlesworth, 120–44. Grand Rapids, Mich.: Eerdmans.

Riesner, Rainer. 1995. "Synagogues in Jerusalem." In *The Book of Acts in Its First-Century Setting.* Vol. 4: *Palestinian Setting*, edited by Richard Bauckham, 179–211. Grand Rapids, Mich.: Eerdmans.

Ritmeyer, Kathleen, and Leen Ritmeyer. 1990. *Reconstructing Herod's Temple Mount in Jerusalem.* Washington, D.C.: Biblical Archaeology Society.

Rohrbaugh, Richard L. 1991. "The Pre-industrial City in Luke-Acts: Urban Social Relations." In *The Social World of Luke-Acts*, edited by Jerome H. Neyrey, 121–49. Peabody, Mass.: Hendrickson. Reprinted in *The New Testament in Cross-Cultural Perspective*, 147–74. Matrix. Eugene, Ore.: Cascade Books, 2007.

————. 1993. "A Peasant Reading of the Parable of the Talents/Pounds: A Text of Terror?" *BTB* 23:32–39. Reprinted in *The New Testament in Cross-Cultural Perspective*, 109–23. Matrix. Eugene, Ore.: Cascade Books, 2007.

———. 1996. "The Preindustrial City." In *The Social Sciences and New Testament Interpretation*, edited by Richard L. Rohrbaugh, 107–25. Peabody, Mass.: Hendrickson.

———, editor. 1996. *The Social Sciences and New Testament Interpretation*. Peabody, Mass.: Hendrickson.

———. 2007. *The New Testament in Cross-Cultural Perspective*. Matrix. Eugene, Ore.: Cascade Books.

Rostovtzeff, Michael. 1941. *Social and Economic History of the Hellenistic World.* 3 vols. Oxford: Clarendon.

Rousseau, John J., and Rami Arav. 1995. *Jesus and His World: An Archaeological and Cultural Dictionary.* Minneapolis: Fortress Press.

Safrai, Shmuel. 1969. "Pilgrimage to Jerusalem at the End of the Second Temple Period." In *Studies in the Jewish Background of the New Testament*, edited by Otto Michel et al., 12–21. Assen: Van Gorcum.

———. 1976a. "Home and Family." In *The Jewish People in the First Century: Historical Geography, Political History, Social, Cultural and Religious Life and Institutions*, edited by S. Safrai and M. Stern, 728–92. CRINT 2. Philadelphia: Fortress Press.

———. 1976b. "The Temple." In *The Jewish People in the First Century: Historical Geography, Political History, Social, Cultural and Religious Life and Institutions*, edited by S. Safrai and M. Stern, 865–907. CRINT 2. Philadelphia: Fortress Press.

Sahlins, Marshall. 1966. *Tribesmen.* FMAS. Englewood Cliffs, N.J.: Prentice-Hall.

———. 1972. *Stone Age Economics.* Chicago: Aldine.

Saldarini, Anthony J. 1988. *Pharisees, Scribes and Sadducees: A Sociological Approach.* Reprint, Grand Rapids, Mich.: Eerdmans, 2001.

Saller, Richard P. 1982. *Personal Patronage under the Empire.* New York: Cambridge University Press.

———. 1989. "Patronage and Friendship in Early Imperial Rome: Drawing the Distinction." In *Patronage in Ancient Society*, edited by A. Wallace-Hadrill, 49–62. LNSAS 1. London: Routledge.

Sanders, E. P. 1985. *Jesus and Judaism.* Philadelphia: Fortress Press.

———. 1992. *Judaism: Practice and Belief, 63 B.C.E.—66 C.E.* Philadelphia: Trinity.

———. 1993a. *The Historical Figure of Jesus.* London: Penguin.

———. 1993b. "Jesus in Historical Context." *ThTo* 50:429–48.

———. 2002. "Jesus' Galilee." In *Fair Play: Diversity and Conflicts in Early Christianity; Essays in Honour of Heikki Räisänen*, edited by Ismo Dunderberg, 3–41. NovTSup 103. Leiden: Brill.

Sanders, Irwin T. 1977. *Rural Society.* Englewood Cliffs, N. J.: Prentice-Hall.

Sant Cassia, Paul. 1993. "Banditry, Myth, and Terror in Cyprus and Other Mediterranean Societies." *CSSH* 35:773–95.

Sawicki, Marianne. 1994. *Seeing the Lord: Resurrection and Early Christian Practices*. Minneapolis: Fortress Press.

————. 2000. *Crossing Galilee: Architectures of Contact in the Occupied Land of Jesus*. Harrisburg, Pa.: Trinity.

Schaberg, Jane. 1987. *The Illegitimacy of Jesus: A Feminist Theological Interpretation of the Infancy Narratives*. San Francisco: Harper & Row.

Schalit, Abraham. 1969. *König Herodes: Der Mann und Sein Werk*. Translated by J. Amir. Studia Judaica 4. Berlin: de Gruyter.

Scheid, John. 1996. "Genius." In *Oxford Classical Dictionary*, edited by Simon Hornblower and Antony Spawforth, 630. 3rd ed. Oxford: Oxford University Press.

Schlegel, Alice, and Rohn Eloul. 1988. "Marriage Transactions: Labor, Property, Status." *AmAnth* 90:291–309.

Schmidt, S. W., J. C. Scott, C. Lende, and L. Guasti, editors. 1977. *Friends, Followers, and Factions: A Reader in Political Clientelism*. Berkeley: University of California Press.

Schmidt, Thomas E. 1992. "Taxes." In *Dictionary of Jesus and the Gospels*, edited by Joel B. Green et al., 804–7. Downers Grove, Ill.: InterVarsity.

Schürer, Emil. 1979. *The History of the Jewish People in the Age of Jesus Christ (175 B.C.– A.D. 135)*. A New English Version. Edited by G. Vermes, F. Millar, M. Black, and M. Goodman. Edinburgh: T. & T. Clark.

Schwartz, Daniel R. 2005. "Herodians and *Ioudaioi* in Flavian Rome." In *Flavius Josephus and Flavian Rome*, edited by Jonathan Edmondson, Steve Mason, and James Rives, 63–79. Oxford: Oxford University Press.

Schwartz, Seth. 1994. "Josephus in Galilee: Rural Patronage and Social Breakdown." In *Josephus and the History of the Greco-Roman Period*, edited by F. Parente and Joseph Sievers, 290–306. Leiden: Brill.

Scott, Bernard Brandon. 1989. *Hear Then the Parable: A Commentary on the Parables of Jesus*. Minneapolis: Fortress Press.

Scott, James C. 1985. *Weapons of the Weak: Everyday Forms of Peasant Resistance*. New Haven: Yale University Press.

Shaw, Brent D. 1984. "Bandits in the Roman Empire." *P&P* 102:3–52.

————. 1990. "Bandit Highlands and Lowland Peace: The Mountains of Isauria." *JESHO* 33:199–233; 237–70.

————. 1993. "Tyrants, Bandits and Kings: Personal Power in Josephus." *JJS* 44:176–204.

Smallwood, E. Mary. 1981. *The Jews under the Romans from Pompey to Diocletian: A Study in Political Relations*. 2nd ed. SJLA 20. Leiden: Brill.

Sperber, Daniel. 1968. "Some Observations on Fish and Fisheries in Roman Palestine." *ZDMG* 118:265–69.

————. 1976. "Objects of Trade between Palestine and Egypt in Roman Times." *JESHO* 19:113–47.

Ste. Croix, G. E. M. de. 1954. *"Suffragium:* From Vote to Patronage." *BJS* 5:33–48.

Stegemann, Ekkehard K., and Wolfgang Stegemann. 1999. *The Jesus Movement: A Social History of Its First Century*. Translated by O. C. Dean Jr. Minneapolis: Fortress Press.

Stegemann, Wolfgang. 1984. *The Gospel and the Poor*. Translated by Dietlinde Elliott. Philadelphia: Fortress Press.

Stegemann, Wolfgang, Bruce J. Malina, and Gerd Theissen, editors. 2002. *The Social Setting of Jesus and the Gospels*. Minneapolis: Fortress Press.

Stemberger, Giinter. 1994. *Jewish Contemporaries of Jesus: Pharisees, Sadducees, Essenes*. Minneapolis: Fortress Press.

Stendahl, Krister. 1962. "Biblical Theology: Contemporary." In *IDB* 1:418–32.

Stern, Menachem. 1974a. "Judea as a Roman Province." In *The Jewish People in the First Century*, edited by S. Safrai and M. Stem, 308–76. CRINT 1. Philadelphia: Fortress Press.

————. 1974b. "The Reign of Herod and the Herodian Dynasty." In *The Jewish People in the First Century*, edited by S. Safrai and M. Stem, 216–307. CRINT 1. Philadelphia: Fortress Press.

Stewart, Edward C., and Milton J. Bennett. 1991. *American Cultural Patterns: A Cross-Cultural Perspective*. Rev. ed. Yarmouth, Maine: Intercultural.

Strange, James F. 1976. "Crucifixion, Method of." In *IDBSup,* 199–200.

Sullivan, R. D. 1977. "The Dynasty of Judaea in the First Century." In *ANRW* II.8:296–354. Berlin: de Gruyter.

Sussmann, Ayala, and Ruth Peled, editors. 1993. *Scrolls from the Dead Sea*. Library of Congress Exhibition Volume. Washington, D.C.: Archetype.

Theissen, Gerd. 1976. "Die Tempelweissagung Jesu: Prophetic im Spannungsfeld von Stadt und Land." *ThZ* 32:144–58.

————. 1991. *The Gospels in Context: Social and Political History in the Synoptic Tradition*. Translated by Linda M. Maloney. Minneapolis: Fortress Press.

Theissen, Gerd, and Annette Merz. 1998. *The Historical Jesus: A Comprehensive Guide*. Translated by John Bowden. Minneapolis: Fortress Press.

Todd, Emmanuel. 1985. *The Explanation of Ideology: Family Structures and Social Systems*. Translated by D. Garrioch. Family, Sexuality, and Social Relations in Past Times. Oxford: Blackwell.

Torjesen, Karen Jo. 1993. *When Women Were Priests: Women's Leadership in the Early Church and the Scandal of Their Subordination in the Rise of Christianity*. San Francisco: HarperSanFrancisco.

Turkowski, L. 1968. "Peasant Agriculture in the Judean Hills, Part 1." *PEQ* 100:21–33.

————. 1969. "Peasant Agriculture in the Judean Hills, Part 2." *PEQ* 101:101–12.

Turner, Jonathan, and Leonard Beeghley. 1974. "Current Folklore in the Criticisms of Parsonian Action Theory." *SocInq* 44/1:47–55.

Udoh, Fabian Eugene. 1996. "Tribute and Taxes in Early Roman Palestine (63 B.C.E.–70 C.E.): The Evidence from Josephus." Ph.D. dissertation, Duke University Press.

———. 2005. *To Caesar What Is Caesar's: Tribute, Taxes and Imperial Administration in Early Roman Palestine (63 B.C.E.–70 C.E.)*. BJS. Providence, R.I.: Brown Judaic Studies.

Vaage, Leif E. 1994. *Galilean Upstarts: Jesus' First Followers according to Q*. Valley Forge, Pa.: Trinity.

Wachsman, Shelley. 1988. "The Galilee Boat." *BAR* 14/5:18–33.

———. 1995. *The Sea of Galilee Boat: An Extraordinary 2,000-Year-Old Discovery*. New York: Plenum.

Wachsman, Shelley, et al. 1990. "Excavations of an Ancient Boat in the Sea of Galilee." *'Atiqot* (Eng. series) vol. 19.

Wallace-Hadrill, Andrew, editor. 1989. *Patronage in Ancient Society*. LNSAS 1. London: Routledge.

Weber, Max. 1963. *The Sociology of Religion*. Introduction by Talcott Parsons. Translated by Ephraim Fischoff. Boston: Beacon.

Weiss, Zeev. 2007. "Josephus and Archaeology on the Cities of the Galilee." In *Making History: Josephus and Historical Method*, edited by Zuleika Rodgers, 385–414. JSJSup 110. Leiden: Brill.

White, K. D. 1977. *Country Life in Classical Times*. Ithaca, N.Y.: Cornell University Press.

White, L. Michael, editor. 1988. *Semeia 48: Social Networks and Early Christianity*. Atlanta: Scholars.

Williams, Robin M. Jr. 1970. *American Society*. 3rd ed. New York: Knopf.

Willis, Wendell, ed. 1987. *The Kingdom of God in Twentieth-Century Interpretation*. Peabody, Mass.: Hendrickson.

Wilson, Robert R. 1975. "Old Testament Genealogies in Recent Research." *JBL* 94:169–89.

———. 1977. *Genealogy and History in the Biblical World*. Yale Near Eastern Researches 7. New Haven: Yale University Press.

Winter, Bruce W. 1994. *Seek the Welfare of the City: Christians as Benefactors and Citizens. First-Century Christians in the Graeco-Roman World*. Grand Rapids, Mich.: Eerdmans.

Wire, Antoinette. 2005. "Women's History from Birth-Prophecy Stories." In *Christian Origins*, edited by Richard A. Horsley, 71–93. PHC 1. Minneapolis: Fortress Press.

Wolf, Eric R. 1966. *Peasants*. FMAS. Englewood Cliffs, N.J.: Prentice-Hall.

Wuellner, Wilhelm H. 1967. *The Meaning of "Fishers of Men."* NTL. Philadelphia: Westminster.

Yadin, Yigael. 1966. *Masada: Herod's Fortress and the Zealots' Last Stand.* Translated by Moshe Pearlman. New York: Random House.

Zangenberg, Jürgen. 2006. "Between Jerusalem and the Galilee: Samaria in the Time of Jesus." In *Jesus and Archaeology*, edited by James H. Charlesworth, 393–432. Grand Rapids, Mich.: Eerdmans.

Zangenberg, Jürgen, Harold W. Attridge, and Dale B. Martin, editors. 2007. *Religion, Ethnicity, and Identity in Ancient Galilee: A Region in Transition.* WUNT 1/210. Tübingen: Mohr/Siebeck.

Zias, Joe, and James H. Charlesworth. 1992. "Crucifixion: Archaeology, Jesus and the Dead Sea Scrolls." In *Jesus and the Dead Sea Scrolls*, edited by James H. Charlesworth, 273–89. ABRL. New York: Doubleday.

INDEX 1

Index of Ancient Sources

Old Testament

GENESIS	28, 31, 48
1–3	29
2:7-23	24
5:1—9:29	27
5:1-32	27
9:28-29	27
11:10-26	48
12:1—25:11	48
12:1-3	29
23:6	48
24	31
24:53	38, 183
24:59-61	37–38
29:24-29	38
30:20	36
31:14-16	36
34:12	38
38:26	51
38:27-30	51
40:20	78
EXODUS	
12	136
20:12	25
20:24	145
22:17	179
23:16	136
28:1	28
29:1-46	165
35:35	179
LEVITICUS	127, 134, 178
1:1-17	135
2:1-16	135
3:1-17	135
4:1—5:13	135
5:14—6:7	135
7:11-14	135
9:1-24	161
12:8	135
16:1-34	28, 136
16:32	28
18	31

19:20-22	135
20	31
23:5-8	136
23:15-21	136
23:27-32	136
23:34-36	136
25	111
25:10	111
NUMBERS	43
27:3-4	43
27:8-11	43–44
29:7-11	136
36:6-12	36
DEUTERONOMY	134
8:8	98
15	111
15:1-2	142
15:2	111
16:1-8	136
16:9-12	136
16:13-15	136
16:16	143
21:17	43, 183
22:5	26
24:1-4a	41
24:1	41
JOSHUA	
2:12	51
6:25	51
15:18-19	36, 38
JUDGES	81
5:7	185
5:11	185
11:1-3	187
11:3	81
RUTH	
1:8	51
1:16-17	51
2:10-12	30
3:10	51
4:13-22	51

1 SAMUEL	
9:1	28
9:16	163
13:19-21	179
18:17-29	34
18:25	179
18:27	30
22:1-2	187
22:2	83
2 SAMUEL	
3:2-5	28
3:3	75
3:12-16	54
5:13-16	28
7:4-17	79
7:7	88
7:14-15	163
9:6	28
11:1—12:25	51
12:1-15	79
12:24-25	51
1 KINGS	
1:3	75
1:11-21	51
1:28-31	51
1:33-35	88
1:34	138
1:39	163
2:13-25	51
2:13	30
2:19	51
3:15	135
4:25	98
5	127
9:16	36, 181
9:26-28	103
10:14-22	103
13:2	28
21	79
22	79
2 KINGS	
12:16	135
25:9	127

215

Index of Subjects

INDEX 3

Index of Authors

3408568

Made in the USA